WTO Trade Remedies in International Law

World Trade Organisation (WTO) trade remedies (antidumping, anti-subsidy and safeguard agreements) are instruments used by WTO members to counter the economic injury caused by dumping, subsidies and the sudden and unforeseen increased imports. They are exceptions to the WTO principle of free trade and to the prohibition for States to react unilaterally to protect their own rights and interests, and as a result they have been accused by some as being the new tools of protectionism.

This book analyses of the role and principles of WTO trade remedies in international law. In particular, it focuses on their aims, their structure, and their position within the WTO and more in general, the international legal system. The book considers trade remedies in light of fragmentation theories of international law and addresses the question how, and to what extent WTO law reflects and influences public international law.

Roberto Soprano is Visiting Professor at the Vrije Universiteit Brussel and the Brussels Diplomatic Academy in Belgium.

Routledge Research in International Economic Law

Available:

International Investment Law and the Right to Regulate
A human rights perspective
Lone Wandahl Mouyal

International Investment Law and Policy in Africa
Exploring a Human Rights Based Approach to Investment Regulation and Dispute Settlement
Fola Adeleke

Forthcoming:

A Chinese Perspective on International Investment Law
Guiguo Wang

Culture and International Economic Law
Valentina Vadi and Bruno de Witte

Defences in International Investment Law
Francis Botchway

WTO Trade Remedies in International Law
Roberto Soprano

Cohesion and Legitimacy in International Investment Law
Public International Law and Global Administrative Law Perspectives
Chisomo Kapulula

International Challenges in Investment Law and Arbitration
Mesut Akbaba and Giancarlo Capurro

State Interest and the Sources of International Law
Doctrine, Morality, and Non-Treaty Law
Markus P. Beham

Trade Facilitation in the Multilateral Trading System
Genesis, Course and Accord
Hao Wu

WTO Trade Remedies in International Law

Their Role and Place in a Fragmented International Legal System

Roberto Soprano

Routledge
Taylor & Francis Group
LONDON AND NEW YORK

First published 2019
by Routledge
2 Park Square, Milton Park, Abingdon, Oxon OX14 4RN

and by Routledge
52 Vanderbilt Avenue, New York, NY 10017

First issued in paperback 2020

Routledge is an imprint of the Taylor & Francis Group, an informa business

British Library Cataloguing in Publication Data
A catalogue record for this book is available from the British Library

Library of Congress Cataloging in Publication Data
Names: Soprano, Roberto, author.
Title: WTO trade remedies in international law : their role and place in a fragmented international legal system / Roberto Soprano.
Description: Abingdon, Oxon [UK] ; New York, NY : Routledge, 2018. | Series: Routledge research in international economic law | Includes bibliographical references and index.
Identifiers: LCCN 2018008810 | ISBN 9781138729230 (hardback)
Subjects: LCSH: World Trade Organization. | Foreign trade regulation. | Tariff–Law and legislation. | General Agreement on Tariffs and Trade (Organization)
Classification: LCC K4610 .S67 2018 | DDC 343.08/7–dc23
LC record available at https://lccn.loc.gov/2018008810

ISBN 13: 978-0-367-58811-3 (pbk)
ISBN 13: 978-1-138-72923-0 (hbk)

Typeset in Galliard
by Taylor & Francis Books

Contents

Foreword

This book comes at a timely moment.

The WTO is currently facing one of the most crucial phase of its life since its creation. The outcome of the Buenos Aires Ministerial Conference confirmed that it is still a critical time for the multilateral trade regime and for the WTO as a forum for negotiations. Emerging economies and developed countries continue to diverge on NAMA and agricultural reforms that would be necessary to update current legislation and tariff concessions. Such an impasse risks to jeopardize the multilateral system and to lead states to find bilateral, plurilateral or sectorial solutions to achieve further trade liberalization and to create new standards and rules for the world trade.

Most recently, the United States administration scepticism about WTO, culminated with the reluctance to reappoint Appellate Body members whose terms are expiring, has also become a major concern for its Members. The attitude of President Trump towards the WTO revealed a changing approach of the United States towards the multilateral trade system that could open new scenarios in the trade diplomacy. In fact, the United States will no longer take the lead in negotiations but would also obstruct the discussion among Members potentially leading to the creation of new coalitions among Members and the development of new strategies.

In addition, the disputes relating to the Market Economy Status of China and the compatibility of autonomous sanctions regimes with WTO commitments poses serious threats to the WTO that could exacerbate the discussion about its role and limits and risks to undermine the whole trade legal system.

The WTO needs new stimulus and ideas to reform internally and to continue to impede to countries to fall into the darkness of protectionism. Roberto Soprano's analysis on the relations between international law and WTO law could led to interesting amendments of WTO trade remedies and ensure that those instruments would not serve protectionist purposes.

Kim Van der Borght
Full Professor of International Economic Law
Centre for Economic Law & Governance
Vrije Universiteit Brussel

WTO and GATT Dispute Settlement Reports

WTO

Short title	*Full case title and citation*
Argentina – Footwear (EC)	Panel Report, *Argentina – Safeguard Measures on Imports of Footwear*, WT/DS121/R and Appellate Body Report WT/DS121/AB/R (adopted 12 January 2000).
Argentina – Poultry Anti Dumping Duties	Panel Report, Argentina – Definitive Anti-Dumping Duties on Poultry from Brazil, WT/DS241/R, adopted 19 May 2003, DSR 2003:V
Brazil – Aircraft	Panel Report, *Brazil – Export Financing Programme for Aircraft*, WT/DS46/R and Appellate Body Report WT/DS46/AB/R (adopted 20 August 1999).
Brazil – Aircraft (Article 21.5 – Canada)	Panel Report, *Brazil – Export Financing Programme for Aircraft – Recourse by Canada to Article 21.5 of the DSU*, WT/DS46/RW and Appellate Body Report WT/DS46/AB/RW (adopted 4 August 2000).
Brazil – Aircraft (Article 21.5 – Canada II)	Panel Report, *Brazil – Export Financing Programme for Aircraft – Second Recourse by Canada to Article 21.5 of the DSU*, WT/DS46/RW/2, (adopted 23 August 2001).
Canada – Aircraft	Panel Report, *Canada – Measures Affecting the Export of Civilian Aircraft*, WT/DS70/R and Appellate Body Report WT/DS70/AB/R (adopted 20 August 1999).
Canada – Aircraft (Article 21.5 – Brazil)	Panel Report, *Canada – Measures Affecting the Export of Civilian Aircraft – Recourse by Brazil to Article 21.5 of the DSU*, WT/DS70/RW and Appellate Body Report WT/DS70/AB/RW (adopted 4 August 2000).
Brazil – Desiccated Coconut	Panel Report, *Brazil – Measures Affecting Desiccated Coconut*, WT/DS22/R (adopted 20 March 1997) and Appellate Body Report, WT/DS22/AB/R (adopted 20 March 1997).
Canada – Aircraft Credits and Guarantees	Panel Report, *Canada – Export Credits and Loan Guarantees for Regional Aircraft*, WT/DS222/R and Corr.1 (adopted 19 February 2002).

Short title	*Full case title and citation*
Canada – Renewable Energy / Canada – Feed-in Tariff Program	Panel Reports, *Canada – Certain Measures Affecting the Renewable Energy Generation Sector / Canada – Measures Relating to the Feed-in Tariff Program*, WT/DS412/R and Add.1 / WT/DS426/R and Add.1, adopted 24 May 2013, and Appellate Body Reports, WT/DS412/AB/R / WT/DS426/AB/R (adopted 24 May 2013).
Canada – Patent Term	Panel Report, *Canada – Term of Patent Protection*, WT/DS170/R, adopted 12 October 2000, and Appellate Body Report, WT/DS170/AB/R (adopted 12 October 2000).
Canada – Aircraft Credits and Guarantees	Panel Report, *Canada – Export Credits and Loan Guarantees for Regional Aircraft*, WT/DS222/R and Corr.1 (adopted 19 February 2002).
Canada – Autos	Panel Report, *Canada – Certain Measures Affecting the Automotive Industry*, WT/DS139/R, WT/DS142/R and Appellate Body Report WT/DS139/AB/R, WT/DS142/AB/R (adopted 19 June 2000).
Chile – Price Band System	Panel Report, *Chile – Price Band System and Safeguard Measures Relating to Certain Agricultural Products*, WT/DS207/R and Appellate Body Report WT/DS207AB/R (adopted 23 October 2002).
China – Cellulose Pulp	Panel Report, *China – Anti-Dumping Measures on Imports of Cellulose Pulp from Canada*, WT/DS483/R and Add.1 (adopted 22 May 2017)
China – HP-SSST (Japan) / China – HP-SSST (EU)	Panel Reports, *China – Measures Imposing Anti-Dumping Duties on High-Performance Stainless Steel Seamless Tubes ("HP-SSST") from Japan / China – Measures Imposing Anti-Dumping Duties on High-Performance Stainless Steel Seamless Tubes ("HP-SSST") from the European Union*, WT/DS454/R and Add.1 / WT/DS460/R, Add.1 and Corr.1 (adopted 28 October 2015) and Appellate Body Reports, WT/DS454/AB/R and Add.1 / WT/DS460/AB/R and Add.1 (adopted 28 October 2015)
EC – Bananas III	Appellate Body Report, *European Communities – Regime for the Importation, Sale and Distribution of Bananas*, WT/DS27/AB/R (adopted 25 September 1997).
EC – Bed Linen	Panel Report, *European Communities – Anti-Dumping Duties on Imports of Cotton-Type Bed Linen from India*, WT/DS141/R and Appellate Body Report WT/DS141/AB/R (adopted 12 March 2001).
EC – Countervailing Measures on DRAM Chips	Panel Report, *European Communities – Countervailing Measures on Dynamic Random Access Memory Chips from Korea*, WT/DS299/R (adopted 3 August 2005)
EC – Fasteners (China)	Panel Report, *European Communities – Definitive Anti-Dumping Measures on Certain Iron or Steel Fasteners from China*, WT/DS397/R and Corr.1 (adopted 28 July 2011) and Appellate Body Report, WT/DS397/AB/R (adopted 28 July 2011).
EC – Hormones	Appellate Body Report, *EC Measures Concerning Meat and Meat Products (Hormones)*, WT/DS26/AB/R, WT/DS48/AB/R (adopted 13 February 1998).

Short title	*Full case title and citation*
EC and Certain Member States – Large Civil Aircraft	Appellate Body Report, *European Communities and Certain Member States – Measures Affecting Trade in Large Civil Aircraft*, WT/DS316/AB/R (adopted 1 June 2011) Panel Report, *European Communities and Certain Member States – Measures Affecting Trade in Large Civil Aircraft*, WT/DS316/R (adopted 1 June 2011), as modified by Appellate Body Report WT/DS316/AB/R,
EC – Sardines	Panel Report, *European Communities – Trade Description of Sardines*, WT/DS231/R and Corr.1 (adopted 23 October 2002) and Appellate Body Report, WT/DS231/AB/R, (adopted 23 October 2002).
EC – Tariff Preferences	Panel Report, *European Communities – Conditions for the Granting of Tariff Preferences to Developing Countries*, WT/DS246/R (adopted 20 April 2004) and Appellate Body Report, WT/DS246/AB/R (adopted 20 April 2004).
EC – Tube or Pipe Fittings	Panel Report, *European Communities – Anti-Dumping Duties on Malleable Cast Iron Tube or Pipe Fittings from Brazil*, WT/DS219/R and Appellate Body Report WT/DS219/AB/R (adopted 18 August 2003).
Guatemala – Cement I	Panel Report, *Guatemala – Anti-Dumping Investigation Regarding Portland Cement from Mexico*, WT/DS60/R and Appellate Body Report WT/DS60/AB/R (adopted 25 November 1998).
Guatemala – Cement II	Panel Report, *Guatemala – Definitive Anti-Dumping Measures on Grey Portland Cement from Mexico*, WT/DS156/R (adopted 17 November 2000).
India – Solar Cells	Panel Report, *India – Certain Measures Relating to Solar Cells and Solar Modules*, WT/DS456/R and Add.1 (adopted 14 October 2016) and Appellate Body Report, WT/DS456/AB/R and Add.1 (adopted 14 October 2016).
Indonesia – Iron or Steel Products	Panel Report, *Indonesia – Safeguard on Certain Iron or Steel Products*, WT/DS490/R, WT/DS496/R, and Add.1, circulated to WTO Members 18 August 2017.
Japan – Alcoholic Beverages II	Panel Report, *Japan – Taxes on Alcoholic Beverages*, WT/DS8/R, WT/DS10/R, WT/DS11/R and Appellate Body Report WT/DS8/AB/R, WT/DS10/AB/R, WT/DS11/AB/R (adopted 1 November 1996).
Korea – Dairy	Panel Report, *Korea – Definitive Safeguard Measure on Imports of Certain Dairy Products*, WT/DS98/R and Corr. and Appellate Body Report WT/DS98/AB/R (adopted 12 January 2000).
Mexico – Steel Pipes and Tubes	Panel Report, *Mexico – Anti-Dumping Duties on Steel Pipes and Tubes from Guatemala*, WT/DS331/R (adopted 24 July 2007), DSR 2007:IV, p. 1207.
Thailand – H-Beams	Panel Report, *Thailand – Anti-Dumping Duties on Angles, Shapes and Sections of Iron or Non-Alloy Steel and H-Beams from Poland*, WT/DS122/R and Appellate Body Report WT/DS122/AB/R (adopted 5 April 2001).

Short title	*Full case title and citation*
Ukraine – Passenger Cars	Panel Report, *Ukraine – Definitive Safeguard Measures on Certain Passenger Cars*, WT/DS468/R and Add.1, (adopted 20 July 2015).
US – 1916 Act (EC)	Panel Report, *United States – Anti-Dumping Act of 1916, Complaint by the European Communities*, WT/DS136/R and Corr.1and Appellate Body Report WT/DS136/AB/R, WT/DS162/AB/R (adopted 26 September 2000).
US – Anti-Dumping and Countervailing Duties (China)	Panel Report, *United States – Definitive Anti-Dumping and Countervailing Duties on Certain Products from China*, WT/DS379/R (adopted 25 March 2011) and Appellate Body Report, WT/DS379/AB/R (adopted 25 March 2011).
US – Carbon Steel (India)	Panel Report, *United States – Countervailing Measures on Certain Hot-Rolled Carbon Steel Flat Products from India*, WT/DS436/R and Add.1 (adopted 19 December 2014) and Appellate Body Report, WT/DS436/AB/R (adopted 19 December 2014).
US – Continued Zeroing	Panel Report, *United States – Continued Existence and Application of Zeroing Methodology*, WT/DS350/R and Appellate Body Report WT/DS350/AB/R (adopted 19 February 2009).
US – Cotton Yarn	Panel Report, *United States – Transitional Safeguard Measure on Combed Cotton Yarn from Pakistan*, WT/DS192/R (adopted 5 November 2001) and Appellate Body Report, WT/DS192/AB/R (adopted 5 November 2001).
US – Export Restraints	Panel Report, *United States – Measures Treating Exports Restraints as Subsidies*, WT/DS194/R and Corr.2 (adopted 23 August 2001).
US – Countervailing Duty Investigation on DRAMS	Panel Report, *United States – Countervailing Duty Investigation on Dynamic Random Access Memory Semiconductors (DRAMS) from Korea*, WT/DS296/R (adopted 20 July 2005) and Appellate Body Report, WT/DS296/AB/R, (adopted 20 July 2005).
US – DRAMS	Panel Report, *United States – Anti-Dumping Duty on Dynamic Random Access Memory Semiconductors (DRAMS) of One Megabit or Above from Korea*, WT/DS99/R (adopted 19 March 1999)
US – Customs Bond Directive	Panel Report, *United States – Customs Bond Directive for Merchandise Subject to Anti-Dumping/Countervailing Duties*, WT/DS345/R (adopted 1 August 2008) and Appellate Body Report WT/DS343/AB/R / WT/DS345/AB/R (adopted 1 August 2008).
US – Gasoline	Panel Report, *United States – Standards for Reformulated and Conventional Gasoline*, WT/DS2/R (adopted 20 May 1996) and Appellate Body Report, WT/DS2/AB/R (adopted 20 May 1996).
US – FSC	Panel Report, *United States – Tax Treatment for "Foreign Sales Corporations"*, WT/DS108/R and Appellate Body Report WT/DS108/AB/R (adopted 20 March 2000).
US – Gambling	Appellate Body Report, *United States – Measures Affecting the Cross-Border Supply of Gambling and Betting Services*, WT/DS285/AB/R, (adopted 20 April 2005).
US – Hot-Rolled Steel	Panel Report, *United States – Anti-Dumping Measures on Certain Hot-Rolled Steel Products from Japan*, WT/DS184/R and Appellate Body Report WT/DS184/AB/R (adopted 23 August 2001).

Short title	*Full case title and citation*
US – Lamb	Panel Report, *United States – Safeguard Measures on Imports of Fresh, Chilled or Frozen Lamb Meat from New Zealand and Australia*, WT/DS177/R, WT/DS178/R and Appellate Body Report WT/DS177/AB/R, WT/DS178/AB/R (adopted 16 May 2001).
US – Line Pipe	Panel Report, *United States – Definitive Safeguard Measures on Imports of Circular Welded Carbon Quality Line Pipe from Korea*, WT/DS202/R and Appellate Body Report WT/DS202/AB/R (adopted 8 March 2002).
US – Offset Act (Byrd Amendment)	Panel Report, *United States – Continued Dumping and Subsidy Offset Act of 2000*, WT/DS217/R, WT/DS234/R and Appellate Body Report WT/DS217/AB/R, WT/DS234/AB/R (adopted 27 January 2003).
US – Shrimp	Panel Report, *United States – Import Prohibition of Certain Shrimp and Shrimp Products*, WT/DS58/R and Corr.1 and Appellate Body Report WT/DS58/AB/R (adopted 6 November 1998).
US – Shrimp (Article 21.5 – Malaysia)	Panel Report, *United States – Import Prohibition of Certain Shrimp and Shrimp Products – Recourse to Article 21.5 of the DSU by Malaysia*, WT/DS58/RW and Appellate Body Report WT/DS58/AB/RW (adopted 21 November 2001).
US – Shrimp (Ecuador)	Panel Report, *United States – Anti-Dumping Measure on Shrimp from Ecuador*, WT/DS335/R (adopted 20 February 2007).
US – Shrimp (Thailand)	Panel Report, *United States – Measures Relating to Shrimp from Thailand*, WT/DS343/R and Appellate Body Report WT/DS343/AB/R, WT/DS345/AB/R (adopted 1 August 2008).
US – Softwood Lumber V	Panel Report, *United States – Final Dumping Determination on Softwood Lumber from Canada*, WT/DS264/R and Appellate Body Report WT/DS264/AB/R (adopted 31 August 2004).
US – Softwood Lumber V (Article 21.5 – Canada)	Panel Report, *United States – Final Dumping Determination on Softwood Lumber from Canada – Recourse to Article 21.5 of the DSU by Canada*, WT/DS264/RW, and Appellate Body Report WT/DS264/AB/RW (adopted 1 September 2006).
US – Stainless Steel (Korea)	Panel Report, *United States – Anti-Dumping Measures on Stainless Steel Plate in Coils and Stainless Steel Sheet and Strip from Korea*, WT/DS179/R (adopted 1 February 2001).
US – Stainless Steel (Mexico)	Panel Report, *United States – Final Anti-Dumping Measures on Stainless Steel from Mexico*, WT/DS344/R and Appellate Body Report WT/DS344/AB/R (adopted 20 May 2008).
US – Tax Incentives	Panel Report, *United States – Conditional Tax Incentives for Large Civil Aircraft*, WT/DS487/R and Add.1 (adopted 22 September 2017) and Appellate Body Report, WT/DS487/AB/R and Add.1 (adopted 22 September 2017).
US – Upland Cotton	Panel Report, *United States – Subsidies on Upland Cotton*, WT/DS267/R, Corr.1, and Add.1 to Add.3 and Appellate Body Report WT/DS267/AB/R (adopted 21 March 2005).

Short title	*Full case title and citation*
US – Wheat Gluten	Panel Report, *United States – Definitive Safeguard Measures on Imports of Wheat Gluten from the European Communities*, WT/DS166/R and Appellate Body Report WT/DS166/AB/R (adopted 19 January 2001).
US – Washing Machines	Panel Report, *United States – Anti-Dumping and Countervailing Measures on Large Residential Washers from Korea*, WT/DS464/R and Add.1 (adopted 26 September 2016) and Appellate Body Report, WT/DS464/AB/R and Add.1 (adopted 26 September 2016).
US – Zeroing (EC)	Panel Report, *United States – Laws, Regulations and Methodology for Calculating Dumping Margins ("Zeroing")*, WT/DS294/R and Appellate Body Report WT/DS294/AB/R (adopted 9 May 2006).
US – Zeroing (Japan)	Panel Report, *United States – Measures Relating to Zeroing and Sunset Reviews*, WT/DS322/R and Appellate Body Report WT/DS322/AB/R (adopted 23 January 2007).

GATT

US – Fur Felt Hats	*Report on the Withdrawal by the United States of a Tariff Concession under Article XIX of the General Agreement on Tariffs and Trade, GATT/CP/106, (adopted 22 October 1951).*
Norway – Textiles	GATT Panel Report, *Norway – Restrictions on Imports of Certain Textile Products, L/4959, BISD 27S/119* (adopted 18 June 1980).

Arbitration Awards

-Air Service Agreement of 27 March 1946 between the United States of America and France, Award of 9 December 1978, R.I.A.A VOLUME XVIII, 1978

-Tacna-Arica question (*Chile v. Peru)* Award of 4 March 1925, R.I.A.A. Vol. II, 1925

-Award in the arbitration regarding the delimitation of the maritime boundary between Guyana and Suriname, Award of 17 September 2007, R.I.A.A. vol. XXX, 2007

-Responsibility of Germany for damage caused in the Portuguese colonies in the south of Africa, R.I.A.A. Vol. II, 1928

-Opinion in the Lusitania Cases, Award of 1 November 1923, R.I.A.A VII, 1923

-Case concerning the difference between New Zealand and France concerning the interpretation or application of two agreements concluded on 9 July 1986 between the two States and which related to the problems arising from the Rainbow Warrior Affair, Decision of 30 April 1990, RI.A.A Vol. 20, 1990

International Criminal Tribunal for the Former Yugoslavia

-Prosecutor v. Galić, No. IT-98–29-A, (30 November 2006).

European Court of Human Rights

-Golder v. United Kingdom, ECHR, Series A, (1995) no. 18;

Permanent Court of International Justice and International Court of Justice

PCIJ

-*S.S. Wimbledon*, Permanent Court of International Justice, Collection of Judgments Ser. A01, (17 August 1923)

-*Case Concerning the Factory at Chorzow*, Permanent Court of International Justice, Collection of Judgments, Series A09, (26 July 1927)

-*Lotus*, Permanent Court of International Justice, Collection of Judgments, Ser. A10, (7 September 1927)

-*The Mavrommatis Palestine Concession*, Permanent Court of International Justice, Collection of Judgments, Ser. A02, (30 August 1924)

-*Factory at Chorzów*, Germany v Poland, Judgment, Claim for Indemnity, Merits, Judgment No 13, (1928) PCIJ Series A No 17, (13 September 1928)

ICJ

-*Corfu Channel case*, Judgment, I.C.J. Reports 1949, (9 April 1949)

-*Armed Activities on the Territory of the Congo* (Democratic Republic of the Congo v. Uganda), Judgment, I.C.J. Reports 2005

-*Fisheries Jurisdiction* (Federal Republic of Germany v. Iceland), Merits, Judgment, I.C.J. Reports 1974

-*Legal Consequences of the Construction of a Wall in the Occupied Palestinian Territory*, Advisory Opinion, I.C.J. Reports 2004

-*Territorial Dispute* (Libyan Arab Jamahiriya/Chad), Judgment, I.C.J. Reports 1994

-*Barcelona Traction, Light and Power Company,* Limited, Judgement, I.C.J. Reports 1970, (5 February 1970)

-*United States Diplomatic and Consular Staff in Tehran*, Judgment, I.C.J. Reports 1980, (24 May 1980);

-*Continental Shelf* (Libyan Arab Jamahiriya/Malta), Judgment, I.C.J. Reports 1985, (3 June 1985);

-*Military and Paramilitary Activities in und against Nicaragua* (Nicaragua v. United States of America). Judgment, *I.C.J. Reports*, 1986, p. 14, (27 June 1986);

-*Gabčíkovo-Nagymaros Project* (Hungary/Slovakia), Judgment, I. C. J. Reports 1997 (25 September 1997)

Introduction

This is not a(nother) book about the WTO rules and jurisprudence on trade remedies. It does not contain technical details on how to conduct anti-dumping, anti-subsidy or safeguard investigations. This study focuses on the place and role of trade remedies within public international law. It is aimed at describing how the WTO and public international rules are deeply interlinked and influence each other.

WTO trade remedies are widespread instruments used by WTO Members to counter the economic injury caused by dumping, subsidies and the sudden and unforeseen increased imports. According to many scholars, trade remedies have become the new tools of protectionism. Their wide use has political and economic motivations, as they increase the price of foreign goods and offer protection to domestic industries. Although they were not created with protectionist intent, they can create barriers to imports. Unilateral actions and in particular unilateral reactions or *"beggar-thy-neighbour"* policies which were so disastrous to world trade and economics during the interwar periods have always been condemned by the new multilateral economic system. The risk of an increase in the use, *rectius* abuse, of trade remedies is particularly high during periods of crisis when domestic producers pledge governments for protection from foreign competitors. This is confirmed by the surge in trade remedies and other non-tariff barriers adopted since the rise of the financial crisis and by the fact that trade remedies are the first cause of disputes among WTO Members.

As described in the first chapter, in international law and in particular in WTO law, unilateral reactions have been replaced by multilateral efforts and judicial processes. Accordingly, WTO rules were partially developed to limit the possibility for States to discriminate and react unilaterally. However, some forms of unilateralism still exist. These exceptions to the WTO multilateral approach are strictly limited and regulated by the WTO system. An example is represented by trade remedies which allow Member States to react unilaterally to injurious practices against their domestic industries and impose trade restrictive measures.

Although WTO trade remedies show many differences among each other and address different problems and have different goals, they share a similar structure: They address specific actions that cause injury to the domestic industry of the importing State and that give to the importing country the right to react by adopting trade restrictive measures. This is due to the fact they are aimed at counteracting a practice causing injury to their domestic industries.

Some scholars have compared WTO trade remedies with countermeasures as they share similar characteristics by being the limited and regulated right under which States are allowed to take unilateral measures for the purpose of safeguarding their rights or interests. Trade remedies constitute an attempt to redress an injurious act by a Member State's own action rather than through the WTO multilateral (quasi) judicial process. However, they differ substantially from classical forms of countermeasures as they allow States to react against lawful but injurious acts committed by private firms.

Drawing from the studies of these scholars and the analysis of fragmentation theories, the second part of the book analyses whether WTO trade remedies may be considered as a modern sub-set of self-help. It then searches whether and to what extent new theories on reactions of States against non-State actors as well as general principles of international law applicable to self-help measures (proportionality, discretion, reversibility, temporary character, etc.) are incorporated into WTO relevant agreements or can be used to promote their reforms.

The book attempts to demonstrate the interrelation between public international law and WTO law by enlightening their reciprocal influence. It also shows that their coherent application would contribute to achieve WTO objectives. As underlined by the former WTO Director-General Lamy, the WTO is both a product and a vehicle of the evolution of international law. The WTO does not only comply with general international law but adapts it to the realities of international trade. This proves that the modern and old international legal systems are strictly interlinked and do not preclude each other. The latter, more than prevailing over the former, completes and fulfils the shortcomings of the old system and improves and adapts it to the needs and challenges of the modern international community.

It is the opinion of the author that analysing and defining the legal nature of trade remedies could be of utmost importance for their teleological interpretation and their reform. The study of their aims, principles and characteristics underlines that particular aspects of the rules currently in force could provide WTO Members with instruments that look more like protectionist measures than reactions for the injury suffered. Reforming trade remedies in such a way to reduce the possibility to create unnecessary or disproportionate barriers to trade is important to guarantee the effective functioning of free trade. The comparative analysis with other forms of self-help will provide new arguments for theories aimed at reforming trade remedies and reducing their possible misuse which is in conflict with the purposes of the WTO.

This book offers a different point of view to reflect upon the possible amendments of trade remedies with the aim to eliminate their possible misuse and enact new rules which better reflect their role of reactions of injured States. It does not merely focus on the technical aspects of the relevant WTO agreements but analyse them in the light of fragmentation theories and the need for increased coherence in international law.

1 Unilateral reactions within the multilateral WTO context

The case of WTO trade remedies

1.1. Introduction

Before analysing the role and place of WTO trade remedies in the international legal order, it is of utmost importance to broadly describe the history and evolution of self-help and unilateral reactions in international law. Such an approach will contribute to highlight the role of international law in limiting unilateralism in international relations.

Since the end of World War II, the international community has undergone significant changes. New players such as international organizations, non-governmental organizations, multinational enterprises as well as groups and individuals have played a more active role in the new scenario of our 'global society'. States are no longer the only participants in the international community. Furthermore, interdependence among national economies and politics has increased intensively and States understand that 'the flutter of a butterfly's wings in China could, in fact, actually effect weather patterns in New York City, thousands of miles away'.

Such a modification of the international community has affected international relations and their legal framework and has led States to work together to find global solutions to global problems. As international players have got closer, unilateral actions and reactions have been replaced by multilateral efforts to avoid unilateral measures that could alter the equilibrium of the modern society and spread domino effects worldwide. However, in the field of WTO law, some forms of unilateralism still exist. These exceptions to the WTO multilateral approach are strictly limited and regulated by the WTO system. WTO rules limit the policy space of States to act and react unilaterally to protect their own interests.

1.2. Limiting unilateralism in international relations: from coexistence through cooperation towards a global community

Since the end of World War II, the international community has undergone significant changes. From a system primary based on individualism, force and wars, States created international organizations and decided to cooperate to achieve common ends.

States act daily on a unilateral basis and their acts produce effects, positive or negative, on other States and individuals. On the one hand, such unilateralism entails the influence of powerful States over smaller States, the imposition of policies and values and actions and reactions to defend or support own rights and interests. According to Sands, what is considered 'unilateral' is the action or the reaction which intrudes upon the interest of third persons to an inappropriate extent.[1] On the other hand, unilateralism has also positive effects in international law as it might ensure its enforcement in the absence of an effective sanctioning system. For the purpose of this study, unilateralism is considered as a form of reaction of States to defend their own rights and interests.

Cooperation and unilateralism have diverging objectives. As professor Dupuy noted,

> a little as in football the state regarded as guilty of unilateralism is the one that does not play the collective game; the one that 'plays personally'; in short, the one that puts the triumph of its interests before that of the collective interest, without even speaking of the 'common good'.[2]

Cooperation has been the main objective of the evolution of international community and its legal system in the last centuries and was originally aimed at maintaining peace. It is probably one of the pillars of the modern idea of the international legal system as it is recognized in the UN Charter and several other binding and non-binding instruments[3] to the extent that scholars considered it as the essence of contemporary international law.[4]

The transformation of international relations from bilateral to multilateral during the last century is one of the main reasons why cooperation prevailed over unilateralism. Historically, State relationships before 1945 were mainly regulated through normal diplomatic channels in the form of treaties. They provided bilateral rules by which States generally agreed to recognize reciprocal rights and duties and ensured peaceful coexistence among themselves.[5] As society expanded and the links between States strengthened, international relations followed similar trends and responded to the needs of States to overcome eventual impasses caused by

1 Philippe Sands, '"Unilateralism", Values, and International Law' (2000) 11.1 *European Journal of International Law* 291, 292.
2 Pierre Marie Dupuy, 'The Place and Role of Unilateralism in Contemporary International Law' 11.1. (2000) *European Journal of International Law* 19.
3 UN General Assembly, Declaration of Principles of International Law Concerning Friendly Relations and Co-operation Among States in Accordance with the Charter of the United Nations, 24 October 1970.
4 According to Dupuy, it is the Alpha and Omega of the United Nations law and more in general of international law. Respectively, in Dupuy, 'The Place and Role of Unilateralism in Contemporary International Law' (n. 2) 23. See also, Wolfgang Friedmann, *The Changing Structure of International Law* (Columbia University Press 1964).
5 Clive Archer, *International Organizations* (Routledge 2001) 10.

bilateralism. This was part of a greater idea based on which States should cooperate with each other within an institutionalized framework.[6]

A first step towards this direction was made through the founding of the League of Nations.[7] Following the end of World War I, the United States, *in primis*, pushed for the creation of a permanent worldwide organization aimed at maintaining international peace and security through efficient and legally binding safeguards. One of Wilson's 14 points was related to the creation of an international organization which should have constituted a centralized authority dedicated to achieving the 'grand design' of perpetual peace.[8] In Wilson's opinion, States had to create a *forum* where they could discuss and find solutions to their problems through peaceful means. Despite its very ambitious aims, the League of Nations faced limitations in its structure and political, economic and military discrepancies among participating countries that couldn't stop the decline of international relations leading the world into another dark period of conflict. As pointed out by Cede, 'the longing for peace and the prohibition of war as a means of international politics, although revolutionizing the minds, were not decisive by themselves'.[9] The maintenance of peace required States to make real efforts to cooperate with each other in order to achieve common goals and avoid conflicts among themselves.[10]

However, in the inter-wars period, unilateralism in its broadest terms prevailed over multilateralism and cooperation and the interests of individual countries took

6 International Organizations were created in the nineteenth century. The first two International Organizations were the International Telegraph Union (1865) and the International Postal Union (1874). However, many scholars recognized that International Organizations are phenomena of the twentieth century. On International Organizations, see generally, Pitman B. Potter, *Introduction to the Study of International Organization* (The Century 1922); Paul Reuter, *Institutions Internationales* (Presses Universitaires de France 1969); Riccardo Monaco, *Scritti di diritto delle organizzazioni internazionali* (Giuffrè 1981); Derek W. Bowett, *The Law of International Institutions* (Sweet & Maxwell 1982); Clause A. Colliard, *Institutions des relations internationales* (Dalloz 1985); Clive Archer, *International Organizations* (Routledge 2001); Jan Klabbers, *An Introduction to International Institutional Law* (Cambridge University Press 2002).

7 On the League of Nations, see, for example, Frederick Pollock, *The League of Nations* (Stevens and Sons 1929 reprinted 2003); Willem Rappard, 'Vues rétrospectives sur la Societé des Nations' (1947) 71 *Recueil des Cours de l'Académie de Droit International de La Haye* 111–225; Charles Howard-Ellis, *The Origin Structure & Working of the League of Nations* (The Lawbook Exchange 2003); William H. Taft, *Taft Papers on League of Nations* (Ohio University Press 2004).

8 Felix Morley, *The Society of Nations – Its Organization and Constitutional Development* (The Brookings Institution 1932) 3.

9 Franz Cede, 'Historical Introduction', in Franz Cede and Lilly Sucharipa-Behrmann (eds.), *The United Nations: Law and Practice* (Martinus Nijhoff Publishers 2001) 4; Benedetto Conforti, *The Law and Practice of the United Nations* (Martinus Nijhoff Publishers 2005) 1–6.

10 According to Reinalda and Veerbeek, this is the approach followed by functionalism and neo functionalism theories. Bob Reinalda and Bertjan Verbeek, *Autonomous Policy Making by International Organizations* (Routledge 1998) 12.

over common interests. The start of World War II revealed the weaknesses of an international system which allowed States to act autonomously and independently in political, economic and military fields. This was exactly the opposite of what John Maynard Keynes stated in 1919. In Keynes' opinion, the world needed a new system of international relations which would favour a global advantage and preclude the isolationism and protectionism that had been adopted by States in the period between the two wars.[11]

Although the League of Nations failed in its goals, it represented an experience of infinite value for the creation of the United Nations. The idea of a global organization itself, the creation of the International Labour Organization and the Permanent Court of International Justice were examples of a form of cooperation among States that enabled countries to discuss, address and solve regional or widespread problems which could undermine the common purpose of maintaining peace and security. As remarked by eminent scholars, the institutionalized organization of the cooperation among States was not in a complete rupture with previous systems of international relations but it improved and evolved international cooperation itself.[12] The League of Nations did not want to transform international relations but develop them to achieve further integration among States.[13] The outstanding lesson from the inter-wars period was that countries 'cannot merely stand together, in a kind of negative passivism, but they must make real efforts to achieve common purposes'.[14]

At the end of World War II, global political and economic interdependence was high and the demand for future security and stability was expressed by all the participants in the conflict. A cooperative effort was necessary to end the war and it was clear even before the conclusion of the conflict that the management of peace afterwards had to rely on cooperation.[15] In addition to enhancing relations among States, cooperation discourages States from acting unilaterally to pursue their advantages in disregard of the interests of other States. In line with these new theories, the founding of the United Nations marked an important stepping stone

11 John M. Keynes, *The Economic Consequences of the Peace* (MacMillan 1919 reprinted 1971) chapter II.

12 Mario Giuliano, Tullio Scovazzi and Tullio Treves, *Diritto internazionale, parte generale* (Giuffrè 2005) 117. See also: Akira Iriye, *Global Community: The Role of International Organizations in the Making of the Contemporary World* (University of California Press 2002) 10.

13 By citing Sir Alfred Zimmern, Goodrich reported that: '[T]he League of Nations was never intended to be, nor is it, a revolutionary organization. On the contrary, it accepts the world of states as it finds it and merely seeks to provide a more satisfactory means for carrying on some of the business which these states transact between one another. It is not even revolutionary in the more limited sense of revolutionizing the methods for carrying on interstate business. It does not supersede the older methods. It merely supplements them'. Leland M. Goodrich, 'From League of Nations to United Nations' (1947) 1.1 *International Organizations* 3, 5 citing Alfred Zimmern, *The League of Nations and the Rule of Law* (MacMillan 1936) 4.

14 Arthur Sweetser, 'The Framework of Peace', in Harriet Eager Davis (ed.), *Pioneers in World Order: An American Appraisal of the League of Nations* (Ayer Publishing 1970) 9.

15 Cede (n. 9) 6.

in the history of international relations through the creation of a permanent organization with universal character that had to ensure a system of collective security and a forum for international cooperation.[16]

Since then, international relations took place prevalently within an organized context and multilateral fora took over bilateral and plurilateral relations.[17] International organizations were perceived as the best means to make States cooperate with each other in order to achieve common ends.[18] As stated by Peter Sutherland, 'the most important means available to secure peace and prosperity into the future is to develop effective multilateral approaches and institutions'.[19] This form of multilateralism has been defined by Ruggie as 'an institutional form that coordinates relations among three or more states on the basis of generalized principle of conduct'. This system 'urges the governments to cooperate, to be in constant communication, to enforce the consistent, agreed upon international regulations and to take into consideration the effects of their policies on other states'.[20] As Vicuña underlined, such changes in international society during the past century have established 'a pattern of evolution from the traditional forms of interstate relations to an increasingly institutionalized community of nations'.[21]

In the past decades, the form of multilateralism described above has been challenged by new economic theories, technological developments and political events that have modified the structure of the international community. The fall of the Socialist countries, the decolonization process, the growing importance of new industrialized countries such as Brazil, South Africa, India and China, internet, new technologies and means of transport have challenged at the basis the

16 *Ibid.*

17 Robert S. Jordan, *International Organizations: A Comparative Approach to the Management of Cooperation* (Greenwood Publishing Group 2001) 26.

18 The US had a leading role in establishing international organizations such as the UN and NATO. According to Tudorache, from a US perspective multilateralism had some advantages such as a shared responsibility in maintaining peace and security, good cooperation for economic development, ensuring common defence and sharing of information among States. Ioan Tudorache, 'Multilateralism and the Maintenance of International Peace and Security' (2003) 9.2 *Romanian Journal of International Affairs* 89. See also, Rosemary Foot, S. Neil MacFarlane and Michael Mastanduno, *US Hegemony and International Organizations: The United States and Multilateral Institutions* (Oxford University Press 2003).

19 Peter D. Sutherland, 'Beyond the Market a Different Kind of Equity' *International Herald Tribune* (New York, 20 February 1997).

20 John Gerard Ruggie, 'Multilateralism the Anatomy of an Institution' (1992) 46.3 *International Organizations* 561. See also Blum who stated: 'when collaboration is required among a large number of states, multilateral regimes help states to cooperate effectively by increasing incentives for compliance, reducing fears of defection by others, and generally overcoming collective action problems'. Gabriella Blum, 'Bilateralism, Multilateralism, and the Architecture of International Law' (2008) 49.2 *Harvard International Law Journal* 356.

21 Francisco Orrego Vicuña, *International Dispute Settlement in an Evolving Global Society – Constitutionalization, Accessibility, Privatization* (Cambridge University Press 2004) 1.

international community.[22] Professor Jackson underlines that the terrorist attacks on 11 September 2001 seem to have created an 'international relations atmosphere that demands greater international cooperation. Perhaps, some might say, this is a wakeup call to nations that might otherwise be tempted to indulge in unilateral measures without consideration of impacts on foreign societies'.[23] New players such as non-governmental organizations, multinational enterprises as well as groups and individuals have a more active role in the new scenario of our 'global society'. States are no longer the only participants in the international community.

This modification of the international community has affected international relations and their legal framework. In fact, States and other entities should work together to find global solutions to global problems. Most of the pressing problems linked to the protection of the environment, terrorist attacks, immigration and human rights policies have obtained a global dimension. For example, the credit crunch in the United States caused unemployment in Europe and contributed to the food crisis in Africa. Similarly, the failures of States in former Yugoslavia caused immigration in Europe. Yet, wars in Iraq, Libya and Syria raised the price of oil around the world. In such an interdependent community, global problems require global solutions and global institutions and the place for unilateralism is even more limited.[24] Unilateralism simply cannot achieve global aims and the actual form of multilateralism requires a deeper and active involvement of the 'global community'.[25]

As noted by Iriye, the term global community is based upon a 'global consciousness, the idea that there is a wider world over and above separate states and national societies, and that individuals and groups, no matter where they are, share certain interests and concerns in that wider world'.[26] In the absence of

22 See in general, Antonio Cassese, *International Law in a Divided World* (Clarendon Press 1986).

23 John H Jackson, 'Perception about the WTO Trade Institution' (2002) 1.1 *World Trade Review* 103.

24 Jackson pointed out that globalization 'connotes conditions of interdependence in world economy and political relationship, which means that events and circumstances in one part of the world can have remarkably large and often swift effects in other distant parts of the world'. John H Jackson, *Sovereignty, the WTO and Changing Fundamentals of International Law* (Cambridge University Press 2006) 8. See also, Peter Van den Bossche and Iveta Alexovi⊠ová, 'Effective Global Economic Governance by the World Trade Organization' (2005) 8.3 *Journal of International Economic Law* 667.

25 See generally, Malcolm Waters, *Globalization* (Routledge 2001); Dani Rodrik, *Has Globalization Gone Too Far?* (Peterson Institute 1997); Jagdish N. Bhagwati, *In Defense of Globalization* (Oxford University Press 2007); Bob Milward, *Globalisation? Internationalisation and Monopoly Capitalism. Historical Processes and Capitalist Dynamism* (Edward Elgar Publishing 2003).

26 According to Iriye such a global consciousness should be termed internationalism, the idea that 'nations and peoples should cooperate instead of preoccupying themselves with their respective national interests or pursuing uncoordinated approaches to promote them'. Iriye (n. 12) 10.

global government, global governance manages global processes.[27] The question that should be answered is whether or not current institutions can be the backbone of this new global society. Are they prepared to face the new challenges? As remarked by Kofi Annan, '[o]ur post-war institutions were built for an international world, but now we live in a global world'.[28] Global society needs global governance and global rules.[29] Current structures and laws are often limited to particular aspects of international cooperation. They are purposed to address specific challenges within specific fields.

In a global society there is a need for a global approach. Rules and policies developed within the framework of trade and financial institutions cannot be addressed, for example, without taking into consideration their impact on environmental or development policies that are managed by different organizations. Such a fragmented universe of international cooperation hampers the international community to act globally. Many scholars underlined the need for 'a new accountable and proper structure to cope with globalization'.[30] The international community is faced with the new challenge to create common structures and policies to address different problems under a common framework. Thus, no longer individual States to act autonomously but a global community that acts with a global mind.

1.3. The evolving idea of cooperation in the international economic context

International economic and financial cooperation was not excluded from the trend briefly described above.[31] Despite the fact that the United Nations was considered as a global international organization, the number of matters on which the new

27 Rosenau used the term 'governance' to 'denote the regulation of interdependent relations in the absence of overarching political authority, such as in the international system. Some now speak of the development of 'global public policy'. James N. Rosenau, 'Toward an Ontology for Global Governance', in Martin Hewson and Timothy J. Sinclair (eds.), *Approaches to Global Governance Theory* (Suny Press 1999) 45.

28 The Secretary-General's Millennium Report cited in Jackson, *Sovereignty, the WTO* (n. 24) 60.

29 Gordon Brown stated 'and if we learn from our experience of turning unity of purpose into unity of action, together we can seize this moment of profound change to create, for the first time, the age of the truly global society, one where progressive multilateralism, not narrow unilateralism, is the norm'. Gordon Brown, *The Change We Choose: Speeches 2007–2009* (Random House 2011). See also, Giuliana Ziccardi Capaldo, 'The Law of the Global Community: An Integrated System to Enforce "Public" International Law', in Giuliana Ziccardi Capaldo (ed.), *The Global Community. Yearbook of International Law and Jurisprudence 2001* (Oceana Publications/ Oxford University Press, vol. 1, 2001) 71–120. Giuliana Ziccardi Capaldo, *The Pillars of Global Law* (Ashgate 2008).

30 David Held, Anthony McGrew, David Goldblatt and Jonathan Perrathon, *Global Transformations* (Polity Press 1999) 180.

31 Emile-Robert Perrin, *Les grand problème internationaux* (Masson 1995) 94.

organization had to deal with and the technicality of many of those issues effectively required the creation of specialized institutions.[32] Many UN agencies or international organizations (under or outside the umbrella of the UN) were created in specific fields of international relations.[33]

In the economic and financial fields, States recognized the need for international institutions to prevent *beggar-thy-neighbour* policies that had been 'so disastrous to world trade and economics during the interwar period and which, in the minds of many leaders, were responsible to a great degree for World War II itself'.[34] According to Krueger, 'to their enormous credit, the founders of the post-war international economic system knew, and understood, the importance of multilateralism'. In fact, they did not merely knew it in theory, 'but they also knew it because they had all experienced the enormous cost of individual actions taken outside a multilateral framework in the 1930s'.[35]

In the nineteenth century, free trade ideas inspired trade policies. Under those theories States abandoned mercantilist approaches and reduced their import tariffs and other trade barriers in order to maximize the gain of trade. *Laissez faire, laissez passer* was thus the 'motto' which characterized trade policies until 1870s.[36] However, free trade theories usually reveal their weaknesses in periods of crises when States easily take cover in protectionism; for example, in 1870, in 1919 and also in 2009 during the recent financial crisis.

32 Rosenne stated that 'in the twentieth, especially since 1945, this phenomenon has taken on an entirely new character, exemplified in the notion of a specialized agency set out in Article 57 of the Charter and agencies established by intergovernmental agreement having wide international responsibilities, as defined in their basic instruments, in economic, social, cultural, educational, health and related fields'. Shabtai Rosenne, *The Perplexities of Modern International Law* (Martinus Nijhoff Publishers 2004) 250.

33 Examples of specialized agencies of the UN are: the Food and Agriculture Organization (FAO), the Educational, Scientific and Cultural Organization (UNESCO), the World Health Organization (WHO) and the World Metereological Organization (WMO).

34 John Jackson, *World Trade and the Law of GATT* (Bobbs-Merrill 1969) 159.

35 Anne O Krueger, 'An Enduring Need: The Importance of Multilateralism in the 21st Century' (Singapore, September 19, 2006) available at: http://www.imf.org/external/np/speeches/2006/091906a.htm (accessed 30 November 2017).

36 Cottier and Oesch reported that 'international trade has a long history. It dates back a long time and substantially contributed to political and cultural developments in different eras. [T]he process has by no means been linear and homogeneous but accompanied by struggle and cycles, and trade policy ever since has navigated by between liberalism and mercantilism in its different forms. Like today it was dominated by diverging interests. Foremost, it shows that eras of free trade were the exception rather than the rule or even a natural principle'. Thomas Cottier and Matthias Oesch, *International Trade Regulation: Law and Policy in the WTO, the European Union and Switzerland. Cases, Materials and Comments* (Stämpfli Publishers 2005) 9. For a deeper analysis on trade policies since nineteenth century see, e.g., Paul Bairoch, *Economics and World History: Myths and Paradoxes* (University of Chicago Press 1993); Raj Bhala, 'Assessing the Modern Era of International Trade' (1998) 21.4 *Fordham International Law Journal* 1647.

Following the Great Depression, World War I disrupted international trade relationships and unsettled frictions among States after the war did not help the recovery of international trade. The limitations and weak efforts of the League of Nations could not prevent the adoption of protectionist measures. A typical example of this era is the 1930 Hawley-Smoot Tariffs Act by which the United States raised average tariffs by 51 per cent. Following the adoption of the mentioned act more than 60 nations retaliated against Washington.[37]

Similar disruptions in international economic relations have often been considered as the main causes of disputes between States. In addition to the import restrictive measures taken by the US after 1929 as a response to the Great Depression, the high burden of the reparation policies of the Versailles treaty toward Germany, the autarky period in Italy and many other protectionist measures enacted in the inter-wars period have often been blamed for leading States to World War II.[38] History demonstrated that when nations are left free to pursue their economic objectives without limitations, they could intervene in the market by raising import tariffs, imposing quotas or modifying exchange rates that could affect international trade and, more in general, international relations.

When the World War II came to end, States decided to build international economic and financial institutions and rules which could prevent a new race to the dark bottom of protectionism.[39] In the mind of the winning States, the new economic order had to be inspired by a new form of free trade which should be guaranteed by rules and by international institutions as the benefits of liberal theories can only occur if liberalism is practiced by all nations.[40] Following such theories, States created a multilateral system in which they were obliged to abstain

37 Joseph M. Jones, *Tariff Retaliation: Repercussion of the Hawley-Smoot Bill* (University of Pennsylvania Press, 1934); Charles Kindleberger, 'Commercial Policy Between the Wars', in Peter Mathias and Sydney Pollard (eds.), *The Industrial Economies: The Development of Economic and Social Policies: The Cambridge Economic History of Europe* (Cambridge University Press, Vol. III, 1989) 161; Bruce E. Moon, *Dilemmas of International Trade* (Westview Press 2000).

38 In 1944, Howkins stated that 'trade conflict breeds non-cooperation, suspicion, bitterness. Nations which are economic enemies are not likely to remain political friends for long', cited in Cottier and Oesch (n. 36) 1. See also, Jackson, *Sovereignty, the WTO* (n. 24) 91; Richard N. Cooper, 'Trade Policy as Foreign Policy', in Robert M. Stern (ed.), *US Trade Policy in a Changing World Economy* (MIT Press 1987) 291 and Frederic E. Emery, 'Economic Conflicts in Relation to War', in Victor H. Wallace (ed.), *Paths to Peace: A Study of War, Its Causes and Prevention* (Ayer Publishing 1957) 40.

39 In 1941, the US Undersecretary of State Sumner Wells stated: 'Nations have more often than not undertaken economic discriminations and raised up trade barriers with complete disregard for the damaging effects on the trade and livelihood of other peoples, and ironically enough, with similar disregard for the harmful resultant effects upon their own export trade. The resultant misery, bewilderment, and resentment, together with other equally pernicious contributing causes, paved the way for the rise of those very dictatorships which have plunged almost the entire world into war'. Sumner Wells, *Post-War Commercial Policy*, US Department of State Pub. No. 1660, Commercial Policy Series 71 (1941), cited in Jackson, *World Trade and the Law of GATT* (n. 34) 38.

40 Moon (n. 37) 80.

from adopting mercantilist measures. The new international economic order imposed specific behaviour on States and limited their policy space. Reciprocal control within international institutions could ensure that liberalism would prevail over protectionism as States were aware that their previous inclinations to mercantilist theories were to be disregarded. As Bruce pointed out, 'they were frightened into constructing an international trade system built more upon multilateral liberalism than unilateral mercantilism'.[41]

In line with the general idea of cooperation among States within an institutionalized framework, States led by the United States and Great Britain planned to create new international organizations in charge of economic and financial matters. In the mind of the leaders, it was necessary to conclude international arrangements which would reflect the realities of economic interdependence.[42]

When representatives of States met in Bretton Woods in 1944, they agreed to create a cluster of international organizations and to draft agreements which should provide the framework for international economic relations.[43] For their founding fathers, the International Monetary Fund,[44] the World Bank[45] and the General Agreement on Tariffs and Trade (GATT)[46] had to provide States with the necessary financial resources to restore their economies after years of war and with new rules to prevent States from having recourse to protectionism.[47]

41 *Ibid.*

42 John G. Merrills, *International Dispute Settlement* (Cambridge University Press 1998) 197.

43 *Ibid.* See also: John H. Jackson, 'Reflections on Problems of International Economic Relations', in Michael Young and Yuji Iwasawa (eds.), *Trilateral Perspectives on International Legal Issues* (Transnational Publishers 1996) 263.

44 Hans Aufricht, *The International Monetary Fund: Legal Bases, Structure, Functions* (Stevens and Sons 1964); Keith Horsefield, *The International Monetary Fund 1945–1965: Twenty Years of Monetary Cooperation* (International Monetary Fund 1969); James Boughton and Sarwar Lateef, *Fifty Years After Bretton Woods: The Future of the IMF and the World Bank* (International Monetary Fund and World Bank 1994).

45 For a deeper analysis on the World Bank, see Edward S. Mason and Robert Asher, *The World Bank Since Bretton Woods* (Brookings Institution Press 1973); Michelle Miller-Adams, *The World Bank: New Agendas in a Changing World* (Routledge 1999).

46 The GATT was supposed to be a temporary agreement that had to be replaced by the more comprehensive Havana Charter. Because the point of the new international law was to Americanize, the United States, from its own perspective, did not really need international law (being already American). 'Accordingly, we would lead the world in creating a new international legal order to which we ourselves never fully acceded. The new international institutions would be for the rest of the world, not really for us, and certainly not superior in authority to our own legal system. As a result, in the ensuing decades, the United states frequently found itself championing international law for other countries, while rejecting or resisting it for itself'. Jed Rubenfeld, 'Unilateralism and Constitutionalism' (2004) 79.6 *New York University Law Review* 1971, 1974.

47 The main founding fathers of the Bretton Woods system were: John Maynard Keynes, Harry Dexter White, Sir Percivale Liesching, James Meade, Lionel Robbins, Myron Taylor, Dean Acheson and Harry Hawkins. Richard N. Gardner, 'Balance Sheet of Success and Failure', in Orin Kirshner (ed.), *The Bretton Woods – GATT System, Retrospect and Prospect after Fifty Years* (Sharpe Armonk reprinted in 1994) 621. For socialist authors the Bretton Woods system was also aimed at avoiding the spreading

It cannot be denied that, to a great extent, contemporary international economic interdependence can be attributed to the Bretton Woods ideas which resisted over more than 50 years.[48] However, globalization is threatening the current international economic structure. The credit crunch in the United States, the Asian crisis in 1998, the increase in living standards and food demand in faster growing economies such as China and India, the decision of the OPEC countries to reduce the quantity of petrol, etc. rapidly spread their effects all over the globe. Unilateral policy decisions in one country would trigger a domino effect worldwide as domestic economies are deeply interlinked and are parts of the same global system. Therefore, international rules and institutions should be modernized to be able to provide solutions to new global challenges.

1.4. The WTO and the financial crisis

At the end of 2008, the world dropped into a profound financial and economic crisis. In many countries around the globe stock markets have fallen, financial institutions have collapsed and governments have adopted rescue packages to bail out their financial systems. At the time of writing this book, domestic economies and international trade have not recovered completely from the crisis and several of the so called 'developed' countries are facing risk of defaults due to their huge sovereign debts.[49]

The financial turmoil has been an interesting stress test for international economic rules and international economic organizations. It offered a chance to analyse the role and effectiveness of international economic law and institutions. Since the start of the crisis, governments have adopted several trade and financial measures to counter the negative effect of the crisis which might hide protectionist intents. As the case of Argentina demonstrated in 2002, in periods of crisis countries may more easily be found in breach of trade and investment treaty obligations.

The financial turmoil has challenged the functioning and usefulness of international organizations to provide prompt and effective responses to crises. The 'Bretton Woods institutions' have often been criticized for not having provided solutions to current economic troubles. The World Trade Organization has been

of communism around the world. See for example, Jeremy Brecher and Tim Costello, *Contro il capitale globale: strategie di resistenza* (Feltrinelli 2002) 64. Meier underlined that 'the Fund, the Bank and the GATT were designed to help advanced industrial countries achieve the multiple objectives of full employment, freer and expanding trade, and stable exchange rate'. Gerald M. Meier, 'The Bretton Woods Agreement – 25 Years After' (1971) 39.2 *Stanford Law Review* 235.

48 John H. Jackson, William J. Davey and Allan O. Sykes, *Legal Problems of International Economic Relations: Cases, Materials and Text* (West Group 2002).

49 This paragraph is based on Roberto Soprano, 'Towards a New Bretton Woods? The Financial Crisis, the Doha Round and the Future of the WTO', in Maria Chiara Malaguti, Biagio Bossone and Susanna Cafaro (eds.), *Legitimacy and Effectiveness in Global Economic Governance* (Cambridge Scholar Publishing 2013) 107.

put under scrutiny as its rules should limit States from adopting protectionist measures.

The analysis of the amount and type of trade measures adopted by States since October 2008 provides the opportunity to evaluate whether or not international economic rules had a positive role in limiting the protectionist willingness of governments and to reflect about possible changes of the WTO system. By analysing the type and amount of measures adopted by WTO Members, it seems that WTO contributed to keep markets open even under the stress of the financial crisis. Obviously, it is not possible to assert that all the measures adopted are WTO compliant without a deep case by case evaluation but it seems that Member States have not had recourse to wide economic barriers as in 1929 and used trade policies and instruments within the boundaries set by WTO. WTO covered agreements have contributed to increased legal stability of economic and trading relations.

The financial crisis has put more emphasis on the role of the WTO as an international organization whose primary function, in broad terms, is to provide the common institutional framework for the conduct of trade relations among its Members.[50] The WTO has different functions listed in the Article III of the WTO Agreement: (1) It shall facilitate the implementation, administration and operation, and further the objectives of the WTO agreements; (2) provide a forum for negotiations; (3) administer the Dispute Settlement System and (4) the Trade Policy Review Mechanism and (5) cooperate with other institutions to achieve greater coherence in global economic policy-making. Apart from the first function, which is hampered by the very limited powers of the WTO to adopt legally binding acts, the financial crisis has underlined the relevance of the other mentioned functions to preserve trade openness.

The WTO Director-General has repeatedly stressed the importance of concluding the Doha Round and invited Member States to resume and conclude talks. This is important for speeding the recovery of national economies and in particular as a message of reassurance for world financial markets. Concluding the Doha Round would likely have a positive economic and 'moral' impact. By agreeing on a final text, countries would give a positive message to the markets reaffirming their intentions to overtake the crisis and their willingness to open up their market.

The WTO lost a chance to become a forum for discussion for the civil society.[51] Since the crisis began, the WTO hosted a global forum on the crisis and gave

50 Article II of the Agreement Establishing the WTO. See also, Peter Van den Bossche, *The Law and Policy of the World Trade Organization: Text, Cases and Materials* (Cambridge University Press 2005) 88.

51 Peter Van den Bossche, 'NGOs Involvement in the WTO: A Comparative Perspective' (2008) 11.4 *Journal of International Economic Law* 717; Mara Blue Jeffords, 'Turning the Protestor into a Partner for Development: The Need for Effective Consultation between the WTO and NGOs' (2003) 28 *Brooklyn Journal of International Law* 937 and Seema Sapra, 'The WTO System of Trade Governance: The Stale NGO Debate and the Appropriate Role for Non-state Actors' (2009) 11 *Oregon Review of International Law* 71.

participants the possibility to present their opinions on the role of trade and the financial turmoil.[52] However, apart from this sporadic event, greater openness to NGOs and the general public still remains an issue of concern for the WTO. Since the Ministerial Conference in Seattle the civil society has paid much more attention to WTO issues due to the intrusiveness of WTO in our lives and the highly sensitive topics discussed in Rue de Lausanne 154 for the entire world.[53]

The Trade Policy Review Mechanism (TPRM) increased vigilance during the crisis on all WTO Members as 'protectionist pressures remain and are being generated by stubbornly high levels of unemployment in many countries, persistent global imbalances, and macroeconomic concerns'.[54] The TPRM is mainly aimed at contributing

> to improved adherence by all Members to rules, disciplines and commitments made under the multilateral [and plurilateral] trade agreements [...] and hence the smoother functioning of the multilateral trading system, by achieving greater transparency in, and understanding of, the trade policies and practices of all Members.[55]

It is a good system of 'early warning and allows peer pressure to operate before problems evolve into disputes'.[56] Although the TPRM's main function is to increase transparency of countries' trade policies and not to assess their compliance with WTO law (which can only be done through the Dispute Settlement Mechanism), Member States increasingly used the TPRM to express their concerns over the increase in trade restrictions, and called on the WTO to continue with its regular trade monitoring reports. Since 2009, the WTO also started a very useful monitoring of the trade and trade-related measures adopted by WTO Members and observers, which became a regular function that further strengthens the transparency aims of the TPRM by providing comprehensive information on recent trade policy changes.[57] As for the cooperation with international

52 Global Problems, Global Solutions: Towards Better Global Governance (Geneva, 2009) http://www.wto.org/english/forums_e/public_forum09_e/public_forum09_e.htm (accessed 20 October 2017).

53 Cho observes that 'WTO's engagement and dialogue with NGOs and civil society is a double-edged sword: while it certainly enhances the WTO's legitimacy through nurturing transparency and promoting PRs, it may also strain the WTO's resources, distract the Secretariat from its main responsibilities, and even risk undermining the integrity of the WTO through unnecessary and even harmful over-politicization'. Sungjoon Cho, 'A Quest for WTO's Legitimacy' (2005) 4 *World Trade Review* 391.

54 Pascal Lamy Trade restrictions on the rise (21 June 2011) http://www.wto.org/english/news_e/sppl_e/sppl196_e.htm (accessed 20 October 2017).

55 Annex 3 of the Agreement Establishing the WTO, Trade Policy Review Mechanism, lit. A(i).

56 Cottier and Oesch, *International Trade Regulations* (n. 36) 194.

57 The monitoring exercise further strengthens the transparency aims of the Trade Policy Review Mechanism by providing information on recent policy changes. It is overseen by the Trade Policy Review Body (TPRB), which also conducts detailed reviews of Members individually. Five comprehensive reports on global trade developments in 2010 were prepared by the WTO Secretariat on behalf of the Director-General. Three

organizations with the view of achieving greater coherence, the Marrakesh Agreement establishing the WTO explicitly mentions the World Bank[58] and the IMF.[59] The relations with the IMF on exchange rates have acquired greater importance due to the recent monetary devaluations artificially adopted by some States to enhance domestic export.[60] As mentioned in the Coherence declaration, 'exchange rate stability, based on more orderly underlying economic and financial conditions, should contribute towards the expansion of trade, sustainable growth and development, and the correction of external imbalances'.[61] However, trade related aspects of monetary devaluations remain an issue out of the scope of the WTO rules as the agreement concluded by the WTO and the IMF cannot add or

of these reports, covering trade and investment measures taken by the Group of 20 (G-20) economies, were prepared jointly with the Secretariats of the Organization for Economic Cooperation and Development (OECD) and the United Nations Conference on Trade and Development (UNCTAD). The other two covered relevant measures taken by all WTO Members and observers and were discussed at TPRB meetings. The Director-General stressed at these meetings that the global crisis and the WTO's trade-monitoring exercise underlined the importance of increased transparency for the smooth functioning of the multilateral trading system. *WTO Annual Report* (2011) 78.

58 A good example is the strengthening of the WTO and World Bank (and other donors) relations within the Enhanced Integrated Framework (EIF) for aid for trade in order to achieve Millennium Development Goals. The EIF is the flagship of trade-related assistance programmes specifically dedicated to least developed countries (LDCs). It is an international partnership combining the efforts of the LDCs with those of the six core EIF agencies (the IMF, the International Trade Centre, UNCTAD, the United Nations Development Programme, the World Bank and the WTO), donors and other development partners (such as the United Nations Industrial Development Organization). The EIF sets out to respond to the trade capacity building needs of LDCs and enable them to become full and active players and beneficiaries of the multilateral trading system. Supported by the overarching principle of country ownership, the EIF is the principal mechanism LDCs can call upon to assist them in mapping out their trade priorities, mainstreaming trade into their national development strategies and presenting these to donor partners for funding and implementation. *Ibid.* at 109.

59 Decision adopted by the General Council at its meeting on 7, 8 and 13 November 1996; Agreements between the WTO and the IMF and the World Bank, Doc. WT/L/194, 18 November 1996. See also the negotiating mandate contained in the General Council Decision on the Relationship between the WTO and the IMF and World Bank, Doc. WT/GC/M/5; Declaration on the Contribution of the World Trade Organization to Achieving Greater Coherence in Global Economic Policymaking http://www.worldtradelaw.net/uragreements/coherencedecision.pdf (accessed 20 October 2017); and Marc Auboin, 'Fulfilling the Marrakesh Mandate on Coherence: Ten Years of Cooperation between the WTO, IMF and World Bank', Discussion paper 13, http://www.wto.org/english/res_e/booksp_e/discussion_papers13_e.pdf (accessed 20 October 2017).

60 Provisions referring to the manner in which contracting parties should behave when dealing with monetary issues and the IMF were already included in the GATT 1947, II.6 (a); VII.4 (a and b), XII:2 (a)(i), XII:3 (d), XIV:1, XIV:3, XIV:3, XIV:5 (a), XV:1, XV:2, XV:4, XV:7 (b), XV:8 and XV:9 (a). However, these provisions do not constitute an institutional structure linking the GATT 1947 and the IMF.

61 Coherence Declaration (n. 59) 40.

modify the rights and obligations of Member States under the WTO Agreements or the IMF commitments.[62] In addition, the WTO has often worked with other regional and international organizations including WIPO, WHO and FAO. With the financial crisis the WTO increased its synergies with other organizations such as UNCTAD and OECD to monitor the attitudes of States in using trade and investment measures.[63]

Last but not least, the WTO Director-General Pascal Lamy has been very active during the crisis and should not be considered as a 'mere spokesperson or market executive'.[64] He participated to several meetings and conferences with the aim of recalling to Member States the importance of respecting international trade commitments. He also set up monitoring and surveillance mechanism reports addressing the use of trade restrictive measures during the crisis, alone or jointly with other DGs of other international organizations.[65] Similarly, the WTO Secretariat, by monitoring trade policy measures enacted by Members in compliance with the principles of independency, impartiality and loyalty, had a more active role in contributing to foster the respect of WTO rules.[66]

The influence of the WTO Director-General's words, WTO studies and reports (as well as other reports prepared by other international, NGOs and Think Tanks)[67] that monitored the behaviour of the States during the crisis, contributed to enhance 'peer pressure' on WTO Members and so avoid a rapid escalation of the use of protectionist measures.

The crisis offered an opportunity to reflect about the role and functioning of WTO. The financial turmoil had offered an opportunity to transform the crisis into a chance to better the WTO. There is a need to update the WTO system by

62 Appellate Body Report, *Argentina – Footwear*, paras. 70–73.

63 WTO/UNCTAD/OECD, 'Report on G20 Trade and Investment Measures (April 2009 – August 2009)', http://www.unctad.org/en/docs/wto_oecd_unctad2009_en.pdf; WTO/UNCTAD/OECD, 'Report on G20 Trade and Investment Measures (September 2009 – February 2010)', available at: http://www.unctad.org// en/docs/wto_oecd_unctad2010d1_en.pdf (both accessed 20 October 2017).

64 Reports of the Consultative Board on the Future of the WTO, available at http://www.ipu.org/splz-e/wto-symp05/future_WTO.pdf (accessed 20 October 2011) 74. See also, WTO Secretariat, *Analytical Index: Guide to WTO Law & Practice* (Cambridge University Press, Vol. 2, 2007) 27.

65 Director-General of the World Trade Organization, 'Report to the TRPB from the Director-General on the Financial and Economic Crisis and Trade Related Developments', WT/TPR/OV/W/2 (15 July 2009).

66 Shaffer stated that 'there are reasons to favour enhancing an independent role for the WTO secretariat, at least incrementally. Yet significant checks on such a development remain on account of the WTO's more politically sensitive policy coverage, its more prominent public profile, and ongoing challenges to the legitimacy of its decisions'. Gregory C. Shaffer, 'The Role of the WTO Director-General and Secretariat' (2005) 4.3 *World Trade Review* 438 and Mary E. Footer, *An Institutional and Normative Analysis of the World Trade Organization* (Martinus Nijhoff Publishers 2006) 306.

67 See for example, the Global Trade Alert whose objective is to provide real-time information on state measures taken during the current global downturn that are likely to affect foreign commerce, and to identify the trading partners likely to be harmed by these measures, the EU Commission reports, or the Global Antidumping Database.

enabling it with needed powers to tackle the new challenges of global society. After a period of shock, it is time to reflect about the role of the WTO in the globalized era.[68]

1.5. Ubi societas ibi ius. The role of international economic law in the international society

As described by Wright, law is a bulk of policies, principles, rules and standards which reflect the society within they have been created. In his opinion, law and society reciprocally influence each other.[69] Similarly to any form of law, international law reflects the system in which it emerged. It is influenced by economic, philosophical as well as legal theories and should, in turn, influence the community and lead its subject towards the achievement of its purposes.[70] In that respect, international law played and continues to play an important role in building the international community and preserving peace and prosperity.[71]

68 Roberto Soprano, 'WTO and the Financial Crisis: What Lessons Should We Learn?' (2011) 12.1 *Journal of World Investment and Trade.*

69 Quincy Wright, *The Role of International Law in the Elimination of War* (Manchester University Press 1961) 31.

70 Minor summarised the evolution of a legal system as follows: 'In the first stages of every primitive society there is a period during which the laws protecting individual rights are vaguely defined and weakly enforced. Each man's ability to hold his own depends upon his strength or cunning or upon the alliances he can form with others for common protection. But as society becomes more stable and civilised, influences begin to work which materially improve the condition of mankind. A spirit of cooperation and of mutual aid and dependence takes the place of the former spirit of rapacity; common interests makes men more friendly; suspicion and distrust give way to mutual confidence; selfish ambition and cupidity yield more or less to an appreciation of the rights of others; and violence surrenders dominion to the gentler arts of reason and peace. What is the cause of this great change in the general attitude of men? It is the rise and development of law [...]'. Raleigh G. Minor, *A Republic of Nations: A Study of the Organization of a Federal League of Nations* (Oxford University Press 1918). Basic realist and neorealist theories believed that international relations started in a situation of international anarchy when States are self-interested and competitive actors. See also, Ruth B. Russel and Jeannette E. Muther, *A History of the United Nations Charter: The Role of the United States, 1940–1945* (Brookings Institution 1958); Clarck Eichelberger, *Organizing for Peace: A Personal History of the Founding of the United Nations* (Harper & Row 1977); Evan Luard, *A History of the United Nations* (Macmillan 1989); Stanley Meisler, *United Nations: The First Fifty Years* (Atlantic Monthly Press 1997) 1–20.

71 In 1943 Kelsen pointed out that: 'the next step on which our efforts must be concentrated is to bring about an international treaty concluded by as many as states as possible – victors as well as vanquished – establishing an international court with compulsory jurisdiction [...]. To eliminate war, the worst of all social evils, from interstate relations by establishing a compulsory jurisdiction, the juridical approach to an organization of the world must precede any other attempt at international reform. Among the two aspects of the post war problem, the economic and the legal, the latter has a certain priority over the former [...]. It is not true that war is the consequence of unsatisfactory economic condition; on the contrary, the unsatisfactory

During the last century international law has been subject to continuous modification in order to adapt to new challenges.[72] In fact, at the beginning of the twentieth century, international law was merely perceived as a rudimental instrument to regulate bilateral relations and designed to maintain peaceful coexistence among States.[73] In the international trade field, the years following the end of World War I were characterized by the absence of international discipline. The Treaty of Versailles and the League of Nations, 'failed to address economic issues, leaving trade policy and law to unilateralism and thus high risks of protectionism'.[74]

Drawing from new political theories developed after the end of World War II, States have strengthened the role of a 'rule oriented' system of international relations.[75] International rules became the backbone of international relations and at the same time supported the work of supra national institutions in achieving global results.[76] Such new theories had a positive impact on the proliferation of

situation of world economy is the consequence of war. If the history of the last thirty years has taught us anything, it is the primacy of politics over economics. Hence the elimination of war is our paramount problem. It is a problem of international policy and the most important means of international policy is international law'. Hans Kelsen, 'Compulsory Adjudication of International Disputes' (1943) 397.37 *American Journal of International Law* 397–398.

72 Malcolm N. Shaw, *International Law* (Cambridge University Press 2003) 27.

73 According to Shaw, International law in the twentieth century became Eurocentric and thus reflected European values. *Ibid.*

74 Cottier and Oesch, *International* (n. 36) 13.

75 For example: The four Geneva Treaties on the law of the sea (1958) replaced by the United Nations Convention on the Law of the Sea (1982); the Vienna Convention on the Law of Treaties (1968), the Vienna Convention on Diplomatic Relations (1961); Vienna Convention on Consular Relations (1963).

76 Rudiger Wolfrum, 'International Law of Cooperation', *Encyclopedia of Public International Law*, Vol. II (1995) 1242–1247. Bedjaoui goes further, underlining how international law evolved from a law of coordination to a law of finalities. According to the scholar, 'the democratization of the international legal order, which used to be – and remains – an objective itself, would be purposeless if it did not provide a means of putting the international legal order at the service of goals which address the needs of the human race. This is a matter involving the assessment of the priorities which the international community should set itself'. Mohammed Bedjaoui, *International Law: Achievements and Prospects* (Martinus Nijhoff Publishers 1991) 14. According to Malanczuk, 'the process of change in international law from a system of coordination of the international intercourse of mainly European states in limited areas, such as diplomatic relations and war, to a universal system of cooperation in numerous fields between quite different entities reflects the advances of natural sciences and technology, increasing global economic and political interdependence and the need to address problems which can no longer be properly dealt with within a national framework such as in the fields of communications, international trade, economics and finance, environment and development or the massive problem of refugee flows'. Peter Malanczuk, *Akehurst's Modern Introduction to International Law* (Routledge, seventh edition, 1997) 7. On the relationship between development in natural sciences and technology and the process of globalization see Manfred Lachs, 'Views from the Bench: Thoughts on Science, Technology and World Law' (1992) 86 *American*

international rules as many new treaties were concluded in this period and most of them were projected within international organizations.[77] This trend was further demonstrated by the creation of the International Law Commission (ILC) which was established by the United Nations General Assembly in 1948 for the 'promotion of the progressive development of international law and its codification'.[78] According to Lachs, it is in this period that the concept of 'international legal community' emerged.[79]

However, such a development of international law was not without any consequences. In particular, it has been considered as the main cause of the erosion of the Westphalian concept of sovereignty on which the whole classical international legal system was based. It could be argued that the Westphalian system has been taken over by changes, *rectius* developments in international law that have complicated the ability of States to exercise their sovereign authority.[80] In fact,

Journal of International Law 673; Held, McGrew, Goldblatt and Perrathon (n. 30) 170–171.

77 As Friedmann remarked, in the past century international law 'has developed from a structure of coordination to one of cooperation'. Wolfgang Friedmann, *The Changing Structure of International Law* (Columbia University Press 1964). McWinney stated that 'co-operation as an international law term emerged only after II World War'. Edward McWinney, 'The Concept of Co-Operation', in Bedjaoui (n.76), 425. Professor Vicuña pointed out that: In a cooperation system 'the attainment of common goals is more actively pursued'. Vicuña, *International Dispute Settlement in an Evolving Global Society* (n. 21) 1. Elias divided international law developments after World War II into three periods: 'from 1945 to 1960 which may be regarded as formative years in which the UN Organization was trying to find its feet, so to speak, and to map out a program of future action and experiment with a number of approaches to post-war problems; from 1960 to about 1969, in which the greatest developments concerned the phenomenal growth of new states and the preoccupation of the world body was the problem of self-determination of peoples and the battle against racial discrimination [...] and the period since 1970, often referred as the decade of development, especially regarding economic and social growth for the world community in general and the Third World in particular'. Taslim O. Elias, *New Horizons in International Law* (Martinus Nijhoff Publishers 1979) 4.

78 United Nations General Assembly, *Resolution* A-RES-174(II) (21 November 1947). See also United Nations Secretariat, *The Work of the International Law Commission* (United Nations Publications 2007).

79 Manfred Lachs, 'Legal Framework of an International Community' (1992) 6.2. *Emory International Law Review* 329. See also Herman Mosler, 'International Legal Community', *Encyclopaedia of Public International Law*, Vol. II (1995) 1251–1255.

80 Eric K. Leonard, *The Onset of Global Governance: International Relations Theory and the International Criminal Court* (Ashgate Publishing 2005) 163. Globalization is provoking an erosion of States' sovereignty. Although many scholars tried to define the concept of sovereignty without agreeing on a common definition it is quite recognized that globalization limits sovereignty of States and leads to a different perception of the concept of sovereignty in international law. According to Mahmud, 'L'état est ainsi amené à renoncer à sa qualité de souverain pour se transformer en un simple agent du processus de mondialization'. Salah M. Mahmud, 'Mondialisation et souveraineté de l' Etat' (1996) 123.3 *Journal de Droit International* 611, 620. For a deeper analysis on the concept of sovereignty see: Charles E. Merriam, *History of the Theory of Sovereignty since Rousseau* (Columbia University Press 1900); Paul Ward,

international cooperation requires States to be bound by rules and not to claim that sovereignty allows them to reject regulations.[81] Such new theories allow interventions within the boundaries of a sovereign State, to impose States to comply with international Courts rulings, to amend internal disciplines in conformity with international rules and request countries to abstain from taking unilateral actions and reactions. As a consequence, the erosion of the traditional Westphalian system led to deep modifications in the structure and purposes of international law. International rules, traditionally considered as instruments for coordinating sovereignties, have been invested with the task of transforming the international community and have been applied in the service of finalities such as peace, development, human happiness and the ecological preservation of the planet.[82]

In the field of international economic law,[83] rules were mainly codified and developed within the context of the Bretton Woods system but covered only a limited part of international economic relations.[84] While the IBRD (International Bank for

Sovereignty: A Study of a Contemporary Political Notion (George Routledge and Sons 1928); Eelco N. Van Kleffens, 'Sovereignty in International Law' (1953) 82 *Recueil des Cours de l'Académie de Droit International de La Haye* 5–131; Bertrand De Jouvenel, *De la souveraineté* (Génior 1955); Marek S. Korowicz, 'Some Present Aspects of Sovereignty in International Law' (1961) 102 *Recueil des Cours de l'Académie de Droit International de La Haye* 7–33 and Rolando Quadri, *Diritto internazionale pubblico* (Liguori 1968) 604; Jens Bartelson, *A Genealogy of Sovereignty* (Cambridge University Press, 1995).

81 Henry Schermers, 'Different Aspects of Sovereignty', in Gerald Kreijen *et al.* (eds.), *State Sovereignty and International Governance* (Oxford University Press 2001) 185. See also, Nerina Boschiero, 'Stato e sovranità nel diritto internazionale', in Bruno Montanari (ed.), *L'Europa e la cultura del postmoderno* (Luiss edizioni 2001) 29.

82 Bedjaoui (n. 76) 14.

83 Van den Bossche affirmed that 'international economic law can be defined, broadly, as covering all those international rules pertaining to economic transactions and relations as well as those pertaining to governmental regulation of economic matters'. Van den Bossche, *The Law and Policy of the World Trade Organization* (n. 50) 38.

84 After the foundation of the UN, trade negotiations were conducted within the framework of the UN Economic and Social Council (ECOSOC). In 1946 a resolution on the creation of the International Trade Organization (ITO) was adopted by the ECOSOC. Negotiations in Lake Success, New York, Geneva (1947) and Havana were held with the purpose of drafting an ITO charter, preparing a schedule of tariffs reductions and preparing a multilateral treaty containing general principles of trade the *General Agreement on Tariffs and Trade* (GATT). In order to bring the tariff cuts and the GATT into force without waiting for the final and more troublesome agreement on ITO, States adopted in 1947 the Protocol of Provisional Application of the General Agreement on Tariffs and Trade. With World War II only recently ended, States tried to boost trade liberalization, and began to correct the legacy of protectionist measures which remained in place from the early 1930s. The lack of support by the US and UK for the creation of ITO, which was supposed to be the third of the Bretton Wood institutions, opened the door wide to the provisory GATT. Although negotiators considered the text to be revised soon in order to comply with the ITO chart, the GATT regulated with few and general rules, the basis of international trade. Adopting a general principle of non-discrimination (MFN and national treatment), it

Reconstruction and Development) was more oriented to lending and reconstruction operations, the IMF provided few rules on currency devaluation and other monetary policies and the GATT the basic principles to regulate international trade. However, the GATT provided only few and not very specific rules to regulate international economic relationships, did not create an international organization and did not contain specific procedures for settling trade disputes. Only at a later time, in 1994, were new rules adopted. Some of them improved existing ones whereas others broke entirely new ground.[85] Other agreements instituted dispute settlement procedures to achieve peace and security but also social and economic objectives[86] as 'peace today should be grasped in all its aspects and must not be reduced simply to the idea of the absence of war'.[87]

Since then, international economics rules became 'a necessary precondition for the proper functioning of markets and for avoiding both market failures as well as government failures directly at their source'.[88] As Petersmann remarked, 'there is today worldwide consensus among economists and governments that liberal trade tends to enhance consumer welfare, individual freedom of choice, competition, efficiency, productivity, innovation and monetary stability'.[89]

In Van den Bossche's opinion, international economic rules are necessary in our society for four reasons.[90] First, States refrain from adopting trade restrictive measures, so they avoid using mercantilist approaches as they can be attracted to adopt trade restrictive measures to protect domestic industry from international competition. As Petersmann remarked, international law gives States a chance to resist the 'song of Sirens' of internal interest groups and lobbies asking for protection.[91] During periods of crisis it is difficult for politicians not to listen to proclaims of entrepreneurs about possible falls in employment and production.

also provides general provisions to regulate other issues such as binding tariffs, freedom of transit for ships, grandfather clause, the use of anti-dumping and countervailing measures, custom valuation, rules of origin, prohibition of quota, subsidies, state trading enterprises and other general regulations and exceptions. However, negotiating countries did not find an agreement on competition and labour standards. Thus, the GATT became the basic legal text for international trading. Mitsuo Matsushita, Thomas Schoembaum and Petros C. Mavroidis, *The World Trade Organization: Law, Practice, and Policy* (Oxford University Press 2006).

85 Malanczuk (n. 76) 31. According to Petersmann, international economic law has proven to be 'the most important tool for transforming the anarchic international law of coexistence' into a peaceful 'international law of cooperation'. Ernst-Ulrich Petersmann, *The GATT/WTO Dispute Settlement System: International Law, International Organizations, and Dispute Settlement* (Martinus Nijhoff Publishers 1997) 2.

86 Edward Krauland, 'The Challenge of Enhancing Global Security through Multilateral Legal Architecture', in Marco J. Bronckers and Reinhard Quick (eds.), *New Directions in International Economic Law: Essays in Honour of John H. Jackson* (Kluwer Law International 2000) 103.

87 Bedjaoui (n. 76) 14.

88 Petersmann, *The GATT/WTO Dispute Settlement System* (n. 85) 2.

89 *Ibid.* 9.

90 Van den Bossche, *The Law and Policy of the World Trade Organization* (n. 50) 36.

91 Petersmann, *The GATT/WTO Dispute Settlement System* (n. 85) 36.

Furthermore, other countries could exhibit similar behaviour and thus could begin a race to the bottom of protectionism measures. The Nobel laureate Ronald Coase stated that 'it is evident that, for their operation, markets [...] require the establishment of legal rules governing the rights and duties of those carrying out transactions. [T]o realize the gains of trade [...] there has to be a legal system and political order'.[92] Secondly, international economic law gives security and predictability to traders and investors. In fact, businessmen 'will be able to predict better how that country will act in the future on matters affecting their operations in that country'.[93] Thirdly, rules are necessary because governments alone cannot face the new challenges of globalization. The protection of the environment, labour standards, consumer protections, sustainable development and the rising of living standards are not only dependant on internal policies but are strictly linked to decisions taken outside of the domestic border.[94] Last but not least, the fourth argument in favour of international economic law is the possibility to achieve a greater measure of equity in international economic relations. International rules ensure that the rights of nonpowerful States are respected by more powerful (economic or military) States.[95]

It should be stressed that WTO law has moved centre stage in the development of international law. As remarked by Jackson,

> it spearheads what we increasingly call global law: principle of rules which are no longer restricted to delimiting sphere of influence (coexistence), or bringing about cooperation, but actually entail elements of integration as trade law is being partly or fully harmonised.[96]

International trade law is playing an important role in the global society. It does not only involve principles and rules delimiting national sovereignty (negative integration) but also increasingly describe rules which nations should enact (positive integration).[97]

The financial crisis has stimulated a debate about the role of international law in the global society. The lack of rules has been blamed by many lawyers, economists and heads of states and ministers as being one of the main causes of the credit crunch.[98] In the globalization era, the international society and markets developed faster than their rules. While markets are global their legal frameworks are not. International law is now called to regulate new aspects of international economics

92 Ronald Coase, *The Firm, the Market and the Law* (The University of Chicago Press 1960 reprinted in 1988) also quoted in John H. Jackson, 'Global Economies and International Economic Law' (1998) 1.1 *Journal of International Economic Law* 4.
93 Van den Bossche, *The Law and Policy of the World Trade Organization* (n. 50) 36. See also: Jackson, 'Global Economies and International Economic Law' (n. 92) 5.
94 Van den Bossche, *The Law and Policy of the World Trade Organization* (n. 50) 37.
95 *Ibid.*
96 Cottier and Oesch, *International* (n. 36) 2.
97 *Ibid.*
98 Sabino Cassese, *Oltre lo Stato* (Editori Laterza 2006) 4.

and also to modify itself in order to face new challenges brought by globalization.[99] After the situation of disorder the world needs new global economic rules. As remarked by Cottier and Oesch, 'trade regulation is at the forefront of this process'.[100]

1.6. Dispute Settlement Systems and unilateral reactions

The concept of 'dispute' in international law has been deeply analysed by scholars and courts. From a legal point of view, in the 1924 *Mavrommatis case*, the Permanent Court of International Justice stated that 'un différend est un désaccord sur un point de droit ou de fait, une contradiction, une opposition de thèses juridiques ou d'intérêts entre deux personnes'.[101] However, the legal definition does not provide a complete description of the concept of disputes as, quoting Merrills, disputes among subjects of international law and in particular among sovereign States are also an *'inevitable part'* of State relations.[102]

In the past centuries, in order to settle their disputes, States had recourse to different means such as negotiation, good offices, mediation, inquiries, conciliation and arbitration. However, they also referred to the use of force and unilateral measures that have been highly criticized; in particular, since the end of the World War II,[103] war, as a mean to settle disputes, appeared to be in disaccord with political and social theories and very risky for the survival of mankind.[104]

The codification of dispute settlement means by the 1989 Hague Convention of Settlement of Disputes by which States agreed 'to use their best efforts to insure the pacific settlement of international differences'[105] was one of the first efforts made by States towards the pacific settlement of international disputes. Similarly, another important step towards the elimination of the recourse to war was made in 1945, when the UN Charter came into effect. In the preamble of the Charter, States agreed to unite their 'strength to maintain international peace and

99 David W. Leebron, 'Linkages' (2002) 96 *American Journal of International Law* 5.

100 Cottier and Oesch (n. 36) 25. Lamy stated that 'the WTO is an engine, a motor energizing the international legal order. This is, in my view, the place and role of the WTO and its legal order in the international legal order: a catalyst for international mutual respect towards international coherence and even for increased global governance, which I believe is needed if we want the world we live in to become less violent, be that social, political, economic or environmental violence'. Pascal Lamy, 'The Place of the WTO and its Law in the International Legal Order' (2006) 17.5 *European Journal of International Law* 969, 984.

101 The Mavrommatis Palestine Concessions, Publications of the Permanent Court of International Justice. Series A – A 2 (August 30th, 1924) 11.

102 Merrills (n. 42) 1.

103 Giuliano, Scovazzi and Treves (n. 12) 52.

104 *Ibid.*

105 The article 1 of the 1899 Convention for the Pacific Settlement of International Disputes sets forth that: 'with a view to obviating, as far as possible, recourse to force in the relations between states, the Signatory Powers agree to use their best efforts to insure the pacific settlement of international differences'.

security'.[106] Under this principle States are precluded from using force to settle their disputes although they are free to choose any alternative peaceful means.[107] According to Merrills, the mentioned principle was set up 'to prevent self-help and to enable disputes to be settled without disruption of the social order'.[108] Although negotiation is still the main means of peaceful dispute settlement, many international courts or tribunals have been set up during the past 50 years. In this period,scholars observed the proliferation of judicial and 'quasi-judicial' bodies specialized *ratione materiae, personarum* and *loci* before which States may claim (and defend) violations of rights and interests.[109] As Petersmann pointed out,

> one of the most important lessons from the 20th century has been that in international relations [...] rule of law and peaceful settlement of disputes can often be secured only to the extent that agreed rule making is supplemented by administrative rule-application and judicial rule-enforcement in the framework of national and international organizations.[110]

The International Court of Justice, the International Tribunal of the Law of the Sea, the International Criminal Court and the EU Court of Justice are examples of international and regional courts which have been created since the end of the second conflict.

The creation of peaceful and judicial or quasi-judicial means of dispute settlement reflects the progress made by international law to contribute to reduce unilateral reactions and forms of self-help.[111] As a rudimentary legal system, international law allows a State to react unilaterally in reply to violations of its rights or interests. However, the rise of new dispute settlement means had a 'confining impact upon the right of states to resort to unilateral measures of self-help'.[112]As stressed by Noortman, the concepts of 'self-help' and 'consensual

106 Art. 1.1 of the UN Charter sets forth: 'to maintain international peace and security, and to that end: to take effective collective measures for the prevention and removal of threats to the peace, and for the suppression of acts of aggression or other breaches of the peace, and to bring about by peaceful means, and in conformity with the principles of justice and international law, adjustment or settlement of international disputes or situations which might lead to a breach of the peace'.

107 For an overview of dispute settlement methods see Merrills (n. 42); Gaetano Morelli, *Soluzione pacifica delle controversie internazionali, Ciclo di Lezioni* (Jovene 1991); Shaw (n. 72) 914–925; John Collier and Vaughan Lowe, *The Settlement of Disputes in International Law* (Oxford University Press 1999); Federico Ortino and Ernst-Ulrich Petersmann, *The WTO Dispute Settlement System, 1995–2003* (Kluwer Law International 2004).

108 Merrills (n. 42) 1.

109 Tullio Treves, *Le controversie internazionali: nuove tendenze, nuovi tribunali* (Giuffrè 1999) 33–36.

110 Ortino and Petersmann (n. 107) 5.

111 Malanczuk (n. 76) 264.

112 Math Noortmann, *Enforcing International Law: From Self-help to Self-contained Regimes* (Ashgate Publishing 2005) 3.

dispute settlement' should be considered strictly linked.[113] Leaving aside the doctrinal debate on whether self-help should prevail over consensual dispute settlement (or *vice versa*), it is important to underline that, in the field of international economic law, the WTO law preferred and thus adopted a 'quasi-judicial'[114] Dispute Settlement System which confines self-help to specific, limited and regulated circumstances.[115] WTO Members injured by (lawful or unlawful) behaviours of other Members cannot, in principle, adopt unilateral measures against the wrongdoing Member. States must not act unilaterally by reacting against another Member which is not acting in compliance with WTO rules.

According to certain scholars, the Dispute Settlement System of the WTO is arguably the most important international tribunal.[116] By adopting the Understanding on Rules and Procedures Governing the Settlement of Disputes (hereafter the 'DSU'), and in particular article 23 thereof, states agreed to exclusively[117] settle their WTO disputes through the WTO Dispute Settlement Body. The principle of exclusivity of the DSU precluded the possibility for States to act unilaterally to solve their disputes. It is not a coincidence that Article 23 is titled 'strengthening of the multilateral system'. As remarked by Picone and Ligustro, Article 23 of the DSU makes the WTO Dispute Settlement System a 'partial self-contained' system and thus allows States to partially derogate public international rules regarding States' responsibility and sanctions.[118]

The creation of the Dispute Settlement Body is one of the main results of the Uruguay Round which overcame many shortcomings of the GATT

113 *Ibid.* 104.

114 Judith Hippler Bello, 'The WTO Dispute Settlement Understanding: Less Is More' (1996) 90.3 *American Journal of International Law* 416.

115 Azhar M. Khansari, 'Searching for the Perfect Solution: International Dispute Resolution and the New World Trade Organization' (1996) 20 *Hastings International Law & Comparative Law Review* 183.

116 Noortmann (n. 112) 104.

117 When Members seek the redress of a violation of obligations or other nullification or impairment of benefits under the covered agreements or an impediment to the attainment of any objective of the covered agreements, they shall have recourse to, and abide by, the rules and procedures of this Understanding. In such cases, Members shall: (a) not make a determination to the effect that a violation has occurred, that benefits have been nullified or impaired or that the attainment of any objective of the covered agreements has been impeded, except through recourse to dispute settlement in accordance with the rules and procedures of this Understanding, and shall make any such determination consistent with the findings contained in the panel or Appellate Body report adopted by the DSB or an arbitration award rendered under this Understanding.

118 However, such a derogation is available to the extent that there is no failure or ineffectiveness of the WTO Dispute Settlement System. Paolo Picone and Aldo Ligustro, *Diritto dell'Organizzazione Mondiale del Commercio* (Cedam 2004) 667–669. See also Aldo Ligustro, *Le controversie tra Stati nel diritto del commercio internazionale, dal GATT all'OMC* (Cedam 1996) 1066.

system.[119] In fact, the ineffectiveness of the GATT Dispute Settlement System[120] and the frequent use of unilateral measures to settle disputes pushed States to reform the dispute settlement mechanisms.[121]Under the GATT, disputes were simply addressed to the chairman and the working parties and then, at a later stage, to a 'panel of experts' composed to settle a particular dispute.[122] However, the adoption of the panel reports was subject to the *consensus* of all contracting parties, including the losing parties. In other words, the losing party in the dispute had a 'veto' power on the adoption of the panel report.[123] Along with this, the lack of procedural rules, the possibility of *forum shopping* and the system's own ineffectiveness, led States to enact new laws governing the settlement of disputes. During the Uruguay Round, WTO Members agreed to adopt new rules, introduce a *negative consensus*, the principle of exclusivity of the DSB to settle disputes on WTO law, an Appellate Body and improved and clarified procedural norms.

By adopting the DSU, Member States shifted the GATT dispute settlement mechanism from a *power oriented* to a *rule oriented* approach and thus enhanced credibility and reliability of the whole system.[124] The effectiveness of the DSB is of foremost importance for the credibility of the whole WTO system as its deficiencies could affect the goals achieved so far. From a legal point of view, by

119 Scott Mcbride, 'Dispute Settlement in the WTO: Backbone of the Global Trading System or Delegation of Awesome Power? (2000) 32 *Law & Policy International Business* 643.

120 Kim Van der Borght, 'The Review of the WTO Understanding on Dispute Settlement: Some Reflections on the Current Debate' (1999) 14.4 *American University International Law Review* 1223, 1224.

121 John H. Jackson, *Restructuring the GATT System* (Taylor & Francis 1990) 61–80.

122 The first dispute was brought by the Netherlands against Cuba and related to the application of Article I to consular taxes.

123 Picone and Ligustro (n. 118), 576; David Palmeter and Petros Mavroidis, *Dispute Settlement in the World Trade Organization: Practice and Procedure* (Cambridge University Press 2004) 7. The GATT dispute settlement has been described more as diplomatic rather than legal. Thomas Cottier and Matthias Oesch, 'WTO Law, Precedents and Legal Change' (2001) 3.1 *Turku Law Journal* 27. Jackson pointed out that 'a reasonable, nuanced approach by the WTO panels is important for the credibility of the WTO dispute settlement system, and such an approach will lessen the dangers of inappropriate reactions by governments and citizen constituencies of nation-state members of the WTO'. John H. Jackson, *The Jurisprudence of GATT and the WTO: Insights on Treaty Law and Economic Relations* (Cambridge University Press 2000) 160.

124 The GATT experience also showed that there was a gradual evolution from a rather diplomatic form of dispute settlement culture to one premised on the rule of law. Jackson affirmed that the rule oriented approach has the important advantage of leading to 'greater certainty and predictability – essential in international affairs, particularly economic affairs, driven by market oriented principles of decentralization decision making, with participation of millions of entrepreneurs'. John H. Jackson, *The World Trade Organization. Constitution and Jurisprudence* (Royal Institute of International Affairs 1998) 60. See also Petersmann, *The GATT/WTO Dispute Settlement System* (n. 85) 1189.

limiting unilateral reactions, the WTO Dispute Settlement System preserves and fosters the multilateral trade regime and helps enforce WTO law. From an economic point of view, by barring States from having recourse to *self-help*, WTO avoids mercantilism and protectionism which could occur if states were left free 'to retaliate' against each other. In addition, from a political point of view, the stipulation against retaliation in the economic field mitigates international frictions and contributes to the preservation of peace and security.

Despite the huge efforts made by international law directed at shifting, *rectius* developing, international relations from coexistence to cooperation (and more recently moving them towards a global community) some form of limited and regulated unilateral reactions still exists within the WTO context. For example, unilateral measures can be taken by WTO Members if a Member fails to comply with the recommendations included in the DSB report. When the DSB 'condemns' a disputing party, such a party should adopt all necessary measures to comply with the DSB recommendations. In the case where the losing party does not comply with the recommendations within a reasonable period of time the winning party may ask the DSB to allow it to 'retaliate' by imposing countermeasures (in the trade field) against the non-complying State. This is a form of unilateral measures which can be adopted by WTO Members. However, as opposed to countermeasures in international law, WTO Members have to be authorized by the DSB which also sets the limits for measures to be adopted.[125]

As illustrated in the next chapter, another possibility for Member States to use unilateral measures to defend their interest is represented by WTO trade remedies (Antidumping, Countervailing and Safeguard measures). They are measures that have been included in WTO agreements and imported from States' trade practice. They are measures that, if they were not explicitly excused by the relevant WTO Agreements, would conflict with the obligations of the States under WTO law. For those reasons, their use and limits should be strictly defined in the relevant WTO covered agreements.

125 Article 22.2 of the DSU. See also, Petros Mavroidis, 'Remedies in the WTO Legal System: Between a Rock and a Hard Place' (2000) 11 *European Journal of International Law* 763; Andreas F. Lowenfeld, 'Remedies with Rights: Institutional Reform in the New GATT' (1994) *American Journal of International Law* 477.

2 The relationships between international law and WTO law

2.1. WTO law and public international law

WTO law is part of the broader discipline of international economic law which in turn is part of public international law. This assumption may appear evident and even obvious but has only recently been admitted by scholars.[1] According to Van den Bossche, international economic law was generally excluded from the purview of international law.[2] Scholars did not mention international economic regulations in their books and manuals. The subject was considered closer to the field of economics or as the hunting ground of a few specialists'.[3]

It is also true that the creation of the GATT and WTO legal system is not the mere design of lawyers and the ambivalence about their role was also raised at the time of negotiating the agreement after World War II.[4] Only some of the GATT negotiators were lawyers. Furthermore, it has also been reported that Keynes, one of the architects of the Bretton Woods system, was not keen to leave lawyers to take the lead in negotiations and to build the structure of the new international

1 John H Jackson, *The World Trading System: Law and Policy of International Economic Relations* (MIT Press 1997) 25; John H. Jackson, 'Global Economics and International Economic Law' (1998) 1.1 *Journal of International Economic Law* 1, 8–9; Joost Pauwelyn, 'The Role of Public International Law in WTO Law: How Far We Can Go?' (2001) 25.3 *American Journal of International Law* 535, 538–540; Ernst-Ulrich Petersmann, 'Dispute Settlement in International Economic Law: Lessons for Strengthening International Dispute Settlement in Non-Economic Areas' (1999) 2.2 *Journal of International Economic Law* 189 and Giorgio Sacerdoti, 'The Role of Lawyers in the WTO Dispute Settlement System', in Rufus Yerxa and Bruce Wilson (eds.), *Key Issues in WTO Dispute Settlement. The First Ten Years* (Cambridge University Press 2005) 125

2 Van den Bossche (Ch. 1 n.50) 59.

3 Donald McRae, 'The Contribution of International Trade Law to the Development of International Law' (1996) 260 *Recueil des Cours de l'Académie de Droit International de La Haye* 114–115. See also, Georg Schwarzenberger, 'The Principles and Standards of International Economic Law' (1996) 117 *Recueil des Cours de l'Académie de Droit International de La Haye.*

4 Gabrielle Marceau (ed.), *A History of Law and Lawyers in the GATT/WTO: The Development of the Rule of Law in the Multilateral Trading System* (Cambridge University Press 2015) 4.

economic organizations. Moreover, according to Marceau, the United States and the European Economic Communities (EEC) differed widely in their managing and shaping of the international trade relationship and the role of GATT. While Americans were seeing the GATT as a treaty, the EEC was considering it as a forum for negotiations. These different points of view caused the reluctance of States to include lawyers in negotiations and the organizations for a number of years.[5]

This patchwork of minds involved in the laying of the foundations of the GATT also influenced the background and mentality of the GATT and then WTO law and lawyers. Differently from other forms of international law, its understanding cannot be merely based on legal principles. Economics and political theories play an important part. It is the case that WTO lawyers, both scholars and practitioners, must include economics and political science in their preparation. As correctly noted by the WTO Director-General Roberto Azevêdo, the rule of law is not merely a technical concept solely of relevance to lawyers. Rather it is the defining principle of the multilateral trading system and a guiding light for everyone who is involved in it.[6]

Despite the mixed nature of WTO law, it cannot be denied that the WTO is part and parcel of international law. This is also confirmed by the fact that today, in almost all international law books, there is a section or a reference to international economic law. The subject is taught in almost all law schools as a specific subject or as a part of international law. The proliferation of Masters and scholarships in this field also confirms that WTO law is a specialization of international law. It should also be pointed out that international economic law is raising many new, interesting and stimulating challenges which legal scholars want to deal with. The increasing relevance of globalization, interdependence of economies and sustainable development theories, the role of trade in the wealth of nations combined with the importance of rules to lead and regulate the transformation of our society have captured the attention of international lawyers.

2.2. The applicability of public international law in the WTO Context

Generally speaking, there are three main points of view from which the relationship between public international law and WTO law can be analysed and the first one is the *applicability* of public international rules in the WTO context.

This argument is strictly linked to the concept of *self-contained* regimes, which has been the subject of in-depth analysis by scholars. The academic discussion, always rejected by panels and the Appellate Body,[7] is concentrated on whether WTO law could be considered a self-contained regime and completely separate from international public law and thus read in clinical isolation from mainstream international law. The ILC group supervised by Koskenniemi suggested that no

5 *Ibid.* 20.
6 *Ibid.*, XXVI.
7 Appellate Body Report, *US – Gasoline*, p. 17.

specialized international legal regime can be created outside the framework of general international law. The group underlined that the notion of self-contained regimes 'is simply misleading' and that 'there is no support for the view that anywhere general law would be fully excluded'. The group concluded by suggesting that 'special regimes' is a more appropriate term than 'self-contained'.[8] In its conclusion, the study group of the ILC stated that

> international law is a legal system. Its rules and principles (*i.e.* its norms) act in relation to and should be interpreted against the background of other rules and principles. As a legal system, international law is not a random collection of such norms. There are meaningful relationships between them.[9]

This reasoning also applies to the WTO. Although WTO law is to be considered as a *lex specialis* which may contract out from non-peremptory norms of public international law, it cannot be read in 'clinical isolation' from general international law.[10] First of all, it should be stressed that the GATT, and all the other agreements covered by the WTO, should be considered international rules. The rules negotiated by States, primary actors in the international legal system, are international treaties, binding on WTO Members and containing norms sanctioning their violations.[11] Marceau stressed that the conclusion of the WTO Agreement as a formal treaty and the creation of the WTO as an international organization are 'developments that had the effect of subjecting the WTO fully to international law'.[12] Pauwelyn considered that the WTO is, without doubt, part of the international law.[13]

Secondly, the repeated use of principles of international law in the WTO context is another example of the strict applicability of international law. As an example, in the *US – Shrimp* case, the Appellate Body stressed that, 'the chapeau of Article XX is, in fact, but one expression of the principle of good faith. This principle, at once a general principle of law and a general principle of international law, controls the exercise of rights by states'.[14] Similarly, in many other cases, the

8 Marti Koskenniemi, 'Study on the Function and Scope of the *Lex Specialis* Rule and the Question of 'Self-Contained Regimes', UN Doc. ILC(LVI)/SG/FIL/CRD.1/Add.1 (2004), para 134.

9 Conclusions of the work of the Study Group on the Fragmentation of International Law: Difficulties arising from the Diversification and Expansion of International Law, *Yearbook of the International Law Commission* (2006) II, Part Two, para 1.

10 Appellate Body Report, *US – Gasoline*, p. 17.

11 The Appellate Body held that 'we must assume that Members of the WTO will abide by their treaty obligations in good faith, as required by the principle of *pacta sunt servanda* articulated in Article 26 of the Vienna Convention. Appellate Body Report, *EC – Sardines*, para. 278.

12 Gabrielle Marceau, 'Conflicts of Norms and Conflicts of Jurisdictions: The Relationship between the WTO Agreement and MEAs and Other Treaties' (2001) 35 *Journal of World Trade* 1081.

13 Joost Pauwelyn, *Conflict of Norms in Public International Law: How WTO Law Relates to Other Rules of International Law* (Cambridge University Press 2003) 27.

14 Appellate Body Report, *US – Shrimp*, para. 158. See also Appellate Body Report *US – Cotton Yarn*, para. 81

WTO DSB has recognized the applicability of international law principles in WTO law such as, for example, *jura novit curia*, [15] non-retroactive effects of treaties[16] and proportionality.[17]

Thirdly, the relationship and applicability of international law and WTO law is particularly evident in the interpretation of WTO rules. The explicit reference by Article 3.2 of the DSU to the general principles of interpretation (*i.e.* customary principles of interpretation codified in the Vienna Convention on the Law of Treaties)[18] demonstrates the fact that WTO law is part of public international law. Despite the intensive use of certain dictionaries to understand the ordinary meaning of terms of provisions, WTO rules are subject to the same rules and principles of interpretation as any other international treaty. Their provisions shall be interpreted in good faith in accordance with the ordinary meaning to be given to the terms of the treaty in their context and in the light of its object and purpose. According to Trebilcock and Howse, the coherence of the international legal system would be put at risk if WTO DSB could interpret WTO rules 'in abstraction from the practice surrounding those agreements, including dispute rulings'.[19]

Moreover, the repeated use of rulings of international courts to interpret WTO rules demonstrates that WTO and public international law should be considered part of the same group of norms. It is in fact common for panels and the Appellate Body to have recourse to cross-references and quotations from different fora. They often rely on definitions or interpretations used in other international courts. This approach is not *sense unique* and only followed by WTO panels. It is quite common for international courts to draw on the jurisprudence of other Courts.[20]

15 Appellate Body Report, *EC – Tariff Preferences*, para. 105.

16 Appellate Body Report, *Brazil – Desiccated Coconut*, paras. 179–180; Appellate Body Report, *EC – Bananas III*, paras. 235 and 237; Appellate Body Report, *EC – Sardines*, para. 200; Appellate Body Report, *Canada – Patent Term*, para. 72.

17 Appellate Body Report, *US – Cotton Yarn*, paras. 119–120; Appellate Body Report, *US – Line Pipe*, para. 257.

18 The general rule of interpretation has attained the status of a rule of customary international law. See, *Territorial Dispute (Libyan Arab Jamahiriya/Chad)*, Judgment, I. C.J. Reports 1994; *Golder v. United Kingdom*, ECHR, Series A, (1995) no. 18 (European Court of Human Rights).

19 Michael J. Trebilcock and Robert Howse, *The Regulation of International Trade* (Routledge, third edition, 2005) 128.

20 Judge Gilbert Guillaume underlined how 'the Inter-American Court of Human Rights has quoted abundantly from the *Chorzów Factory*, *'Lotus'* and *Corfu Channel* cases, whilst the International Criminal Tribunal for the former Yugoslavia has made a number of references to the Court's decision in the *Barcelona Traction* case. The body responsible for settling WTO disputes has made frequent reference to the case-law of our Court. Thus, in its recent decision on *EC – Hormones,* it took account of the Court's findings in the *Gabčíkovo-Nagymaros Project (Hungary/Slovakia)* regarding the existence of the precautionary principle. Finally, the Iran-United States Claims Tribunal has also relied to a substantial extent on our jurisprudence'. Statements by the President, The proliferation of international judicial bodies: The outlook for the international legal order. Speech by His Excellency Judge Gilbert Guillaume, President of the International Court of Justice, to the Sixth Committee of the General Assembly of the United Nations (27 October 2000) http://www.icj-cij.org/files/p

According to Wang, international investment arbitral tribunals have made reference to WTO DSB reports.[21] As will be analysed later, the applicability of international law in the WTO is not merely limited to the applicability of principles and interpretation of the WTO rules but it also permeates its structure and objectives.

Last but not least, the theory of *falls back* also shows the relationship between the WTO and international law. As mentioned above, WTO law is generally seen as a *lex specialis* of international law governing international trade relations. As a *lex specialis*, it *derogat legi generali* and therefore prevails, in case of conflicts, over non-peremptory norms of public international law. In practice, this means that WTO lawmakers may draft, within certain limits, strictly defined rules that do not completely follow international law. *Quid juris* when the special regime of WTO law does not explicitly contract out from general international law? Then, the WTO system falls back on international law to fill in the gaps. As remarked by two scholars, the 'chimera of "self-contained regime" remains a phantom with no legal basis in international law, a notion which, despite its persistent appearance in jurisprudential debate, is best confined to the lively world of myth and fable'.[22]

2.3. The risk of fragmentation of public international law

The second point of view of the relationship between international law and WTO law, strictly linked to the previous one, is the risk of *fragmentation* of public international law.

The proliferation of sectorial legal frameworks has raised questions regarding the relationship between general international law and more specific areas of law. In fact, the growing importance and increase in international relations occasioned the development of numerous specific fields of international law including environment, trade, criminal, monetary and financial laws. Many more rules have been enacted, international organizations built and courts for the settlement of disputes created. The risk that international environmental, labour and other provisions may contrast with WTO rules is not to be discounted as the number of treaties and more general international rules have increased and negotiators in different fora are always different persons with different backgrounds (e.g. the Kyoto protocol and the UNESCO Convention on the protection and promotion of cultural diversity).[23] Those treaties and conventions have very often been developed

ress-releases/1/3001.pdf accessed 29 November 2017. See also the Appellate Body Report, *EC – Hormones*, para. 123.

21 Guiguo Wang, *International Investment Law: A Chinese Perspective* (Routledge 2014) 23.

22 Anja Lindros and Michael Mehling, 'Dispelling the Chimera of "Self-Contained Regimes" International Law and WTO' (2005) 16.5 *European Journal of International Law* 877. See also, Lorenzo Gradoni, *Regime failure nel diritto internazionale* (Cedam 2009).

23 Bradnee Chambers, 'International Trade Law and the Kyoto Protocol: Potential Incompatibilities', in Bradnee Chambers (ed.), *Inter-linkages: The Kyoto Protocol and the International Trade and Investment Regimes* (United Nations University Press 2001) 87.

independently from one another and have been based on the interests of different groups of States. Accordingly, one of the main aims of the abovementioned ILC study was to address the issue of fragmentation

> because of the widespread concern in international legal circles that the expansion of the coverage of international law through the conclusion of multilateral and regional treaties and the growing number of institutions covering specific fields (from trade, to human rights, social economic cultural cooperation, environment, etc.) created the risk that the unity of the system could be impaired.

As remarked by Sacerdoti, the risk was augmented by the increasing number of international tribunals and courts called on to settle disputes in the specific areas of international law without being subject to coordination, review or hierarchical relations.[24] Jenks also noted that the sectorialization of international law is the natural corollary of the extension of its scope. It follows the changing nature of international society and the modification of the role of international law in the achievement of global objectives. In an article published in 1953, Jenks stated that 'the conflict of law making treaties [...] must be accepted as being in certain circumstances an inevitable incident of growth' of international law.[25]As stressed in the ILC report, the diversification of international law does not necessarily entail fragmentation in the sense of incoherence. Fragmentation reflects the collision of fundamentally contradictory rationalities.[26]

The fragmentation issue also raises concerns about the governance of international law issues. The proliferation of international organizations causes a problem of coordination among them in order to maintain a consistent global approach to a specific issue, information sharing and crafting of new rules.[27] Specific issues may now be tackled in different fora and the lack of coordination may become an obstacle to finding solutions. This is reflected in the increasing efforts in cooperation between international organizations. The WTO, for example, strengthened its links with a number of other international organizations to achieve greater coherence. In the *Decision on achieving greater coherence in global economic policy-making*, agreed in Marrakesh in 1994, it is reported *inter alia* that monetary policy and exchange rate stability are supposed to contribute to 'the expansion of

24 Giorgio Sacerdoti, 'WTO Law and the "Fragmentation" of International Law: Specificity, Integration, Conflicts', in Merit E. Janow, Victoria Donaldson and Alan Yanovich (eds.), *The WTO: Governance, Dispute Settlement & Developing Countries* (Juris Publishing 2008) 602.

25 Wilfred Jenks, 'Conflict of Law-Making Treaties' (1953) 30 *British Yearbook of International Law* 401, 405.

26 Andreas Fischer-Lescano and Gunther Teubner, 'Regime-Collisions: The Vain Search for Legal Unity in the Fragmentation of Global Law' (2004) 25.4 *Michigan Journal of International Law* 999.

27 Wilfrid Jenks, 'Coordination in International Organization: An Introductory Survey' (1951) 28 *British Yearbook of International Law* 29.

trade, sustainable growth and development, and the timely correction of external imbalances'. The WTO's Sanitary and Phytosanitary (SPS) Agreement, for example, considers that measures adopted by WTO Members that are based on standards developed in Codex Alimentarius, operated jointly by the WHO and the FAO, the International Office of Epizootics and the International Plant Protection Convention are presumed to be compatible with the WTO agreement. This is only an example of the efforts of States and international organizations to address cross-sectorial issues. This need is even more evident in the trade field as certain problems whose origins lie in fields other than trade cannot be tackled by adopting trade measures alone, as there are interlinkages between the different aspects of economic policy. But coherence in global economic policy-making, as recognized by the WTO itself, goes far beyond the WTO's formal and specific cooperation arrangements with the IMF and the World Bank.

2.4. The reciprocal influence of WTO law and public international law

The third perspective on the relationship between international law and WTO law, the most relevant for the purpose of this book, is the *reciprocal influence* of WTO law and public international law.

This section shall address the question on how, and to what extent, WTO law reflects public international law and how public international law is affected by WTO rules. An interesting study by Professor McRae underlines that there are basically two ways to analyse this relationship: in terms of 'tradition continued' and 'new frontier'.[28] According to the first theory WTO law is 'just' a specialized branch of international law. It is not possible to deny that WTO obligations derive from treaties, that the institutional organization reflects other International Organizations, that they share principles on interpretation, pacific dispute settlement, State responsibility, etc. Under those theories, WTO law is an emerging and growing field of international law. Although it has been argued that negotiators did not even 'think' of public international law when drafting the WTO treaty,[29] WTO law reflects international law. As stated by the WTO Director-General Lamy, it is clear that WTO law is largely a circumstantial application of international law in general.[30] WTO law is the instrument used by international law to cope in the trade field.

On the other hand, the theoretical 'new frontier' approach generally recognizes that WTO law and public international law differ in their fundamental constructs *i. e.* the liberalization of world trade and the concept of sovereignty respectively. According to McRae, international trade law runs counter to sovereignty as it requires States to do exactly the opposite of what a sovereignty-based regime

28 Donald McRae, 'The WTO in International Law: Tradition Continued or New Frontier?' (2000) 3.1 *Journal of International Economic Law* 30.
29 Pauwelyn, 'The Role of Public International Law in the WTO' (Ch.2 n.1) 538.
30 Lamy, 'The Place of the WTO' (Ch.1 n.100) 973.

would require them to do: pursue and protect national interests even at the expense of those of foreigners.[31] According to Petersmann, the objectives of the modern international economy are not the nation State and its national economy, but their global integration and deregulation for the benefit of individual producers, traders and consumers.[32]However, it cannot be denied that the WTO enshrines a concept of sovereignty, though modern sovereignty. As described in the first chapter of this book, the idea of Westphalian sovereignty has been eroded as international law stepped into domestic States. International cooperation and *a fortiori* globalization require States to be bound by international rules which are intrusive in the domestic territory of sovereign States. For example, international criminal law overcomes old rules of State immunity and destroys any expectation of sovereign impunity and international labour rules impose minimum standards for the protection of workers. International law imposes legal constraints on States in order to impede arbitrary actions even against its own citizens.

From the point of view of the continuously changing concept of State sovereignty and the evolution of international law, WTO law is contributing to delimiting the policy space of States in order to preserve free trade and its potential benefits for economic growth and the preservation of peace. WTO law does not completely overtake domestic decision making over internal and international policies but requires States not to adopt barriers to trade merely for protectionist reasons. It leaves States free to decide on levels of technical standards, sanitary and phytosanitary precautionary levels, tariffs and regulation of market access for goods and services. On the other hand, it impedes discrimination between domestic and foreign products and services (and between foreign like products and services), to use particular subsidies or, more in general, to raise barriers to trade for protectionist purposes. Thus, decision making is still left to sovereign domestic authorities but the boundaries of these decisions are drawn by the WTO.

A particular aspect which is evidence of the influence on WTO law of the modern concept of sovereignty, and which reflects the way international law limits the powers of States, is represented by trade remedies. These particular instruments, which implicitly recognize the possibility for States to protect their domestic industries in cases where they have been affected or threatened by the adverse consequences of injurious acts committed by companies, are addressed to

31 McRae divide the new frontier theory into theoretical and practical approaches. The practical is emerging with the evolution of the WTO dispute settlement system. McRae, 'The WTO in International Law' (Ch.2 n.28) 30. According to Petersmann, 'classical international law tends to be state-centred and to focus on the external sovereignty (independence) of governments. Modern international economic law is citizen oriented and aims at limiting the traditional Hobbesian insistence on sovereign rights of governments, border controls, mercantilist protections of domestic industries and nationalist discrimination against foreigners which, as shown by economic theory, hinder mutually beneficial cooperation among citizens across frontiers'. Ernst-Ulrich Petersmann, 'From the Hobbesian International Law of Coexistence to Modern Integration Law: The WTO Dispute Settlement System' (1998) 1.2 *Journal of International Economic Law* 179.

32 *Ibid.* 179–180.

sovereign states and aimed at limiting the sovereign right to protect the interests of their domestic producers. The structure of trade remedies generally reflects the international law approach to the regulation of unilateral reactions taken by States.

They represent 'a significant incursion into core WTO disciplines created to liberalise trade'.[33] As noted by Voon, anti-dumping and countervailing measures would in principle conflict with the MFN rule, due to the less favourable treatment given to the targeted imports than those coming from other countries. Safeguards could also violate the WTO prohibition on quantitative restrictions.[34]

As a consequence of these deep reciprocal relationships, it should be pointed out that public international law is also influenced by WTO law. Classical theories of international law should be reviewed in light of the developments which have occurred in the field of international trade law. From a broader point of view this involves the new challenges faced by international law in dealing with economic globalization, the management of global financial crises, developmental issues and their influence over international rules and policies, and the emerging of new industrialized countries and their weights in the international law making processes, all of which undermine the structure of classic international law.

At a more practical level, international economic law and WTO law influenced public international law on, *inter alia*, the role of individuals and NGOs in dispute settlement (*e.g.* arbitrations, *amicus curiae*) and the law making process, a more effective system of enforcement measures (retaliation and cross-retaliation), procedural aspects in dispute settlement proceedings, the rule of consensus and *negative consensus* in decision making, rights and substantial interest to have access to justice. It is, thus, possible to affirm that WTO law has received the imprinting influence from general international law and it is contributing to adapting international law to new and modern challenges. As with any kind of phase-sensitive learning, in its early period of life WTO law acquired several of its behavioural characteristics from international law and then rapidly moved to developing a sub system that has its own characteristics and behaviours without completely leaving its primordial environment.

33 Tania Voon, 'Eliminating Trade Remedies from the WTO: Lessons from Regional Trade Agreements' (2010) *Georgetown Law Faculty Publications* 226.

34 Voon stressed that 'all three trade remedies could violate individual Members' schedules of tariff bindings (ceilings above which the relevant Member has agreed not to impose tariffs on specific products). In concluding the GATT 1947, negotiators incorporated these exceptions for trade remedies in part because some countries (the United States ('US') in particular) would not otherwise have agreed to other aspects of liberalisation mandated by that agreement. The GATT contracting parties maintained and clarified these exceptions in the GATT 1994 and the related trade remedy agreements upon the creation of the WTO'. *Ibid.* 5 citing also Trebilcock and Howse (n. 144) 312–313 and Kenneth Dam, *The GATT: Law and International Economic Organization* (University of Chicago Press 1970) 99, 106 and WTO, *World Trade Report 2009* (Geneva 2009) 26–30, 39.

2.5. The concept of self-help in international law

Self-help[35] has been a debated concept in international law. Despite the frequent reference to it, scholars have long discussed the meaning of the term and the differences between it and self-defence and other forms of *autoprotection*. [36] For years, the academic debate about self-help focused on the relationship between the injured and wrongdoing states and the consequences of the unlawful act. Scholars also differed on the consideration on the nature of self-help. Some of them consider it a form of dispute settlement (Bryde), whereas others consider it a sanction (Quadri).

At the beginning of the twentieth century, Anzilotti considered that the consequences of an unlawful act were merely the right of the injured State to ask for the *restitutio in integrum* and the duty on the wrongdoer to comply with the request. Kelsen criticized Anzilotti and stated, instead, that retaliation was the only and immediate consequence of the wrongful act. This is in line with Kelsen's opinion which considers sanctions as the characteristic of every legal system. Accordingly, he did not consider self-help as a right held by the injured State but as a coactive action of the legal system.[37]

Self-protection, which gives the faculty to States to unilaterally remedy violations of their rights, is acknowledged to be a 'characteristic feature'[38] of all primitive legal systems which 'in international law has been honed into an art form'.[39] As remarked by Ago, the term correctly reflects

> the fact that in international law … it is the rightful holder of a particular subjective who is at the same time given the faculty of taking measures for the purpose of safeguarding the right in question, to see to it that the right is respected and to exercise it.[40]

In the absence of a central authority in international society which could ensure the coercive enforcement of the law, self-help is the right to 'make justice by one's

35 Self-help, autoprotection and self-protection will be used as synonyms. Werner Levi, *Contemporary International Law: A Concise Introduction* (Westview Press 1979) 23–27; Stanimir Alexandrov, *Self-Defense Against the Use of Force in International Law* (Kluwer Law International 1966) 317–319.

36 Hans Kelsen, *General Theory of Law and State* (Harvard University Press 1945) 339; Benedetto Conforti, *Diritto Internazionale* (Editoriale Scientifica 2002) 374.

37 Kelsen's approach is influenced by his consideration of law as a set of imperative norms where sanctions constitute the crucial component. Benedetto Conforti, *International Law and the Role of Domestic Legal Systems* (Martinus Nijhoff Publishers 1993) 173.

38 Yoram Dinstein, *War, Aggression and Self-Defence* (Cambridge University Press 2001) 159.

39 Yoram Dinstein, 'International Law as a Primitive Legal System' (1986) 19.1 *New York University Journal of International Law and Policy* 12. See also: Malanczuk (Ch.1 n.76) 3.

40 *Addendum to Eighth Report on State Responsibility* by Mr. Roberto Ago, doc. *A/CN.4/318/Add.5–7*, para. 95, reproduced in *Yearbook of the International Law Commission 1980*, Vol. II (Part One) 56. See also, Hans Kelsen, *Principles of International Law* (Holt, Rinehart and Winston 1966) 13–15.

own hands'. According to Bodansky, self-help is a necessary part of any legal system, including the international system that 'lacks strong vertical enforcement'. Scholars stress that 'there is no world policeman to command or coerce obedience to international law rules; instead, states and other actors rely on a combination of other mechanisms such as countermeasures to win respect and compliance for these duties'.[41] According to Arangio-Ruiz, 'in a predominantly inorganic society, in which individual States and groups of States must place so much reliance on the unilateral protection of their rights, the concept of self-help ultimately characterizes the whole range of inter-State relations'.[42]

Classical international law legitimated forms of self-help due to the few restraints on States to pursue domestic policy and the lack of peaceful dispute settlement means in force. Forms of self-help were not limited and were scarcely regulated by international rules.[43] The development of international law and international society, as described in the previous chapter, reduced self-help by restructuring the way States relate to each other and by replacing it with other peaceful methods of international dispute settlement. However, as remarked by Dupuy, the verticalization of international relationships in the framework of International Organizations did not supplant the horizontal structure of the international community.[44] The *model institutionnel* and *model relationnel* coexist dialectically and are mutually conditional.[45] In particular, according to Cassese, the more recent legal institutions are mainly aimed at attenuating 'the most conspicuous deficiencies of the old one'.[46]

Self-help is still allowed under modern international law and still coexists with the institutional structure of the international community, though it is strictly regulated. In modern international law the term has been interpreted as

> the legal theory which describes as, and comprises under, all the different forms taken by the system which in principle grants to the State, as the holder

41 David Bederman, 'Counterintuiting Countermeasures' (2002) 96 *American Journal of International Law*, 817.

42 *Third Report on State Responsibility by Mr. Gaetano Arangio-Ruiz, Special Rapporteur*, doc. A/CN.4/440, para 12, reproduced in *Yearbook of the International Law Commission* (1991) Vol. II (Part One) 9.

43 During the period before the mid-nineteenth century, scholars considered self-help as the right to take any measures against other States for the protection of their rights or interests. The right of self-help was not limited. Dionisio Anzilotti, *Corso di diritto internazionale III* (Athenaeum 1928) 155. According to Lamberti Zanardi, this wide interpretation of self-help was abandoned during nineteenth century following the process of organization and instutionalization of the international community. Pierluigi Lamberti Zanardi, *La legittima disfesa nel diritto internazionale* (Giuffrè 1972) 18.

44 Rene-Jean Dupuy, 'Communauté internationale et disparités de développement' (1979) 165 *Recueil des Cours de l'Académie de Droit International de La Haye* 46, 67.

45 Javier Fernandez Pons, 'Self Help and the World Trade Organization', in Paolo Mengozzi (ed.), *International Trade Law on the 50th Anniversary of the Multilateral Trade System* (Giuffrè 1999) 56.

46 Antonio Cassese, *International Law in a Divided World* (Clarendon Press 1986) 31.

of a subjective right, the faculty of acting in order to protect and safeguard that right in certain circumstances.[47]

Leaving aside the academic debate about the nature of self-help, the term is defined as the heading under which unilateral measures of self-defence, countermeasure (also called reprisal) and retorsion are allowed[48] and excludes the responsibility of the State to the extent such measures are applied in compliance with international rules and principles. Self-protection includes measures with different purposes. They could be aimed at achieving the cessation of the harm as such, enforcement action to induce the wrongdoing State into compliance, preventing the recurrence of the event, exerting pressure in order to obtain compensation for a prejudice suffered, and it has been discussed whether they might have punitive intents.[49] In some cases, the objectives may overlap or their distinction and may appear not to be so evident in practice.[50]

47 According to Ago, this is in contradistinction with the opinions of Morelli and Sereni who believed that what distinguishes self-help from the other circumstances precluding wrongfulness, and particularly from the application of a sanction, is that self-help takes the form of enforcement action for the purpose of exerting pressure on the State that is bound by an international obligation, with the object of securing the performance of that obligation, or the form of action whereby the State holding a subjective right exercises this right directly by substituting itself for the State that owes the obligation. This would mean that self-help could be resorted to even in the absence of any internationally wrongful act on the part of the State forming the object of the action. *Addendum to Eighth Report on State Responsibility* by Mr. Roberto Ago, para. 95, 56. See also Gaetano Morelli, *Nozione di diritto internazionale* (CEDAM 1976) 352; Angelo Piero Sereni, *Diritto internazionale* (Giuffrè vol. III, 1962) 1524. Quadri stressed that self-help is the *faculty* (and not the action) given by international law to the injured State to react against the wrongdoing State. Accordingly, Quadri specifies that self-help is *sanction* of international law. In Quadri's opinion, self-help shall not be perceived as subjective right which oblige the subject of the action to *pati*. Quadri (Ch.2 n.55), 264–265.

48 The Vienna Convention on the Law of Treaties provides rules for dealing with termination and suspension of the operation of treaties, which in effect encapsulate self-help in the form of either partially or completely walking away as a state's main remedy for another state party's breach of the treaty. Christine Bell, 'Peace Agreements: Their Nature and Legal Status' (2006) 100 *American Journal of International Law* 384. According to Conforti, the principle *inadimplenti non est adimplendum* in case of suspension of a treaty is a specification of reprisals while in case of termination it can be included among the causes of termination of treaties. Benedetto Conforti, *Diritto Internazionale* (Ch.2 n.36) 360. For the definition of the terms see, Lassa Oppenheim, *International Law A Treatise*, Vol. II (Longmans 1960) 134–144; Giuliano, Scovazzi and Treves (Ch.1 n.12) 440–445 and 481–482; Lamberti Zanardi (n. 168) 131–135.

49 See Dereck Bowett, 'Reprisals Involving Recourse to Armed Force' (1972) 66.1 *American Journal of International Law* 3; Lamberti Zanardi (Ch.1 n.43) 133–134; Quadri (Ch.1 n.80) 269; Karl Strupp, 'Le regies generates du droit de la paix' (1934) 47 *Recueil des Cours de l'Académie de Droit International de La Haye* 570.

50 Brownlie refers to declaratory judgments involving injunctive relief. Ian Brownlie, *The Rule of Law in International Affairs: International Law at the Fiftieth Anniversary of the United Nations* (Martinus Nijhoff Publishers 1998) 122. Giuliano, Scovazzi and

Under international law, self-defence is a term used to refer to the circumstance precluding the wrongfulness of an act which would otherwise be illegal. As described in Article 21 of the Draft Articles on Responsibility of States for Internationally Wrongful Acts (DARSIWA) the 'wrongfulness of an act of a State is precluded if the act constitutes a lawful measure of self-defence taken in conformity with the Charter of the United Nations'. As a consequence, the resort to force by a State does not constitute a violation of the prohibition set by art. 2 (4) of the UN Charter allowing a State to react in self-defence to the extent that the reaction remains within the limits of the right of self-defence. However, a State that exceeds the necessary or proportionality principles will commit a violation of international law. Similarly, countermeasures are 'a feature of a decentralized system by which injured States may seek to vindicate their rights and to restore the legal relationship with the responsible State which has been ruptured by the internationally wrongful act'.[51] With the term countermeasure, international law refers to the measures that are adopted by an injured state and would be considered in violation of international law if they were not adopted as a reaction to a wrong. Retorsion, on the other hand, refers to reactions of States that are unfriendly and are taken against another unlawful or unfriendly State's actions. The main feature of retorsion is the fact that these reactions do not violate the target State's rights under international law.

Self-help appears to fall within the classical international law approach described in the first chapter and which refers to the regulation of relations among sovereign states. It reflects the classical function of international law that limits recourse to force and unilateral measures against other States. Hudec also reviewed the possibility of using self-help beyond the limits of international trade law as a form of 'civil disobedience' in cases where there is no legal justification for such unilateral countermeasures. He considered that there may nonetheless be a policy justification for breaking the law in certain circumstances. 'That question might be raised, for example, about illegal measures used to break a negotiating impasse over new rules, in circumstances where the adoption of a particular legal reform appears essential for continued political support of the whole legal system'. He considered that

Treves stated that countermeasures had punitive character. White and Abbas deny any punitive aim. Giuliano, Scovazzi and Treves (Ch.1 n.12), 443 and Nigel D. White and Ademola Abass, 'Countermeasures and Sanctions', in Malcolm Evans (ed.), *International Law* (Oxford University Press 2003) 510. In addition, according to Forlati Picchio, 'il apparaît ainsi que la vision traditionnelle selon la quelle les représailles avaient une fonction essentiellement répressive, voir punitive, n'est plus acceptée en droit international contemporain'. Linos Alexandre Sicilianos and Laura Forlati Picchio (eds.), *Les sanctions économiques en droit international* (Martinus Nijhoff Publishers 2002) 15. Critics to the exclusive punitive nature of reprisals have been made by Ago and Bowett. See also Roberto Ago, 'Le delit international' (1939) 68 *Recueil des Cours de l'Académie de Droit International de La Haye* 527; Bowett, *Self Defence in International Law* (Manchester University Press 1958) 13.

51 Arnold Pronto and Michael Wood, *The International Law Commission 1999–2009: Treaties, Final Draft Articles, and Other Materials* (Oxford University Press 1999) 328.

> though such a policy would lack most of the moral qualities of the conduct we know as 'civil disobedience' it would claim a similar kind of justification. The guilty party would agree to suffer the consequences of its illegal act, but still consider it 'justified' for having produced a stronger legal system than would have been the case without it.[52]

Self-help is thus the genus and unilateral measures such as self-defence, retorsion and reprisal are its subordinate species.[53] It is the limited and regulated right under which States are allowed to use various means for the purpose of safeguarding their rights. The fundamental right of a State to seek redress for injuries suffered.[54] This definition is not purely of a semantic nature but is extremely important for the purpose of this book in order to identify the different measures that coexist under the same umbrella and are regulated by similar principles.

52 Robert E Hudec, *Essays on the Nature of International Trade Law* (Cameron May 1999) 207. The fact that a violation of the law could promote a change in existing rules has been examined by scholars and jurisprudence. The International Court of Justice stated that 'the Court does not consider that, for a rule to be established as customary, the corresponding practice must be in absolutely rigorous conformity with the rule' and that 'reliance by a State on a novel right or an unprecedented exception to the principle might, if shared in principle by other States, tend towards a modification of customary international law'. *Military and Paramilitary Activities in and against Nicaragua (Nicaragua vs. United States of America)*, Merits, Judgment. I.C. J. Reports 1986, paras 186 and 207. By reference to the Proclamation of the President of the United States Truman concerning the continental shelf, Weil described it as the 'dialectique subtile, qui fait de la violation d'ajourd'hui le germe de la règle de demain'. Prosper Weil, 'Le droit international en quête de son identité' (1992) 237 *Recueil des Cours de l'Académie de Droit International de La Haye* 168.

53 Georg Schwarzenberger, 'The Fundamental Principles of International Law' (1955) 87 *Recueil des Cours de l'Académie de Droit International de La Haye* 342. For Schachter, self-help cover all the measures taken by an aggrieved (*i.e.* victim) State against the law-breaking State. Oscar Schachter, *International Law in Theory and Practice* (Martinus Nijhoff Publishers 1991) 185. According to Bowett self-help 'is often viewed as the larger concept of which self-defense forms a part'. Derek Bowett, *Self Defence in International Law* (Manchester University Press 1958) 11 and Dinstein, *War, Aggression and Self-Defence* (Ch.2 n.38) 160. In the *Corfu Channel* case, the United Kingdom stated: 'there is recognized in international law the right of a State, when a state of affairs involving a serious and flagrant breach of the law has been brought about by another State or has been permitted to come about, to intervene by direct action. The purpose of such intervention may be to prevent the continuance of the situation which is in breach of the law, or, where the intervening State has suffered an injury of a nature capable of being redressed, to further the administration of international justice by preventing the removal of the evidence'. *Corfu Channel* case, documents of the written proceeding, II, 1950, para. 82 (a), 282. However, the Court could not accept this defence stating that: 'between independent States, respect for territorial sovereignty is an essential foundation of international relations'. *Corfu Channel* case, Judgment of April 9th, 1949: I.C.J. Reports 1949, 35.

54 Albert E. Hindmarsh, 'Self-Help in Time of Peace' (1932) 26.2 *American Journal of International Law* 321.

2.6. The place and role of WTO trade remedies: particular forms of self-help or sui generis measures?

As described in the previous chapter, under classical theories, forms of self-help generally include self-defence, countermeasures (retaliation) and for certain authors, retorsion. They can be employed through different means and might take, for example, the form of interruption of diplomatic relations, declaring a foreign diplomat *persona non grata*, pacific blockades, termination of a treaty or naval demonstration.[55] In the economic field they could also take the forms of withdrawal of aid, import barriers, end of contracts, freezing of assets or nationalization of foreign companies.

As described in the first chapter, possibilities for States to resort to self-help measures in the trade field have been reduced, when not prohibited, by the creation of a 'sub system' of international rules and dispute settlement mechanisms. The WTO system is acknowledged as being a partial 'self-contained system' *rectius* 'special regime' in which primary rules prescribing specific behaviours or prohibitions are linked to special secondary rules which specify the possible means at the disposal of the injured States to counter the violation. In case of a violation of a primary rule the injured State can only resort to specific measures provided by the sub system and cannot resort to any remedy provided by general international law. This form of derogation from State responsibility rules of general international law (based on the principle *lex specialis derogat legi generali*) has been analysed by scholars[56] and jurisprudence[57] and recognized by the ILC.[58] As a consequence, in case of a violation of WTO norms a WTO Member cannot react directly by violating other WTO norms but shall have recourse to the DSU mechanism. No Member can use trade instruments to counter other violations of WTO rules. Under Article 22 of the DSU a Member, where the losing party of a WTO dispute fails to bring its measure found to be inconsistent with a WTO covered agreement into compliance therewith, or does not comply with the recommendations within a reasonable period of time, can request authorization from the DSB to suspend the application to the Member concerned of concession or other obligations under covered agreements. This form of

55 Alexandrov, *Self-Defense* (Ch.2 n.135) 15.

56 Bruno Simma, 'Self Contained Regimes' (1985) XVI *Netherlands Yearbook International Law* 111; Bruno Simma and Dirk Pulkowski, 'Of Planets and the Universe: Self-contained Regimes in International Law' 17 *European Journal of International Law* 483.

57 Permanent Court of International Justice, *S.S. Wimbledon*, Ser. A, No. 1, 23; *United States Diplomatic and Consular Staff in Tehran*, Judgment, I.C.J. Reports 1980, 40, para. 86; *Military and Paramilitary Activities in and against Nicaragua*, 134, para. 267

58 Article 55 of the Draft Articles on Responsibility of States for Internationally Wrongful Acts adopted by the International Law Commission at its fifty-third session (2001).

'countermeasure'[59] is regulated by WTO law and subject to the approval of a WTO body.[60]

While the use of the term 'countermeasures' with reference to trade remedies is often abused or largely misused in relevant literature, a limited number of scholars have analysed whether WTO trade remedies could be considered a form of 'countermeasures' within the meaning of public international law. On this matter, Boisson de Chazournes held that trade remedies cannot be considered countermeasures.[61] When referring to anti-dumping and countervailing measures, the scholar stressed that they are aimed at counteracting the injurious effects resulting from the dumping or the granting of subsidies and suffered by the domestic industry which justify the State's exercise of such rights, rather than the intention to react to a particular state act. She also considered that the practice of dumping is carried out by an undertaking, whether private or public, and not by a State. In relation to safeguard measures, she considered that they cannot be assimilated to countermeasures because of their different *fait generateur*. In fact, safeguard measures are adopted by a State that wants to react to the deterioration of the economic condition of a particular industrial sector due to the surge in imports, or to oppose a significant reduction in its monetary reserves; they are not adopted against the conduct of another State. The adoption of safeguard measures is therefore not linked either to the assessment of the lawfulness or wrongfulness of the conduct of another State, or to the assessment of the advisability of responding to the conduct of a State. It is a matter of a State protecting a market rather than prejudicing the interests of another State.

With reference to countervailing measures, Triggiani refused to use the terms reprisals (when adopted against prohibited subsidies) and retorsion (when adopted against actionable subsidies). Triggiani considers them (in particular the former) as forms of the principle *inadimplenti non est adimplendum.* [62] Yet Mitchell and

59 Laurence Boisson de Chazournes, *Les contre-mesures en droit international économique* (Pedone 1992).

60 According to Palmeter and Alexandrov the purpose of retaliatory measures 'is not to induce compliance, but to maintain the balance of reciprocal trade concessions negotiated in the WTO agreements'. David Palmeter and Stanimir Alexandrov, 'Inducing Compliance in WTO Dispute Settlement', in Daniel Kennedy and James Southwick (eds.), *The Political Economy of International Trade Law: Essays in Honor of Robert E. Hudec* (Cambridge University Press 2002) 646–647. Instead, Charnovitz considers that it 'is conceived primarily as a sanction, while the rebalancing idea retains vestigial influence'. Steve Charnovitz, 'Should the Teeth be Pulled? An Analysis of WTO Sanctions', *Ibid.* 611. For Andrew Mitchell 'the suspension of concessions is intended to induce compliance'. Andrew D. Mitchell, 'Proportionality and Remedies in WTO Disputes' (2007) 17.5 *European Journal of International Law* 998.

61 Boisson de Chazournes (Ch.n.59) 71 footnote n. 10 and 61–62. Similar concerns are shared by Fernandez Pons, in reference to safeguard measures. Fernandez Pons (Ch.2 n.45) 58, footnote 5.

62 Ennio Triggiani, *Gli aiuti statali alle imprese nel diritto internazionale e comunitario* (Cacucci 1989) 285–296.

Canal Forgues considered that trade remedies are close to countermeasures.[63] More precisely, Canal Forgues, stated that they are very close, in their adoption, to classic reprisals. Similarly, Mitchel affirmed that anti-dumping and countervailing measures are 'closest to […] countermeasures in international law, because Members may impose them in response to conduct that is accepted as "unfair" (dumping or certain forms of subsidy)'.[64] Last but not least, Ligustro used the term countermeasures in relation to countervailing and anti-dumping measures.[65]

In relation to WTO jurisprudence, the Appellate Body has also used the term countermeasures with reference to trade remedies. In the *US – Line Pipe* case, it implicitly considered trade remedies as countermeasures that could be adopted by Member States to react to unfair practices or a violation of the treaty and of measures as safeguards that do not entail any allegations of violation or unfair practice.[66]

The WTO trade remedies agreements contain the word countermeasure only with reference to remedies that can be taken under the SCM Agreement. However, the use of the term does not refer to the countervailing duties that can be autonomously and unilaterally adopted by the importing State but merely to the remedies that can be adopted by the importing State only if, and to the extent that, they have been authorized by the DSU.[67]

Following the analysis of the main critics to the relationship between trade remedies and countermeasures it emerges that such critics focus on the lawfulness of the act, the nature of non-State actor of the companies practising the injurious behaviours as well as the aim of the measures. It is important to stress that this study does not focus on the analysis of trade remedies as countermeasures or as a form of retorsion but as particular unilateral measures allowed by international law under the heading of self-help in order for a State to protect its rights and interests. As described previously, self-help covers a wide range of unilateral measures with different purposes, actionable through different means and subject to similar

63 Eric Canal Forgues, *L'institution de la conciliation dans le cadre du GATT: Contribution à l'étude de la structuration d'un mecanisme de règlement des differends* (Bruylant 1993) 222–223.

64 Mitchell, 'Proportionality' (Ch.2 n.60) 996.

65 According to Picone and Ligustro, antidumping and countervailing measures can also be considered as forms of countermeasures. Picone and Ligustro (n. 118) 130, 248 and 266.

66 The Appellate Body considered that 'if the pain inflicted on exporters by a safeguard measure were permitted to have effects beyond the share of injury caused by increased imports, this would imply that an exceptional remedy, which is not meant to protect the industry of the importing country from unfair or illegal trade practices, could be applied in a more trade-restrictive manner than countervailing and anti-dumping duties. On what basis should the *WTO Agreement* be interpreted to limit a *countermeasure* to the extent of the injury caused by unfair practices or a violation of the treaty but not so limit a *countermeasure* when there has not even been an allegation of a violation or an unfair practice?' (*italics added*). Appellate Body Report, *US – Line Pipe*, para. 257.

67 SCM Agreement articles 4.10, 4.11, 7.9, 7.10 and 9.4. See also *US – FSC* (article 22.6 – US), paras. 5.4–5.7.

principles. Countermeasures are only one of the forms of self-help and trade remedies cannot be defined as countermeasures, as will be described later.

In order to understand whether trade remedies could be considered particular forms of an evolving concept of self-help, it is necessary to analyse whether the fact that WTO Members may react against specific injurious practices regardless of the author (public or private firms) and the lawfulness of the action, in addition to their direct and indirect purposes, makes them unsuitable to fit under the umbrella of self-help and its principles. In fact, as will be analysed later, trade remedies are reactions against acts of individuals (*i.e.* corporations) and not of States. Even in the case of countervailing measures, the reaction of the State targets a behaviour of investigated companies exporting subsidized goods. In addition, they also address, except in the case of prohibited subsidies, specific behaviours that are to be considered lawful from an international point of view.

Despite the several differences relating to the content, nature and objectives of trade remedies and self-help measures, such States' unilateral reactions have been analysed all together. Trade remedies differ from each other because they address different behaviours and have different rules to verify the existence of the action taken into consideration (dumping in anti-dumping, subsidies in countervailing and increased imports in safeguard investigations). Other differences appear from the fact that anti-dumping and safeguard measures counteract actions taken by private firms whereas countervailing measures react to acts of companies (exportations) but indirectly attributable to governments (subsidies). Moreover, anti-dumping and countervailing measures differ from safeguards because of the level of injury required to apply these measures (which is higher for safeguards than for the other remedies), the range of products which can be included in the like product definition during investigations and many other procedural and substantive aspects.

Trade remedies have also different purposes and characteristics. While anti-dumping and countervailing measures are responses to *unfair* practices, many scholars consider safeguards as responses to *fair* practices.[68] Fairness is definitely a concept that may be interpreted in different ways depending on the criteria chosen. According to Brown and Stern, fairness is an element in the existence and functioning of the trade system that can best be assessed in terms of two criteria: equality of opportunity and distributive equity. In their view

> other concepts of fairness include commitments that countries make in the global trading system with regard to supporting rules designed to prevent cheating in market access commitments or to facilitate trade flows, those relating to procedures for the settlement of disputes or the use of trade remedy measures, and those relating to governance of the system.

68 Yong S. Lee, *Reclaiming Development in the World Trading System* (Cambridge University Press 2006) 83–84; Jackson, Davey and Sykes (n. 48) 604; Picone and Ligustro (Ch.1 n.118) 304.

Lee instead focused on fairness from the point of view of development theories and in the context of trade relations between developed and developing countries and considered that such an approach is not consistent with the promotion of development.

> If it is our priority to promote the economic development of poor nations, our focus should not be so much on how 'fair' the competition between the industries of developing and developed nations should be, but how we should help poor countries to promote their industries successfully so that they can have viable economies that would bring them out of poverty.

Regardless of the theories of fairness,[69] dumping is generally considered an unfair practice because dumped prices are artificially low due to internal barriers in the exporting country or a firm's predatory intents.[70] Dumped prices do not reflect costs of production and other expenses the firm bears for the production and marketing of the exported good which should determine its *fair value*. Subsidies are considered unfair because subsidized firms practise export prices which are artificially low due to the government's financial contribution. This alters the competition in the market by making the subsidies' recipients more competitive and thus injuring domestic industry in the importing countries. The justification for anti-dumping and countervailing measures is found in the promotion of fair trade.[71] Dumping and subsidies give firms an unfair advantage and therefore the importing country has a right to offset this by applying counter trade remedies.[72] On the other hand, safeguards are considered as responses to fair practices because they are aimed at offsetting a temporary and unforeseen injurious situation for the domestic industry regardless of the fairness of the action of the exporters.

Although trade remedies could be deemed to address different problems, to have different goals and other differences, they share a similar structure: *i.e.* all

69 Andrew Brown and Robert Stern, 'Issues of Fairness in International Trade Agreements', discussion paper No. 554 (18 September 2016) http://www.fordschool.umich.edu/rsie/workingpapers/Papers551-575/r554.pdf accessed 23 November 2017.

70 According to Jackson 'it has been argued that international trade dumping depends heavily on import barriers of the exporting country, and that this is unfair. A counterargument is that the problem in such a case is the import barriers, not the dumping as such, and that the sanctions against dumping are an inefficient way to get at the real problem'. Jackson, *The World Trading System* (n. 126) 254. See for a critique on this issue, Gary Burtless, *Globaphobia: Confronting Fears about Open Trade* (Brookings Institution Press 1998) 102.

71 Lee criticized the fair trade approach (*i.e.* that producers should compete on a level playing field) in trade between developed and developing countries. Lee (n. 193) 85.

72 Lee (n. 193) 84. Bhagwati stated that any free trade regime needs the means of preventing distortive practices and thus permit countervailing and antidumping actions to maintain fair, competitive trade. Jadeshi Bhagwati, *Protectionism* (MIT Press 1988) 35. On this point Palmeter stated: 'but this is the ideal. The reality is that, however legitimate their roles in a free trade regime, these laws have been captured and misused by the forces of protectionism'. Nicholas D. Palmeter, *The WTO as a Legal System: Essays on International Trade Law and Policy* (Cameron May 2003) 14.

trade remedies address a specific action that has to cause injury to the domestic industry of the importing State and which gives the right to the importing country to adopt trade restrictive measures. This is due to the fact that they are aimed at counteracting a practice which is injurious to their domestic industries. Their structure is basically composed of three substantive elements: 1) the existence of a particular action (dumping, subsidy or increased imports), 2) an injury to the domestic industry and 3) a causal link between them.

The study of the structure of trade remedies is of foremost importance to understanding their legitimacy in the WTO legal system and to revealing practices which could shift the role of trade remedies from reactions of injured States to unlawful and protectionist measures. In international law the classical forms of self-help share a common primary-secondary structure starting with a *fait declencheur* that, for self-defence and countermeasure, is a violation of an international norm while for retorsion is an unfriendly behaviour. This is the primary rule that is followed by a reaction of the injured State that would fall under the State responsibility secondary rules of law.

The structure of trade remedies is anomalous within the WTO legal system. They allow Member States to impose trade restrictive measures (*e.g.* import duties or quotas) and unilaterally react to injurious (but lawful) actions under specific circumstances. When a firm in Country A, for example, dumps its product on Country B and affects its domestic industry, Country B can unilaterally react by imposing duties on the dumped imports. In fact, WTO agreements are generally aimed at prohibiting States from using tariffs and non-tariff policies to create obstacles to trade. Most of the WTO norms impose duties on States not to adopt or maintain barriers to trade or to enact domestic rules in order to comply with minimum legal standards. However, trade remedies are part of a different sub group of WTO norms. They allow injured Members to unilaterally adopt trade restrictive measures. If dumping, subsidies or sudden and unforeseen growth in imports affect their domestic industry, they can react unilaterally without referring to the DSB. In theory, this could be considered contrary to the principle of free trade and undermine the basis of the whole WTO system. However, their use is regulated by WTO rules and their violation can be challenged before the DSB.

2.7. Self-help measures and WTO trade remedies

Understanding whether trade remedies are *particular* forms of self-help (excluding countervailing measures adopted to counteract prohibited subsidies) implies an analysis of their main elements as they allow States to react against injurious but lawful acts. In fact, dumping, increased imports and 'actionable' subsidies are not internationally wrongful acts.

According to Article 3 of DARSIWA, the characterization of an act of a State as internationally wrongful is governed by international law. In other words, in order to consider an act of a State as internationally wrong, there must be an international rule which prohibits a State from doing something, or obliges a State to do something, and there must be a violation of that rule.[73] In the absence of such a rule, a State cannot be deemed to be responsible for having committed an internationally wrongful act. No international norms prohibit individual firms from practising dumping, increasing exports or States from granting 'actionable' subsidies. The WTO agreements do not contain any similar prohibition.[74]

As already briefly described, trade remedies are reactions against lawful acts. The Oxford dictionary defines 'lawful' as 'permitted by, conforming to or recognized by the law'. Accordingly, in order to define dumping, subsidies or the surge in imports as lawful practice, it is necessary to verify that no provisions contained in the GATT or WTO covered agreements or elsewhere, prohibit them.

By reading the relevant rules, no prohibition of dumping, subsidies and surge in imports can be found. Those practices are generally not prohibited. As mentioned above, the structure of the WTO norms is to allow them to the extent that they are not causing injury to the domestic industry of the importing State. Only in cases of injury does the importing State have the faculty, though not the obligation, to counter them. This is also linked to the history and rationale of those measures that have been enacted with the twofold aim of recognizing the right of the injured State to react by adopting an act that would otherwise be prohibited whilst on the other hand limiting the use of the reaction. An exception to what has been just described, is represented by prohibited subsidies which are subsidies granted in violation of the WTO SCM Agreement. Under Article 3 of the SCM Agreement a WTO Member is prohibited from granting or maintaining subsidies that are: (a) contingent, in law or in fact,[75] whether solely or as one of several

73 In the *Lotus* case the PCIJ affirmed that the principle of sovereignty requires that what is not positively prohibited to States is permitted to them. The Case of the S.S. Lotus (Fr. v. Turk.), 1927 P.C.I.J., (ser. A) No. 10, 18–19 (Sept. 7). See also *Military and Paramilitary Activities in and against Nicaragua*, p. 135.

74 WTO norms do not regulate dumping or other private practices because they are aimed at regulating measures and actions of WTO Members and not of private companies. See on this issue, Van den Bossche (n. 50), 516 and Petros Mavroidis, *The General Agreement on Tariffs and Trade. A Commentary* (Oxford University Press 2005) 182.

75 This standard is met when the facts demonstrate that the granting of a subsidy, without having been made legally contingent upon export performance, is in fact tied to actual or anticipated exportation or export earnings. The mere fact that a subsidy is granted to enterprises which export shall not for that reason alone be considered to be an export subsidy within the meaning of this provision. (Original footnote). The Appellate Body in *US – Tax Incentives* stated that 'Article 3.1(b) of the SCM Agreement prohibits subsidies the granting of which is "contingent ... upon the use of domestic over imported goods". The Appellate Body has found that the legal standard for establishing the existence of "contingency" under Article 3.1(b) is the same as under Article 3.1(a) of the SCM Agreement. Since the ordinary meaning of "contingent" is "conditional" or "dependent for its existence on something else", a subsidy would be prohibited under Article 3.1(b) if it is "conditional" or "dependent for its existence on" the use of domestic over imported goods. Therefore, a subsidy would be "contingent" upon the use of domestic over imported goods if the use of those goods were a condition, in the sense of a requirement, for receiving the subsidy'. Appellate Body Report, *US – Tax Incentives*, para. 5.7.

other conditions, upon export performance, including those illustrated in Annex I[76]; (b) contingent, whether solely or as one of several other conditions, upon the use of domestic over imported goods. They are prohibited as they distort international trade and thus damage other countries' trade. This provision of Article 3.1 (a) clearly reflects negotiating parties' intentions during the Uruguay Round to differentiate export subsidies from other forms of subsidies. This is due to the nature of export subsidies that for their contingency upon export affect and distort competition in the international market. The proviso of Article 2.3 of the SCM Agreement does not require that in the case of export subsidies a specificity test shall be conducted in order to demonstrate that a subsidy is limited to certain enterprises. Export subsidies are *per se* prohibited. However, not all subsidies granted to exporting firms are prohibited but only those which are *contingent* upon export performance or the use of domestic over imported goods.[77]

As for dumping and increased imports, the rationale comes from the fact that WTO rules are international rules and so addressed to the principal subjects of international law: States.[78] As reflected by the term itself, international law has been perceived as the body of rules regulating State relations. Instead, in reference to 'actionable subsidies', this could generally be explained by the fact that WTO

76 Measures referred to in Annex I as not constituting export subsidies shall not be prohibited under this or any other provision of this Agreement. (Original footnote).

77 Panel Report, *US – FSC (Article 21.5 – EC)*, paras. 8.54–8.55. On this issue, the Panel on *US – FSC (Article 21.5 – EC)* recalled that: '[t]he meaning of "contingent" in that provision is "conditional" or "dependent for its existence upon". We further recall that the legal standard expressed by the word "contingent" is the same for both de jure or de facto contingency. There is a difference, however, in what evidence may be employed to establish that a subsidy is export-contingent. We recall the Appellate Body's [*Canada – Autos*] statement that "de jure export contingency" is demonstrated on the basis of the words of the relevant legislation, regulation or other legal instrument, as opposed to the "total configuration of the facts constituting and surrounding the grant of the subsidy"'. The Appellate Body [in *Canada – Autos*] has also recently stated, 'that a subsidy is also properly held to be de jure export contingent where the condition to export is clearly, though implicitly, in the instrument comprising the measure. Thus, for a subsidy to be de jure export contingent, the underlying legal instrument does not always have to provide *expressis verbis* that the subsidy is available only upon fulfilment of the condition of export performance. Such conditionality can also be derived by necessary implication from the words actually used in the measure'. Appellate Body Report, *Canada-Autos*, para. 118. In order to assist the interpreter in identifying measures that could be considered export subsidies an 'Illustrative List of Export Subsidies' was annexed to the SCM Agreement. In addition, Article 3.1(b) sets forth a prohibition to grant export subsidies which are contingent upon the use of domestic over imported goods. This norm was introduced during the Uruguay Round and made an important step toward free trade. Differing from the Subsidies Code 1979, the norm focuses on the domestic market of the subsidizing States. Subsidies contingent upon the use of domestic products do not only alter competition in the international market but affect foreign competitors in the domestic market of the subsidizing country. Picone and Ligustro (Ch.1 n.118) 243.

78 According to Malanczuk, 'the international legal system is still *primarily* geared towards the international community of states, represented by governments'. Malanczuk (Ch.1 n.76) 2.

Members explicitly designed the SCM Agreement in such a way as to prohibit only some forms of subsidies which could directly affect international trade. Accordingly, they decided not to prohibit other forms of subsidies and leave States with the necessary policy space to pursue their internal objectives. Subsidies may both alter competition and play an important role in economic programmes. Their differentiation is of utmost importance in a system which at the same time shall reduce obstacles to trade, ensure full employment and raise standards of living.

The absence of the wrongfulness element cannot lead the reader to directly exclude trade remedies from forms of self-help. In fact, within the group of self-help measures described before, many scholars agreed to include retorsion which is a form of reaction by a state through a lawful but injurious act against an unlawful or simply injurious action committed by another State. This assumption is, however, not accepted by all scholars. It has also been argued that retorsion 'lives and breathes in the incompleteness of international law where no unambiguous rules of international law prohibit the remedy'. It is considered the unregulated behaviour of States where only the rules of politics, comity and international politeness are the proper measurement for the acceptability of the act.[79] In fact, the ILC decided to exclude retorsion from the scope of Article 22 of the DARSIWA by asserting that such a measure does not conflict with an international obligation and therefore there is no need to excuse the measures to preclude, as an exception, its lawfulness.[80] This approach was also followed by Arangio-Ruiz who stressed that retorsion should not find a place within the framework of a codification of State responsibility. However, other scholars such as Cassese, Shaw or Conforti considered that retorsion is relevant for the analysis of self-help.[81]

While it is true that retorsion does not entail State responsibility (to the extent that it does not constitute a violation of international law) it is generally recognized as a form of reaction of the State and subject to certain principles typical of self-help such as the remedial character,[82] and according to Cassese, proportionality in gravity to the conduct.[83] Measures of retorsion are characterized by the absence of unlawfulness. They react to discourteous or unkind or unfair and inequitable acts by acts of the same kind.[84] They can be adopted to react against a

79 Hjörtur Sverrison, *Countermeasures, the International Legal System, and Environmental Violations* (Cambria Press 2008) 72.

80 Math Noortmann (Ch.1 n.112). See also the debate among members of the International Law Commission, In particular, Pellet, Simma, Rosenstock and Tomka taking a position for the exclusion of retorsion from the scope of the analysis against the position of Lukashuk. International Law Commission, *Yearbook of the International Law Commission* (United Nations Publications 2000) 269.

81 Benedetto Conforti, *International Law and the Role* (n. 162) 186; Malcolm N. Shaw (Ch.1 n.72) 1022; Christopher C. Joyner, *International Law in the 21st Century: Rules for Global Governance* (Rowman & Littlefield 2005) 180; Noortmann (n. 112) footnote 83.

82 Nii Lante Wallace-Bruce, *The Settlement of International Disputes: The Contribution of Australia and New Zealand* (Martinus Nijhoff Publishers 1998) 88.

83 Cassese, *International Law* (Ch.2 n.46) 310.

84 Lassa Oppenheim and Ronald Roxburgh, *International Law: A Treatise, Volume 1* (The Lawbook Exchange, Ltd., 1920) 42.

violation of rights as well as against damaging of interests. Similar to measures of retorsion, trade remedies are to be considered as reactions against lawful but injurious acts.

Classic international law already seems to be confronted with forms of reaction that do not depend on the lawfulness of the action. This does not mean that trade remedies should be considered measures of retorsion. In fact, such measures are not unfriendly acts but measures that would be considered unlawful were they not specifically justified by a relevant WTO agreement.

Another element that should be analysed is the fact that trade remedies are not reactions against behaviours of States, the main subjects of international law. Under Article 2 of the DARSIWA, 'there is an internationally wrongful act of a State when conduct consisting of an action or omission: (a) is attributable to the State under international law; and (b) constitutes a breach of an international obligation of the State'. Accordingly, two elements must be present for the act to be 'wrongful' under international law: the act shall be attributable to a State and the act shall constitute a violation of an international norm. For the first element, the act is imputed to a State when it is committed by its organs or in various other circumstances in which another subject is acting 'on behalf of' the State.[85] In particular, acts of individuals shall be considered acts of a State under international law 'if the person or group of persons is in fact acting on the instructions of, or under the direction or control of, that State in carrying out the conduct'.[86] To prove the link between private individuals and the State is a question of evidence and in the absence of such a proof the State cannot be considered responsible under international law.[87]

Leaving aside subsidies, neither dumping nor increased imports can be attributable to the exporting state. In many economic systems, apart from those mainly controlled by centralized governments, the State does not interfere in the decisions of domestic firms on price strategies and the volume of goods to export.[88] Entrepreneurs are generally left to set their own strategies and thus to decide whether or not to practise dumping or increase their exports toward a specific country. Because those acts are not attributable to the States, it is not possible to use the term internationally wrongful acts in reference to dumping and increased imports.

As already described, one of the main characteristics of trade remedies is that they are considered reactions against acts of individual *rectius* companies and not against acts committed by States. Dumping is in fact a practice of a company that

85 Articles 4–11 of the *DARSIWA*.

86 Article 8 of *DARSIWA*. See also article 9 thereof.

87 This is so to the extent that the State cannot be deemed responsible for having violated a duty to protect or prevent the action of individuals or the government *a posterior* adopt the act of the individual. *United States Diplomatic and Consular Staff in Tehran, Judgment, I.C.J. Reports 1980*, para. 57 and *Military and Paramilitary Activities in and against Nicaragua*, 109–115. Giuliano, Scovazzi and Treves (n. 12) 420; John O'Brien, *International Law* (Cavendish Publishing 2001) 370.

88 Ligustro, *Le controversie tra Stati* (Ch.1 n.118) 302.

decides to set different prices in the export markets than in its own market. Similarly, surge of imports are acts of companies that have increased, for whatever reasons, their exports of a concerned good toward a specific country. Yet, and despite subsidies being granted by public bodies, the reaction of the injured state through the countervailing measures is not, primarily, directed against the State but against the companies that export the subsidized goods towards the injured State. Although under new theories, and for many scholars, individuals and private firms should be considered as new and particular subjects of international law (mainly in international criminal law), it cannot be denied that international rules are primarily concerned with rights and duties of States and in the WTO system individuals do not have legal personality.[89] This means that individuals do not have capacity to enter into legal relations and to have legal rights and duties under WTO law, they cannot sign the WTO Agreements and 'sue' a State or another individual before WTO DSB.[90] Although WTO rules can be made for their benefit (*e.g.* to open markets for private firms, for the benefit of consumers, or generally to safeguard the interest of mankind), WTO rules do not confer any rights on them. In other words, WTO rules are not aimed at prescribing or limiting the actions of individuals but those of States. Accordingly, as described above, the Anti-dumping Agreement, the SCM Agreement and the Safeguard Agreement are aimed at regulating the reaction of the states against dumping, subsidies and increased imports, respectively.

The acts of individuals that cannot be attributed to the State were generally not taken into consideration by international law. It follows, that if the original act cannot be attributed to the state, then the reaction of the injured State cannot be considered as a reaction but an act that may entail its responsibility under international law.[91] This classical interpretation followed by scholars and courts described above has been reviewed with the intent of justifying the reaction against terrorist attacks under the principle of self-defence. Many authors focused on self-defence in response to armed attacks by non-State actors. They questioned

89 Gaetano Arangio Ruiz, *Gli enti soggetti dell'ordinamento internazionale* (Giuffrè 1951). On the status of individuals in International law, see Giuseppe Sperduti, *L'individuo nel diritto internazionale* (Giuffrè 1950); Malanczuck (n. 76) 100–104; Mark Janis, 'Individuals as Subject of International Law' (1984) 61.17 *Cornell International Law Journal* 61 and on firms as subject of international law Philippe Franceskakis (ed.), *L'entreprise multinational face au droit* (Litec 1977).

90 Steve Charnovitz, 'Judicial Independence in the World Trade Organization', in Laurence Boisson de Chazournes, Cesare Romano and Ruth Mackenzie (eds.), *International Organizations and International Dispute Settlement: Trends and Prospects* (Transnational Publishers 2002) 223.

91 *Armed Activities on the Territory of the Congo (Democratic Republic of the Congo v. Uganda)*, Judgment, I.C.J. Reports 2005, at paras. 146 and 147. It is interesting to note that one of the most famous cases defining the principle of self-defence, *Caroline*, was initiated following the reaction of a State against the attack of an armed band and not in the context of a State to State conflict. For a description of the events see James A. Green, *The International Court of Justice and Self-Defence in International Law* (Bloomsbury Publishing 2009) 64–67.

whether the reaction of a state against the act of non-State actors could be considered as falling under the right of self-defence and more precisely under Article 51 of the UN Charter. Such an interpretation would be acceptable, as Article 51 does not require the attribution of the armed attack by non-State actors to a State. In the absence of such a right, a State would be deprived of any means of defence as it would be denied its right to react. According to such an interpretation, in order for the injured State to react against the non-State actor based in another State, the following must be demonstrated: (a) State complicity with or active support to the non-State actor in its armed attack; (b) the territorial State failed to exercise due diligence; (c) the State has exercised due diligence, but has not been able to prevent the attack, or further attacks. Accordingly, the responsibility would be triggered by the fact that the State did not do all that it could reasonably have done to ensure that the non-State actor did not use its territory to start an armed attack against another State. Similar considerations have also been used to justify retaliatory measures taken against cyber-attacks. Accordingly, a State that does not prevent their citizens from conducting cyber-attacks from their territories would fail to exercise due diligence. The injured state would thus be entitled to have recourse to self-defence.[92]

The works of scholars on this matter have mainly been focused on the possibility of finding a link (*e.g.* omission of due diligence) between the conduct of the non-State actors and the State in order to justify State responsibility and consequently the recourse to self-defence by the injured State. In that respect, Ziccardi Capaldo concluded that UN Security Council Resolution 1701 has actually taken a step in the direction of allowing States attacked by non-State actors to retaliate. This statement was based 'upon "acknowledgement and adoption" (with the meaning of "awareness/conscious negligence") – a less rigid standard than the criterion of "effective control," which itself was a more cautious approach than the earlier-espoused standard of "due diligence/mere negligence"'.[93]State practice also seemed to confirm such an interpretation. The military intervention against Al Qaeda in Afghanistan in October 2001 and Security Council Resolutions 1368 (2001) and 1373 (2001) support the interpretation that self-defence is admissible to counter large-scale terrorist attacks.[94]

92 Nicholas Tsagourias, 'Cyber attacks, Self-defence and the Problem of Attribution' (2012) 17.2 *Journal of Conflict and Security Law* 229. On the NATO opinion on this matter see, David Fidler, Richard Pregent and Alex Vandurme, 'NATO, Cyber Defense, and International Law' (2013). Articles by Maurer Faculty. Paper 1672 http://www.repository.law.indiana.edu/cgi/viewcontent.cgi?article=2673&context=facpub (accessed on 05 January 2018).

93 Giuliana Ziccardi Capaldo, 'Providing a Right of Self-Defense against Large-Scale Attacks by Irregular Forces: The Israeli-Hezbollah Conflict' (2007) 48 *Harvard International Law Journal Online* 111.

94 It should however be noted that Security Council resolution 1368(2001) does not settle the matter entirely, as in that case there was already significant evidence of a degree of responsibility of a State (Afghanistan) for the continuing ability of the terrorists to carry out attacks. *Ibid.*

As stressed by Wolfrum, the International Court of Justice apparently did not follow such an interpretation, although its jurisprudence in this respect is not fully conclusive.[95] The Court adopted a very cautious approach on this matter. In the case concerning *Armed Activities on the Territory of the Congo* this question was left open. Even though the Court stated that in the absence of attribution of the armed force to a State there is no right of self-defence against that State.[96] In line with the *Wall Advisory Opinion*, it decided not to rule on whether, and under what conditions, contemporary international law provides for a right of self-defence against large-scale attacks by irregular forces.[97] Eminent scholars stressed that the silence of the ICJ, and in particular of the *Wall Advisory Opinion*, should not be read as suggesting that the use of force in self-defence is not permissible unless the armed attack is by a State.[98]

Other authors have also focused on the possibility to have recourse to self-defence against attacks by non-State actors without proving the link between the non-State actor and host States. According to Paddeu, Article 21 of DARSIWA may extend to the justification of the interference with the rights of third States, as for example the State from which the non-State actors operated. It followed that the right of self-defence may be stretched to include, in certain circumstances, the impairment of the rights of third parties, such as the host State. Under these theories the right of self-defence would permit interference with such a third party without removing the possibility for the injured State to react against the non-State actor under Article 51 and justify the act as a self-help measure.[99] It has also been argued that no words or sentences in the text of Article 51 could be read to suggest or request a limitation on the use of the right of self-defence to State armed attacks alone. No sentences explicitly limit the state's right to protect itself

95 Rüdiger Wolfrum, 'Fighting Terrorism at Sea: Options and Limitations under International Law', in Myron H. Nordquist, Rüdiger Wolfrum and Ronán Long (eds.), *Legal Challenges in Maritime Security* (Brill 2008) 21. It has been noted that 'the European Union statement made upon the adoption of General Assembly resolution ES-10/18 (concerning the Wall Advisory Opinion) suggests that EU member states and the other states associated with the statement would not accept the possible implication of the Opinion that self-defence is not available unless the armed attack is by a state. The European Union will not conceal the fact that reservations exist on certain paragraphs of the Court's advisory opinion. We recognise Israel's security concerns and its right to act in self-defence'. Elizabeth Wilmshurst, 'Principles of International Law on the Use of Force by States in Self-Defence', Working Paper (1 October 2005) reprinted in 'The Chatham House Principles of International Law on the Use of Force in Self-Defence' (2006) 55.4 *The International and Comparative Law Quarterly* 963.

96 *Armed Activities on the Territory of the Congo (Democratic Republic of the Congo v. Uganda)*, Judgment, I.C.J. Reports 2005, at paras. 146 and 147.

97 *Legal Consequences of the Construction of a Wall in the Occupied Palestinian Territory*, Advisory Opinion, I.C.J. Reports 2004.

98 Wilmshurst (Ch.2 n.95) 9.

99 Federica I. Paddeu, 'Self-Defence as a Circumstance Precluding Wrongfulness: Understanding Article 21 of the Articles on State Responsibility' (2015) 85.1 *British Yearbook of International Law* 90–132.

from an attack by another State. The right of self-defence allows the use of force to counter an attack. The source of the attack, whether it is from a State or a non-State actor, is completely irrelevant to the existence of the right.

According to certain scholars, in contemporary international law the State's right to self-defence against attacks by non-State actors is not generally questioned. The inherent right to react against an attack regardless of the nature of the perpetrator is not disputed. Therefore, any state is entitled to react to an attack. But the right to use force in self-defence is an inherent right and is not dependent upon any prior breach of international law by the State on the territory of which defensive force is used.[100] As noted by eminent scholars, what is questioned

> is the right to take action against the state that is the presumed source of such attacks since it must be conceded that an attack against a non-state actor within a state will inevitably constitute the use of force *on* the territorial state.[101]

Therefore, international law is already confronted with reactions of States against acts committed by non-State actors that could be justified under international law. The reaction of the State for a violation of its rights is not questioned. The focus of international law is on the limitations on the reaction.[102]

The UN Convention on the Law of the Sea (UNCLOS) offers other interesting elements to discuss about the reaction of a State against an act committed by non-State actors. Articles 105 of UNCLOS allows States to seize a pirate ship or aircraft, arrest the persons and seize the property on board. According to Treves, seizing a pirate ship under the power granted to all States by UNCLOS implies the possibility of the use of force.[103] This interpretation is fully supported by the wording used by the Security Council which mentions the use of 'all necessary means for repressing acts of piracy and armed robbery' as well as by the EU Council Joint Action explicitly stating in its 'Operation Atalanta' 'all necessary measures, including use of force'.[104] It is worth mentioning that the 'right of self-defence' described in Article 105 of UNCLOS is not limitless as the State is bound by the restricted number of measures that can be taken as well as the principle of self-defence. The reaction of the State could merely take the form of interception and destruction.

100 Wilmshurst (Ch.2 n.95) 10.
101 *Ibid.*
102 *Ibid.*
103 Tullio Treves, 'Piracy, Law of the Sea, and Use of Force: Developments off the Coast of Somalia' (2009) 20.2 *European Journal of International Law* 399.
104 Article 2 of the EU Council Joint Action 2008/851 sets forth: Under the conditions set by the relevant international law and by UNSC Resolutions 1814 (2008), 1816 (2008) and 1838 (2008), Atalanta shall, as far as available capabilities allow: (d) take the necessary measures, including the use of force, to deter, prevent and intervene in order to bring to an end acts of piracy and armed robbery which may be committed in the areas where it is present. EU Council Joint Action 2008/851 (OJEU 200 L 301 12.11.2008) also cited by Treves, 'Piracy' 399.

For the purpose of this study, it is interesting to note that the exceptional use of force would be allowed as a right to react in specific circumstances and that the targets of the reactions would be the pirates' vessels, aircraft or crew and not necessarily the flag State. The reality of our society has led the notion of self-help under classic international law to evolve so as to include reactions of States targeting acts of individuals and justifying such reactions without incurring a violation of international law. Self-help is already being interpreted in such a manner to include unilateral measures taken by a State to counter an injurious act committed by a non-State actor, regardless of whether the act could be imputable to a State. The reaction can directly target the individuals without being directed against any State. Failure to comply with self-help principles and limits would entail state responsibility for the wrongdoing State.

The analysis of international law described so far will be used for the analysis of trade remedies from the point of view of considering them as a species of self-help. The analysis showed that international law is already open to reactions that have been taken by non-State actors and more precisely without any link to a State. However, this study does not claim that under WTO law private individuals become subjects of law nor that the acts of dumped, subsidized or increased imports are acts that can be attributable to a State. Similar to the role of non-State actors in waging wars, as recognized by international law, WTO law recognizes that individual companies have acquired growing importance in international relations.

The fact that international law regulates trade remedies, a reaction of injured States against an action of a private firm, is further evidence of the evolution of international law towards mixed relationships between States and non-State actors. Modern international law pays great attention to the action of individuals. It considers them as important actors in the community and their behaviour is taking up increasing amounts of space in the international legal system.

The inherent right of States to protect themselves against attacks by non-State actors is developing as a common element of the principle of self-help. This is also the case for trade remedies granting Member States the right to react against acts of non-State parties, private or public companies. Furthermore, they empower Member States to target individuals in their reaction without targeting other Member States. Moreover, they allow a Member State to react without the reaction being considered a violation of an international norm. Only the failure to comply with the limitations on such reactions contained in the relevant WTO agreement will entail State responsibility under WTO rules, as it will alter the balance between the reciprocal rights and obligations of Member States.

2.8. A delegation of powers by the WTO legal system to Member States

The legal rationale under which the WTO system allows trade remedies is to give States the possibility of safeguarding their interests (or rights) in specific circumstances in which unilateral measures can better achieve this purpose than multilateral/judicial remedies.

The difference between rights and interests is of foremost importance in these circumstances. It is possible to consider that in cases where trade remedies are applied against prohibited subsidies, the imposing country (the importing country) offsets the injurious consequences of a violation of its rights. In fact it is possible to use the term 'right' because in this case the reaction is against an act which violates an international norm (internationally unlawful act) *i.e.* Article 3 of the SCM Agreement. There is a legal obligation which explicitly prohibits a WTO Member from granting prohibited subsidies. Thus, in cases where a WTO Member grants prohibited subsidies, the Member imposing countervailing measures reacts to an unlawful practice.[105] Conversely, when an international norm imposing or precluding a specific behaviour does not exist it cannot be possible to use the term 'right' and violation thereof. However, as stated by Picone and Ligustro, a similar reaction is admissible when aimed at offsetting lawful but unfair or simply injurious practices for the injured State. In this case there is a violation of interests and not of rights. Member States have an interest in the preservation of their domestic industries and WTO law allows them (in limited circumstances) to intervene in the market in order to offset the injurious effects of dumping, subsidies or the sudden and unforeseen growth of imports. Only in those circumstances can WTO Members preserve the market, and thus their domestic industries, against negative effects of some injurious practices.

From a legal point of view, this is not a general interest in protecting domestic industry against the effects of foreign competition but a strictly limited interest in defending domestic industry under certain specific circumstances. More than the lawfulness of the actions, trade remedies' rules are concerned with their injuriousness. It is their adverse effect on the domestic industry of the importing State and not the lawfulness of the actions which gives the injured State the right to impose trade measures.[106]Injury is a (the) central element which justifies the reaction of the State. It is strictly limited to specific circumstances and does not

105 Picone and Ligustro considered that in this case it could be possible to use the word countermeasures. See Picone and Ligustro (n. 118) 129. For Triggiani this is a form of *inadimplenti non est adimplendum*. Triggiani (n. 187) 285–289. Dam underlined that 'illegality is an uncertain and ambiguous concept when applied to the General Agreement. Although the substantive provisions [...] are drafted in conventional terms, including a rather liberal use of prohibitory language, the remedy provisions are not drawn in terms of sanctions. Rather the organizing principle is [...] a system of reciprocal rights and obligations to be maintained in balance'. Kenneth Dam, *The GATT: Law and International Economic Organization* (University of Chicago Press 1970) 352.

106 This recalls, at least for the countervailing duties, the debated concept of the state responsibility for lawful acts. However, it shall be underlined that dumping and increased imports, as described before, are actions committed by private firms and there are no links with the State. On the issue of the state liability for lawful acts see Pierre-Marie Dupuy, 'Le fait générateur de la responsabilité internationale des états' (1984) 188 *Recueil des Cours de l'Académie de Droit International de La Haye* 61–110; Philippe Cahier, *Le problème de la responsabilité pour risque en droit international, Les Relations internationals dans un monde en mutation* (Sijthoff 1977) 499; Giuliano, Scovazzi and Treves (n. 12) 493–499. For an analysis on this matter, Quadri (Ch.1 n.80) 590–593.

apply in any case where the domestic industry is suffering because of causes other than dumping, subsidies or increased imports.[107] The concept of injury is specifically described in WTO trade remedy Agreements. It coincides with the worsening of the economic situation of the domestic industry caused by dumping, subsidies or increased imports and varies depending on the context and the adjective related to it. It could be *serious* or *material* but always linked and demonstrable through an analysis of the economic factors and indices which can be used to evaluate the State of the industry.[108] In sum, dumping, subsidies and increased imports are not unilaterally counter actionable where they do not cause injury to the domestic industry.[109]

This is strictly linked to the purpose of those norms. They are aimed at offsetting dumping, subsidy and unforeseen growth of imports as they are the cause of injury. Trade remedies are not (or at least should not be) aimed at allowing the complaining domestic industry to improve its economic situation and market position but to eliminate the cause of injury to the domestic industry. Although with some differences, the reaction of the injured State is aimed at counteracting the action which causes injury to the domestic industry. Neither punitive nor protectionist intent is found in trade remedies. Their purpose is specifically aimed at removing the fact which causes injury to the domestic industry.

According to Picone and Ligustro, the structure of trade remedies could be considered a 'reaction of the injured State'.[110] The WTO multilateral system delegates the necessary powers to Member States to eliminate the injury or the threat of injury suffered by their domestic industries in a timely manner.[111] So, the WTO system only allows Member States to impose unilateral trade restrictive measures if they comply with WTO rules. Trade remedies constitute an attempt to redress an injurious act by a Member State's own action rather than through the WTO multilateral (quasi) judicial process. This delegation of powers is also due to the fact that there is no supra-national entity in charge of regulating and sanctioning dumping and countervailable subsidies practices. In order to do this, it would be necessary to build an international body and enact rules addressed to

107 According to Triggiani, injury is a central element because is the element by which a State can demonstrate the breach of the principle of reciprocity which is the real interest protected by the norm. Triggiani (Ch.2 n.62) 293.

108 In reference to countervailing measures Triggiani underlined that it is not injury itself which justifies the reaction of the State but the fact that subsidies alter the overall contractual equilibrium. In his text he quoted Dupuy who, by referring to economic sanctions imposed by the United Nations, affirmed that they are not adopted by Member State 'parce que leur droit subjectif est lésé mais parce q'ils ont un intérêt commun au maintien ou au rétablissement de la Paix international'. Pierre-Marie Dupuy, 'Responsabilité internationale des Etats' (1984) 187 *Recueil des Cours de l'Académie de Droit International de La Haye* 103.

109 In reference to countervailing measures, Benitah defined them as effect-based norms. Marc Benitah, *The Law of Subsidies under the GATT/WTO System* (Kluwer Law International 2001) 11.

110 Picone and Ligustro (Ch.1 n.118) 128.

111 Triggiani (Ch.2 n.62) 235.

firms and private entities which is not a common practice for the WTO legal system.[112] As some scholars have suggested, trade remedies should be replaced by a global competition/antitrust norm and authority.[113] This authority could sanction private enterprises and States for anticompetitive behaviour. However, the project is still far from realization.

The delegation of powers is balanced by the existence of rules which limit the discretionary powers of the investigating authorities and by the dispute settlement mechanism which can review the respect of WTO rules in imposing measures. While the use of trade remedies is allowed by the WTO system, its misuse has become a source of concern for many free traders. The misuse of trade remedies shifts their role from reaction of injured States to protectionist instruments. Their misuse can nullify the results of trade liberalization efforts. When Member States levy anti-dumping, countervailing or safeguard measures which do not comply with WTO rules, they are imposing *de facto* unilateral protectionist barriers to trade. Accordingly, it is not the use or abuse of trade remedies which could be challenged before WTO panels but their misuse.

2.9. Judicial control over the correct use of trade remedies

The imposition of trade remedies which are not in compliance with WTO rules affects the balance between rights and obligations of Members and thus alters the synallagmatic relations between Members. However, the WTO legal system can always rebalance it by evaluating the compliance of such measures with WTO rules. Any international agreement is not very worthy if it cannot be enforced in case of violation of its rules by a party. An effective mechanism to settle disputes increases the practical value of the commitments the signatories undertake in an international agreement.[114]

The DSU is a 'rule oriented' instrument which guarantees the respect and enforcement of WTO law and ensures the 'prompt settlement' of disputes between Members.[115] As laid down in Article 3.3 of the DSU, the fact that a

112 For the role of individuals as subjects in international WTO law see also Michael Laidhold, 'Private Party Access to the WTO: Do Recent Developments in International Trade Dispute Resolution Really Give Private Organizations a Voice in the WTO?' (1999) 12.2 *Transnational Lawyer* 427.

113 Patrick A. Messerlin, 'Should Antidumping Rules be Replaced by National or International Competition Rules?', in Heinz Hauser and Ernst-Ulrich Petersmann (eds.), *International Competition Rules in the GATT-WTO System* (1994) 49 *Aussenwirtschaft* and Ralf Boscheck, 'The Governance of Global Market Relations: The Case of Substituting Antitrust for Antidumping' (2001) 24.1 *World Competition* 41.

114 World Trade Organization Secretariat, *A Handbook on the WTO Dispute Settlement System* (Cambridge University Press 2004) XIX.

115 On the power or rules orientation of the GATT and WTO dispute settlement system see John H. Jackson, *The World Trading System* (n. 126) 109–112. See also Davey who stated that an adjudicatory rule based system is superior to a negotiation power based system. William J. Davey, 'Dispute Settlement in GATT' (1987) 51.11 *Fordham International Law Journal* 67.

Member who considers that a benefit accruing directly or indirectly under the covered agreement is being impaired by measures taken by another Member could sue that Member before the DSB and obtain the prompt settlement of the dispute is 'essential to the effective functioning of the WTO and the maintenance of a proper balance between rights and obligations of Members'. This ensures *inter alia* that the rights of Members protected by the Anti-dumping Agreement, the SCM Agreement and Safeguard Agreement (and respective GATT provisions) are enforced.

When a dispute over an alleged violation of a WTO norm arises between Members, they must attempt to resolve their differences through consultations. Following a diplomatic approach which is common in international law, the DSU imposes on the parties to the dispute a duty of consultation in order to attempt to obtain satisfactory adjustment of the matter.[116] The consultation phase gives the parties the opportunity to find a mutually satisfactory solution without the intervention of the DSB.[117] In the trade remedy field, the dispute arises when a WTO Member considers that another WTO Member has adopted anti-dumping, countervailing or safeguard measures which are not in compliance with the respective WTO rules.[118] During the confidential consultation phase, WTO Members should try to settle the dispute between themselves in a manner which is consistent with the WTO Agreements.[119] In trade remedies' cases, they have led to mutually agreed solutions in several cases and they have had an important role in terminating investigations or in settling the dispute before the composition of the panel. The majority of the disputes involving trade remedies are settled at the end of the (quasi) judicial procedure.

Trade remedy agreements contain some specific rules which differentiate them from the standard procedures of the DSU.[120] Under Article 1 of the DSU, following the principle *lex specialis derogat legi generali*, in case of contrast between the norms of the DSU and those contained in the covered agreements, the latter shall prevail over the former.[121] As pointed out by the Appellate Body, this provision does not allow for the replacing of the whole set of norms in the DSU with specific rules but only the part which is different from the special and additional rules contained in the covered agreements.[122]

Leaving aside the technical details of the functioning of the DSB, for the purpose of this study, it is interesting to highlight the role of the panels and Appellate Body in delimiting the boundaries on the use of trade remedies. In fact, WTO

116 Article 4.5 of the DSU.
117 Good offices, consultation and mediation can also be used to settle the dispute if parties to the dispute agree. Article 5 of the DSU.
118 Before bringing a case, the Member shall exercise its judgement as to whether the action under DSU would be fruitful. Article 3.7 of the DSU.
119 Article 3.6 of the DSU.
120 Anti-dumping Agreement 17.4 through 17.7 and SCM Agreement 4.2 through 4.12, 6.6, 7.2 through 7.10, 8.5, footnote 35, 24.4, 27.7, Annex V.
121 Article 1.2 of the DSU.
122 Appellate Body Report, *Guatemala – Cement*, paras. 51–81.

reports have contributed to interpreting the relevant agreements and clarified rules by giving meaning to words and sentences and delimiting the role and the work of investigating authorities. The decisions of the panel, and in particular those of the Appellate Body, are not only important for the settlement of the specific dispute but for the strengthening of the whole WTO legal system. Although they cannot be considered as precedents, the jurisprudence plays an important role in overcoming shortcomings of the WTO covered agreements and ensuring coherence.[123] In the absence of the principle of *stare decisis*, the reports adopted by the DSB only bind the parties to the dispute.[124] Furthermore, under Article 3 of the DSU, recommendations and rulings of the DSB cannot add or diminish the rights and obligations provided in the covered agreements.[125] According to McNelis, 'it is almost a mantra that WTO dispute settlement reports are not precedents'.[126] However, reports adopted by the DSB are an important part of the GATT *aquis* and therefore should be taken into account where they are relevant to any dispute.[127] The Appellate Body has also underlined that reports are 'part and parcel of the WTO aquis of dispute settlement system'.[128] This is also confirmed by the role of the dispute settlement mechanism of the WTO which is a central element in providing security and predictability to the multilateral trading system.[129]

123 See also article 59 of the ICJ Statute.

124 According to Lauterpacht, the decision of International courts, 'are evidence of the existing rule of law. That does not mean that they do not in fact constitute a source of international law [...] In fact they are to a substantial degree identical with the source of law enumerated in the first three paragraphs of article 38. In form they may be merely a subsidiary means for determining what these sources are. The effect is the same'. Hersch Lauterpacht, *The Development of International Law by International Courts* (Stevens 1958) 117. Other scholars underlined that: 'for jurisprudence to be acknowledged as an autonomous source of law, one would have to acknowledge law making powers to the WTO Judges. This however, would run counter the explicit wording of article 3.2 DSU [...] It is undeniably an interpretative element and not a source of law'. Matsushita, Schoenbaum and Mavroidis (n. 84) 62–63. See also, Picone and Ligustro (n. 118) 581; Lorand Bartels, 'The Separation of Powers in the WTO: How to Avoid Judicial Activism' (2004) 53.4 *International and Comparative Law Quarterly* 861.

125 Article 3 of the DSU.

126 Nathalie McNelis, 'What Obligations Are Created by World Trade Organization Dispute Settlement Reports?' (2003) 37.3 *Journal of World Trade* 652. Professor Jackson stated that: 'a strict "precedent effect" or stare decisis is not operating, even though panels do often cite prior panel reports to support their conclusions. However, there clearly is a de facto precedential effect operating, albeit not strictly'. John H. Jackson, *The Jurisprudence of GATT & the WTO* (Cambridge University Press 2000) 127.

127 Appellate Body Reports, *Japan – Alcoholic Beverages II*, para. 108 and *US – Shrimp* (Article 21.5 Malaysia), para. 109.

128 Appellate Body Report, *US – Stainless Steel from Mexico*, para. 160.

129 In order to maintain coherence, Article 4 of the Working Procedures of the Appellate Body sets forth that 'to ensure consistency and coherence in decision making, and to draw on the individual and collective expertise of the Members, the Members shall convene on a regular basis to discuss matters of policy, practice and procedure. The Members shall stay abreast of dispute settlement activities and other relevant activities of the WTO and, in particular, each Member shall receive all documents filed in an

The jurisprudence clarifies WTO rules. It enforces and clarifies the law, overcomes shortcomings and ensures the evolution of international law.[130] In the field of trade remedies, jurisprudence has played an important role in clarifying existing provisions, filling the gaps and raising new issues for negotiations.[131] In the trade remedies area, the WTO jurisprudence has been largely used to fill in the lacunae of the text and clarify existing provisions. The 'zeroing saga', for example, helped the Member States to clarify the methodology for the calculation of dumping margins. The several reports on the definition of subsidies helped to distinguish between which subsidies are allowed and which are not allowed under the SCM Agreement. The reports on safeguard helped to clarify the standard required for the opening of an investigation. The role of the DSB is therefore extremely important in leading the Member States to adopt measures that are more in line with their role of reactions of injured States.

In addition to the international dispute settlement, the SCM Agreement and the Anti-dumping Agreement request Members whose national legislation contains provisions on anti-dumping and countervailing measures to maintain judicial, arbitral or administrative tribunals or procedures for the purpose, *inter alia*, of the prompt review of administrative actions relating to final determinations and reviews of determinations.[132] The Anti-dumping Agreement and the SCM Agreement also requests those tribunals or procedures to be independent of the authorities responsible for the determination or review in question. The SCM Agreement (but not the Anti-dumping Agreement) obliges mentioned Members to provide all interested parties who participated in the administrative proceedings and are directly and individually affected by the administrative actions with access to review. The evaluation made by the domestic tribunals and by domestic procedures is different from the evaluation of the panels and the Appellate Body. First of all, in domestic proceedings private firms may have standing rights under domestic law and thus can challenge the adoption of an anti-dumping, countervailing measure before the domestic courts. This means that a

appeal in accordance with the objectives set out in paragraph 1, the division responsible for deciding each appeal shall exchange views with the other Members before the division finalizes the appellate Report for circulation to the WTO Members'. On this issue Ehlermann stated: 'the exchange of views [...] have contributed greatly to consistency and coherence of decision making'. Claus Dieter Ehlermann, 'Six Years on the Bench of the World Trade Court' (2002) 36.4 *Journal of World Trade* 655. According to Blanchard, there is 'un effet persuasive découlant d'une forme de jurisprudentialisation des décision'. Dominique Blanchard, 'Les effets des rapports de l'organe de règlement des différends de l'OMC – A la lumière du règlement (CE) 1515/2001 du Conseil de l'Union européenne' (2003) 464 *Revue du Marché Commun et de l'Union Européenne* 42.

130 According to Brownlie, 'a coherent body of jurisprudence will naturally have important consequences for the law'. Brownlie (n. 175) 19. See also Giorgio Sacerdoti, Alan Yanovich and Jan Bohanes (eds.), *The WTO at Ten: The Contribution of the Dispute Settlement System* (Cambridge University Press 2006).

131 Roberto Soprano, 'La rilevanza dei precedenti giurisprudenziali OMC come possibile rimedio al problema dello "zeroing"' (2008) 22.2 *Diritto del Commercio Internazionale* 433.

132 Article 13 of the Anti-dumping Agreement and 23 of the SCM Agreement.

private firm can request that a domestic court, of the country imposing e.g. anti-dumping measures, review the application of such a measure. However, in many countries, in national courts an interested party may invoke a violation of a domestic norm but cannot invoke a breach of WTO law.[133] Most WTO Members' domestic legal systems deny *direct effects* to WTO Agreements.[134] This goes beyond the basic distinction of dualist and monist approaches to international law and means that the WTO does not create any rights for individuals and that parties cannot rely on WTO norms in cases of judicial review of domestic acts involving national legislation. Thus, individuals cannot invoke GATT in a court in order to challenge the lawfulness of a domestic act and courts cannot take into consideration WTO rules to assess the lawfulness of a domestic act in an action brought before them. In conclusion, the WTO system introduces dispute settlement mechanisms which control the use of trade remedies and intervenes in cases of violation of WTO or domestic norms and prevents such instruments from being used for protectionist purposes.

133 Thomas Cottier, 'A Theory of Direct Effect in Global Law', in Armin Von Bogdandy, Petros Mavroidis and Yves Mény (eds.), *European Integration and International Coordination, Studies in Transnational Economic Law in Honour of Claus-Dieter Ehlermann* (Kluwer Law International 2002) 99, 112–15; Cottier and Oesch, 'WTO Law, Precedents and Legal Change' (Ch.1 n.123) 27, 31–3; Thomas Cottier and Krista Nadakavukaren Schefer, 'The Relationship between World Trade Organization Law, National and Regional Law' (1998) 1.1 *Journal of International Economic Law* 83, 120–22; John H. Jackson, *The Jurisprudence of GATT & the WTO* (Cambridge University Press 2000) 328; Judson Osterhoudt Berkey, 'The European Court of Justice and Direct Effect for the GATT: A Question Worth Revisiting' (2000) 9.4. *European Journal of International Law* 626–657; Joel Trachtman, 'Bananas, Direct Effect and Compliance' (1999) 10.4 *European Journal of International Law* 655 and John Barcelo 'The Status of WTO Rules in U.S. Law', in Cornell Law School Research Paper No. 06–004, 2006; Nupur Chowdhury, 'The (Absence of) Direct Effect of WTO Law – Current Developments within the Indian Legal System', in Claudio Dordi (ed.), *The Absence of Direct Effect of WTO in the EC and in Other Countries* (Giappichelli 2010).

134 In the EU, the direct effect of GATT and WTO rules has been examined in several cases by the EU Court of Justice. In particular in the *Nakajima case*, ECJ found that the EU basic regulation on anti-dumping was adopted expressly to comply with the EU's WTO obligations, and that the regulation could be examined for legality with regard to WTO obligations on that basis. See Case C-69/89, *Nakajima All Precision Co. Ltd. v. Council*, 1991 E.C.R. I-2069 as well as Joined Cases C-120/06P & C-121/06P, *Fabbrica Italiana Accumulatori Motocarri Montecchio SpA v. Council*, 2008 E.C.R. I-6513, Case C-94/02, *Etablissements Biret et Cie Safeguard Agreement v. Council*, 2003 E.C.R. I- 10565; Joined Cases C-21/72 & C-24/74, *International Fruit Company NV v. Produktschap voor Groenten en Fruit* 1972 E.C.R. I-1219. See also, John H. Jackson, 'Direct Effect of Treaties in the US and the EU, the Case of the WTO: Some Perceptions and Proposals', in Anthony Arnull, Piet Eeckhout and Takis Tridimas (eds.), *Continuity and Change in EU Law: Essays in Honour of Sir Francis Jacobs* (Oxford University Press 2008) 361, 373–75; Piet Eeckhout, *External Relations of the European Union: Legal And Constitutional Foundations* (Oxford European Community Law Library 2004) 330.

3 Trade remedies in WTO and public international law

3.1. Political and economic rationale of trade remedies

For a long time, trade remedies have been accused of being the new tools of protectionism.[1] They have often been blamed for being the new ways by which first traditional users, and then new users, have justified the imposition of import barriers. In particular, anti-dumping measures have been supported by economic motivations in only a few circumstances (*i.e.* predatory dumping). In all other cases these remedies have been accused of advancing industrial interests whilst impacting negatively on consumers and competition.[2] An interesting study by Zanardi showed that as a consequence of the increase in limits on recourses to tariffs and non-tariff instruments imposed during the Uruguay Round, was that many WTO Members adopted trade remedies (in particular anti-dumping) legislation.[3] It cannot be denied that trade remedies are mostly used in sectors such as steel and chemicals that were subject to tariff elimination or deep reduction in plurilateral treaties concluded during the Uruguay Round. However, arguments in favour of anti-dumping and safeguard have also relied on liberalization of markets as they may promote further liberalization as countries would not agree, in their absence, on treaties on tariff reductions.

The widespread use of trade remedies has political and economic motivations. From an economic point of view trade remedies increase the price of foreign goods and offer protection to domestic industries. Although they have not been created with protectionist intent, they can create barriers to imports. By levying import duties or imposing a quota (as a safeguard) a Member State can exclude

1 Emmanuel Nyahoho, Cédrick Lefebvre and Claire Malbouires, 'Les mesures anti-dumping: un phenomene commercial largement répandu' (2007) 38.3 *Etudes Internationales* 361; David Richardson and Edward M. Graham, *Global Competition Policy* (Peterson Institute 1997) 224; Ibek Debroy and Debashis Chakraborty (eds.), *Anti-Dumping: Global Abuse of a Trade Policy Instrument* (Academic Foundation 2007) and Anne O Krueger and Chonira Aturupane, *The WTO as an International Organization* (University of Chicago Press 2000) 407.

2 Maurizio Zanardi, 'Antidumping: A Problem in International Trade' (2005) 22.3 *European Journal of Political Economy* 591.

3 Maurizio Zanardi, 'Anti-dumping: What are the Numbers to Discuss at Doha?' (2004) 27.3 *The World Economy* 403.

foreign competitors from a domestic market. From a political point of view, it is possible for a State, under the pressure of influential lobbies, to use trade remedies for protectionist purposes.[4] Domestic producers lobby government in order to receive protection from foreign competitors. The risk is particularly high in periods of crisis when entrepreneurs ask governments to support their production and exports. Developing countries have also challenged the use of trade remedies by developed countries.[5] The imposition of duties or quotas on imports from developing countries may seriously affect their developmental needs. In some circumstances these measures can also conflict with other stimulus policies such as aid for industrial development. However, in the last few years, developing countries have become users of trade remedies, and in particular anti-dumping measures, in order to protect their industries.

It cannot be denied that the main target of trade remedies is China and its cheap exports around the world. Since its accession to the WTO, the number of trade measures adopted against Chinese products has increased drastically. Many scholars have accused trade remedies, mainly anti-dumping, of being an instrument to counter cheap Chinese competition. Similarly, States have been criticized for using trade remedies to counter social and environmental Chinese 'advantages' and thus misusing such instruments that are intended for completely different purposes. Yet others, more harshly, have accused trade remedies of protecting sectors which lack investment in innovation or would no longer be competitive.

Another highly debated concern has been the proliferation of the use of trade remedies. In particular the so call 'traditional users' such as the European Union, the United States or Canada have been overtaken by the 'new users' India, Argentina, Brazil, Pakistan or Turkey.[6] The spread of the use of trade remedies by many countries has become a source of concern for companies and economists. The increase in their use has also challenged the Dispute Settlement System of the WTO. In fact, they represent the main cause of disputes and contribute to an increased workload of panellists and Members of the Appellate Body with an impact on the 'length of the trials' in Geneva.

It is true that the misuse of trade remedies could affect the global trading system. However, from a legal point of view, they should not be perceived as protectionist measures *per se* but, as explained previously, they should be regarded as particular and strictly limited unilateral reactions allowed by the WTO system to protect the interests of injured States. Their misuse should, of course, be condemned.

4 According to some scholars, 'etant largement impliquées dans le processus, ces dernières (les enterprises nationales), forment des groups de pression qui incitent les gouvernement à agir en leur faveur et ce, au detriment des consommateurs qui n'ont pas voix au chapitre, et des concurrents étrangers qui l'ont moins'. Nyahoho, Lefebvre and Malbouires (Ch.3 n.1) 365.

5 The United States and the European Community were the major users of trade remedies since a few years ago. Currently, China, India and Turkey are among the major users of trade remedies, mainly anti-dumping duties.

6 The statistics on the use of anti-dumping measures are reported on the WTO web site.

3.2. A brief history of trade remedies' negotiations

Historical developments in trade remedies demonstrate that changes in the trade remedies agreements have been aimed at limiting the possibility of using measures for protectionist purposes and to affect free trade. Since the entry into force of the relevant articles of the GATT, negotiations during GATT and WTO, Rounds have mainly concentrated on the reduction of discretion of the investigating authorities. The different positions of States in negotiations also reflect the different interests of importing and exporting countries, as well as developing countries' perspectives and their changing role and power. The European Union and the United States have historically been the largest users of trade remedies to protect their domestic industries, with exporting countries such as Singapore, Hong Kong, the Nordic Countries and Korea often complaining about the misuse of such trade remedies against their exports. However, the situation partially changed during the Doha Round. The European Union and the United States are no longer the largest users of measures. Since 1995 India, China, Turkey and Argentina emerged as 'new users' of the mentioned measures, addressing both exports from the European Union and United States. However, the situation has not been completely reversed and proposals still deal with the needs of developing countries and reduction of arbitrariness during investigation.

From an historical point of view, the drafting of the GATT/WTO had two approaches: allowing a State to adopt these measures and drawing boundaries for their use. As Zanardi noted, when in 1923 Jacob Viner wrote his masterpiece *Dumping: A Problem in International Trade*, he did not imagine that, almost a century later, the remedies envisaged to alter dumping could become a source of concern for international trade.[7] Similar conclusions can be drawn for countervailing and safeguard measures as their use has been drastically challenged in WTO 'courts'. For many years, trade remedies were based merely on domestic legislation without any international framework to rely upon.[8] States were left free to legislate for the criteria and procedures for adopting trade remedies. This unilateral approach very soon revealed its weakness as it created an obstacle to free trade policies. In fact, these measures create barriers to trade by doing exactly the opposite of what liberalism theories were trying to achieve through bilateral and then multilateral liberalization. States decided to intervene, to gradually introduce common definitions and criteria for the adoption of the measures.

7 Zanardi, 'Antidumping: A Problem in International Trade' (Ch.3 n.2) 592.

8 According to Jackson and others, a first (but limited in scope) international agreement to counteract dumping was signed by Great Britain and the Netherlands in the nineteenth century and after then other 10 European countries adhered to the pact. The agreement referred to dumping of sugar and remained in force for 18 years. However, it has never been enlarged to cover other products. Jackson, Davey and Sykes (Ch.1 n.48) 693.

3.2.1. Anti-dumping measures

In the anti-dumping domain, the first domestic anti-dumping law was enacted by Canada in 1903.[9] Following the Canadian example, many other countries started to unilaterally adopt legislation against dumping to protect domestic industries from a perceived threat of predatory behaviour from abroad.[10] New Zealand, Australia, Great Britain and the United States adopted anti-dumping laws between 1905 and 1921.[11] However, more than to counteract dumping practices, national anti-dumping legislation was already perceived as an instrument to protect domestic enterprises from foreign competition. In the absence of an international discipline, States were free to decide when imports could be considered to have been dumped and match all the other conditions necessary to adopt trade barriers. Put differently, national anti-dumping laws were regarded as legislation allowing States to raise import barriers to trade without infringing MFN (Most Favoured Nation) clauses often included in bilateral agreements. As remarked by Jackson, other 'nations feared that their trading partners would use the laws as protectionist devices, rather than as simple regulatory measures to deal with patently unfair practices'.[12] Domestic legislation was of 'as much concern as the dumping practices themselves'.[13]

A first effort to create an international regulation on anti-dumping was made by the League of Nations in the 1920s. Whilst not taking important decisions, the result of the League of Nations and World Economic Conference in 1933 was the study of Viner's *A Memorandum on Dumping* which described the different forms and effects of dumping.[14] Following the debate, States took a step towards the creation of anti-dumping rules during the negotiations for the conclusion of the GATT 1947. Drawing from the text presented by the United States proposing the introduction of an article containing general principles on anti-dumping and countervailing measures, Parties adopted Article VI of the GATT. That Article, still in force, provides a basic discipline on anti-dumping and countervailing duties, defining dumping as the practice where 'products of one country are introduced into the commerce of another country at less than the normal value of the products'. According to the Article, 'dumping is to be condemned if it causes or

9 Pietro S. Nivola, *Regulating Unfair Trade* (Brookings Institution Press 1993) 31.
10 Jackson, Davey and Sykes (Ch.1 n.48) 694.
11 Greg Mastel, *Antidumping Laws and the U.S. Economy* (Sharpe 1998) 18.
12 Jackson, Davey and Sykes (Ch.1 n.48) 694.
13 *Ibid.*
14 Viner divided dumping in 'sporadic', 'short-run or intermittent' and 'long-run or continuous'. Viner classified dumping according to its duration because of its different economic impact. He condemned only short-run dumping because 'it could induce a maladjustment in the use of productive resource of the importing country', see Viner, *A Memorandum on Dumping* (League of Nations 1926). However, Viner's classification has been accused to be 'too simplistic' and 'misjudging the true costs of resource misallocation in the importing country'. Ivo Van Bael and Jean-Francois Bellis, *Anti-Dumping and Other Trade Protection Laws of the EC* (Kluwer Law International 2004) 30; Gabrielle Marceau, *Anti-Dumping and Anti-Trust Issues in Free-Trade Areas* (Oxford University Press 1994) 14–15.

threatens material injury to an established industry in the territory of a contracting party or materially retards the establishment of a domestic industry'. Contracting Parties also decided to include basic rules relating to the calculation of the margins of dumping, material injury, limits to anti-dumping duties and other general, very general, provisions. However, Article VI of the GATT did not address many concerns. In fact, the adoption of the international GATT norm between all Contracting Parties was drastically limited by the so called 'grandfather clause'.[15] As a result of that clause, bigger users of anti-dumping instruments, such as Canada and the United States, were not bound by GATT rules and could keep using their domestic norms because they predated GATT rules.[16] Furthermore, the very general content of the Article did not cover all the aspects of the investigation and substantive elements for adopting anti-dumping measures. The shortcomings of the norms allowed States to circumvent the rules and use anti-dumping measures to raise restrictive barriers to trade. As remarked by Mastel, 'by the 1960's, antidumping laws were in use worldwide and a new set of concerns began to rise. A number of countries viewed the injudicious or unjust application of antidumping duties as a potential threat to free trade'.[17]

In 1958 a panel of experts was set up to study possible solutions to the abuse of anti-dumping measures. The panel examined different domestic legislation in order to provide a common discipline aimed at harmonizing domestic legislation and at defining the most critical terms which had not been addressed by GATT. Despite its absence of binding effect, the report was of foremost importance during the negotiations of the Kennedy Round. During those negotiations, States continued to express their concerns about the abuse of anti-dumping measures by States and pushed for a reform of Article VI. They all agreed to maintain basic rules and to build up on them. The proposal of Great Britain[18] aimed at limiting discretion in anti-dumping investigations.[19] There were many comments by States with[20] the European Community pushing for a binding

15 The grandfather clause was an exception to GATT rules that allowed Members with an old rule to continue to apply it to existing situations although the new rule was put into force. Marc Hansen and Edwin Vermulst, 'The GATT Protocol of Provisional Application: A Dying Grandfather' (1989) 4.5 *Columbia Journal of Transnational Law* 263.

16 Trebilcock and Howse (Ch.2 n. 19) 233 and Mastel (n. 270) 22.

17 Mastel (Ch.3 n.11) 23.

18 According to Grey, the British authorities wanted more freedom for their exporters to dump in Canada and to compete with the Japanese. In relation to the United States, the British wanted to limit the ability of the Treasury to harass exporters who might be dumping and lead the U.S. Tariff Commission to apply a more meaningful concept of injury. Rodney Grey, *The Development of the Canadian Antidumping System* (Private Planning Association of Canada 1973) 9.

19 Draft International Code on Antidumping Procedure and Practice: Note by the United Kingdom Delegation, GATT, Doc. No. spec. (65) 86 (October 7, 1965).

20 Comments by the European Community, GATT, Doc. No. TN.64/NTB/W/1C/Add. 1, (April 21, 1966); Comments by Japanese Government, GATT, Doc. No. TN.64/NTB/W/4, (January 27, 1966); Note by United States Delegation, GATT

norm and the Canadian delegation proposing new rules on 'sporadic dumping'.[21] After years of debates, negotiating Countries agreed on the 'Agreement on the Implementation of Article VI' (hereafter 'AD Code 1967') introducing a definition of 'domestic industry'[22] and 'like product'[23] and requiring dumping to be the principal cause of injury.[24] However, the AD Code 1967 was not ratified by the United States due to the opposition of the Senate to the modifications of domestic law.

The failure of the AD Code 1967 was still a live topic during negotiations of the Tokyo Round which concentrated more on non-tariff barriers than on anti-dumping. States were afraid that opposition between countries during anti-dumping negotiations would affect the whole *Round*. [25] The negotiations were characterized by the proposals made by developing countries that began to raise their voices in the international community. They increasingly started to participate in debates to protect their economic and developmental interests after having obtained independence from their colonizers.[26]

In that respect, the Egyptian representative made it clear that anti-dumping rules should be subject to reform and also reflect the interests of developing countries.[27] It proposed that rules relating to constructed normal value should not be applied during investigations concerning imports from developing countries and measures should not be imposed in case of negligible volumes

Doc. No. TN.64/NTB/W/3, (January 10, 1966); Comments by Denmark, GATT Doc. No. TN.64/NTB/W/12 Add.7, (July 4, 1966); Comments by Sweden, GATT Doc. No. TN.64/NTB/W/12 Add.8, (July 7, 1966) and Comments by Australia, GATT Doc. No. TN.64/NTB/W/12 Add. 9, (July 8, 1966).

21 The 'sporadic dumping' or 'one-shot-dumping' was defined as a mean whereby exporting producers could dispose of temporary surpluses 'quickly and conveniently without disturbing their regular market'. Terence P. Stewart, *The GATT Uruguay Round: A Negotiating History (1986–1992)*, Vol. 1 (Kluwer Law 1993) 1420.

22 The domestic producers as a whole of the like products or those of them whose collective output of the product constitutes a major proportion of the total of those products. Article 4 of the AD Code 1967.

23 Identical, i.e., alike in all respects to the product under consideration, or in the absence of such a product, another product which although not alike in all respects, has characteristics closely resembling [the dumped product]. Article 2 of the AD Code 1967.

24 The dumping had to be 'demonstrably the principal cause' of the injury. Article 3 of the AD Code 1967.

25 According to Trebilcock and Howse, the EU sought to ensure compliance by the United States in order to reopen the Code during the Tokyo Round. Trebilcock and Howse (Ch.2 n.19) 234.

26 According to Lowenfeld, 'the 1979 AD Code remained for the most part, an agreement among the industrial countries, but India and Brazil, the States that have been the leaders among developing states in the GATT/WTO system, both became original parties to the Anti-Dumping Code, and Egypt, Korea, Mexico, Pakistan, and Singapore signed on subsequently'. Andreas Lowenfeld, *International Economic Law* (Oxford University Press 2003) 249.

27 Statement by the Representative of Egypt, GATT, Doc. No.MTN/NTM/INF/30, (June 30, 1978), paras. 2–3.

of imports.[28] The text agreed upon by Contracting Parties (Agreement on Implementation of Article VI of General Agreement on Tariffs and Trade) modified the previous AD Code 1967 and introduced basic rules for the settlement of disputes concerning anti-dumping.[29]

In 1986 a new Round began. The *Uruguay Round*, in which 125 countries participated, started with the declaration of *Punta de l'Este* and terminated with the adoption of the Marrakesh declaration. The idea of agreeing on a new anti-dumping text was due to a proposal of Korea whose products had been increasingly subjected to anti-dumping cases brought by the European Community, the United States, Canada and Australia.[30] From the beginning of the negotiations, countries divided into three groups. The so called *right wing* (Singapore, Hong Kong and Nordic Countries)[31] mainly exporter countries, pushed for amendments which could give more detailed rules and limited discretion in investigations in order to overcome shortcomings of the text and reduce the possibility for a State to adopt anti-dumping measures for protectionist purposes.[32] The *left wing* (United States and European Community)[33] did not want to modify the text in force and clarified existing provisions. They wanted to maintain Tokyo Round rules which gave them space to adopt anti-dumping measures to protect their domestic industry.[34]Another group was composed of developing countries who pushed for a reform which took into account their developmental needs in the investigations. Only in late 1991 was the text of the Agreement on Implementation of Article VI of the GATT (hereafter 'Anti-dumping Agreement') approved by States and it

28 Stewart (Ch.3 n.21) 1452.

29 According to Trebilcock and Howse, 'the negotiations concentrated mainly on causality and injury determination. [R]ather than requiring that the dumping be demonstrably the principal cause, the 1979 Code only specified that any injuries caused by other factors must not be attributed to the dumped imports. Making it more consistent with the US position'. Trebilcock and Howse (Ch.2 n.19) 234.

30 Gary Horlick and Eric Shea, 'The WTO Antidumping Agreement' (1995) 29.1 *Journal of World Trade* 7.

31 *Amendments to the Antidumping Code*, Nordic Countries, GATT, Doc. MTN. GNG/NG8/W/64, (December 22, 1989); *Amendments to the Antidumping Code*, Hong Kong, GATT, Doc. MTN. GNG/NG8/W/51, (December 22, 1989). See also, *Amendments to the Antidumping Code*, Japan, GATT, Doc. MTN. GNG/NG8/W/48, (August 3, 1989).

32 The Group of exporting countries wanted 'antidumping rules as tight and explicit as possible'. Stewart (Ch.3 n.11) 1499.

33 *Communication from the European Communities to GATT Uruguay Round-Anti-dumping Code*, GATT, Doc. MTN.GNG/NG8/W/63, (December 20, 1989) and *Amendments to the Antidumping Code*, United States, GATT, Doc. MTN. GNG/NG8/W/50, (December 20, 1989).

34 According to Lowenfeld, 'dumping and antidumping became seriously contested, with the European Community and the United States determined to plug "loopholes" and the target countries, notably Japan, Hong Kong, and Korea, seeking both to revisit the basic concepts embodied in the 1967 and 1979 codes and to eliminate practices that seemed to tilt the required price comparison against imports'. Lowenfeld (Ch.3 n.26) 249.

entered into force in 1995 with the ratification of the Marrakesh Agreement.[35] This was recognized as a milestone achieved in the development of an international discipline on anti-dumping and[36] provided new detailed rules and regulates many new aspects of the anti-dumping regime.

In 2001 the WTO Ministerial Conference decided to begin a new Round of negotiations called the *Doha Developmental Round.* Although WTO Doha negotiations concentrated more on the Agreement on Agriculture and NAMA (Non-Agricultural Market Access), they also focused on the reform of anti-dumping provisions.[37] Countries had different positions and the EC, and in particular the US, faces the interests of the 'Friends of Anti-dumping Negotiations'.[38] During the negotiations conducted so far, countries have discussed new rules to limit what are still considered the main causes of abuse of the anti-dumping instruments such as a mandatory 'lesser duty rule';[39] 'price undertakings' for developing countries involved in the investigations;[40] the prohibition of 'zeroing'; the calculation methods of

35 For the Carlisle texts, *Report of the Acting Chairman of the Informal Group on Anti-dumping*, GATT, Doc. No. Mtn.GNG/NG8/W/83/Add.5 (July 23, 1990) and Stewart (Ch.3 n.21) 1519.

36 According to Mastel, 'the Uruguay Round transformed the GATT rules on anti-dumping from general guidelines to what is now essentially a fully detailed international system to control dumping'. Mastel (Ch.3 n.21) 23. See also, Harald Sander and Andras Inotai, *World Trade after the Uruguay Round: Prospects and Policy Options for the Twenty-first Century* (Routledge 1996) 43.

37 The Ministerial Council sets that 'in light of experience and of the increasing application of these instruments by members, we agree to negotiations aimed at clarifying and improving disciplines under the Agreements on Implementation of article VI of the GATT 1994 and on Subsidies and Countervailing Measures, while preserving the basic concepts, principles and effectiveness of these Agreements and their instruments and objectives, and taking into account the needs of developing and least-developed participants. In the initial phase of the negotiations, participants will indicate the provisions, including disciplines on trade distorting practices, that they seek to clarify and improve in the subsequent phase'. World Trade Organization Ministerial Declaration. WT/MIN (01)/DEC/1, (November 14, 2001), para. 28. See also, William Kerr and Laura Loppacher, 'Anti-dumping in the Doha Negotiations: Fairy Tales at the World Trade Organization' (2004) 38.2 *Journal of World Trade* 211.

38 The "Friends of Anti-dumping Negotiations" (FAN) is a group of Member States that was created in 2003 and included Brazil, Chile, China, Columbia, Costa Rica, Hong Kong, Israel, Japan, Korea, Norway, Mexico, Singapore, Switzerland, Thailand, Turkey, and the Separate Customs Territory of Taiwan, Penghu, Kinmen, and Matsu. It was created from the initiative of a coalition of countries brought together to oppose U.S. legislation on the Byrd Amendment in 2001.. They want to change WTO rules to prevent abuse of anti-dumping measures and burdensome or unnecessary investigations. Linda M. Young and John Wainio, 'The Anti-dumping Negotiations: Proposals, Positions and Anti-dumping Profiles' (2005) 6.1 *The Estey Centre Journal of International Law and Trade Policy* 30.

39 World Trade Organization. Negotiating Group on Rules. Note by the Chairman. Compilation of Issues and Proposals Identified by Participants in the Negotiating Group on Rules, TN/RL/W/143, (August 22, 2003), para. 49.

40 *Ibid.* para. 46.

'injury' and the concept of 'domestic industry';[41] as well as the adoption of a 'cost saving' and a 'swift control mechanism' which, respectively, reduce the costs of the investigations and the negative effects produced by their initiation.[42]

3.2.2. Safeguard measures

The historical evolution of the regulation of safeguard is also fundamental for highlighting the reasons for adopting more stringent legislation. Similar to anti-dumping and countervailing measures, the first multilateral safeguard clause was included in Article XIX of the GATT 1947 and brought from the 1943 Trade Agreement between the United States and Mexico. According to Jackson, Article XIX *'was a result of United States desires'.* [43]

Prior to GATT rules, safeguards or emergency mechanisms had been contemplated by many trade agreements.[44] According to Cottier and Oesch, the reasons for their inclusion in international agreements are that they are vital for the trading system and inherently accompany the process of liberalization and of structural adjustment that goes along with enhancing market access for imported products.[45] Similar views have been shared by Trebilcock and Howse who considered that the rationale for the inclusion of a safeguard provision was twofold: to encourage greater liberalization and to increase the trade regime's flexibility.[46] They allow countries to take trade restrictive measures in cases where liberalization causes prejudice to their domestic industry.[47] The rationale for their inclusion in international agreements may seem, at first glance, a bit odd as trade agreements are aimed at enhancing international trade and therefore are also 'expected to

41 *Ibid.* paras.15–20.

42 World Trade Organization. Negotiating Group on Rules, Paper by Brazil; Colombia; Costa Rica; Hong Kong, China; Israel; Korea; Japan; Mexico; Norway; Separate Customs Territory of Taiwan, Penghu, Kinmen and Matsu; Singapore; Switzerland; Thailand and Turkey. TN/RL/W/46, (January 24, 2003), para. 15.

43 Jackson, *The World Trade and the Law of GATT* (n. 34) 553.

44 William Clayton, *GATT: An Analysis and Appraisal of the General Agreement on Tariffs and Trade* (US Council of the International Chamber of Commerce 1995) 36 also quoted in Trebilcock and Howse (n. 144) 300.

45 Cottier and Oesch (Ch.1 n.36) 486. Free trade thinking suggests that attempts to restrict import surges based on fair trade should be prevented as such surges are not resulting from any market failure but is on the contrary a result of the normal operation of a free market.

46 Trebilcock and Howse (Ch.2 n.19) 301. On this point Cottier and Oesch stated that safeguard instruments are 'politically necessary in order to undertake liberalization in the first place and find the necessary majorities to do so at home'. Cottier and Oesch (n. 36) 486.

47 The Appellate Body précised that 'Not any measure suspending, withdrawing or modifying a GATT obligation or concession will fall within the scope of Article XIX:1 (a). Rather, it is only measures suspending, withdrawing, or modifying a GATT obligation or concession that a Member finds it must be temporarily released from in order to pursue a course of action necessary to prevent or remedy serious injury that will constitute "safeguard measures"'. Appellate Body Report, *Indonesia – Iron or Steel Products (Viet Nam)*, para. 7.14.

increase import flows by mutually advantageous concessions'.[48] However, it should be considered that liberalization may enhance import flows more than the expected level thereby affecting the domestic industry of an importing country party to the agreement. In this situation the Parties face the option of maintaining import flows and injury to the domestic industry but respecting treaty obligations or withdrawing the agreement and saving the domestic industry but reducing the overall level of liberalization. This is generally the rationale for having a 'safety valve' in trade agreements.[49] From a political point of view, this will give more confidence to States and provide arguments for overcoming internal criticism of the risks of liberalization that are often raised before the conclusion of free trade agreements. Despite the fact that GATT Contracting Parties were aware of the risks of trade restrictive application of the mentioned provisions and laid down in Article XIX other conditions under which safeguard measures may be imposed, they could not impede the heavy recourse by states to those instruments. In fact, during the GATT period around 150 safeguard measures were notified to the Contracting Parties to the GATT 1947.

The lack of precise rules for regulating many aspects of the imposition of safeguard measures led to disputes on, for example, whether the principle of non-discrimination (*i.e.* to apply safeguard measures on all exporters) should have been applicable to Article XIX. While developed countries pushed for the measures to be 'selective' and applicable only against countries considered responsible for affecting domestic industry, developing countries wanted the measures to be general and non-discriminatory. On this point, by settling the *Norwegian Restriction on Imports of Certain Textile Products* case, the panel ruled that safeguard measures should be applied in a non-discriminatory manner.[50] The adoption of the report caused Contracting Parties to have recourse to so called 'grey area' measures other than Article XIX in order to face import surges considered to be injurious: *i.e.* Voluntary Export Restraints (VERs), Voluntary Restraint Arrangements (VRAs) and Orderly Marketing Arrangements (OMAs). These measures were not formally adopted by the importing country but taken by the exporting country and avoided all the difficulties and compensation required by GATT Article XIX.[51]

During the Tokyo Round, negotiations were conducted to put into force new rules on safeguards but, despite the efforts of the Contracting Parties, they did not lead to a conclusion. The first specific agreement on safeguard, the Agreement on Safeguard (hereafter the 'Safeguard Agreement') was only adopted during the Uruguay Round and entered into force in 1995.[52]

48 UNCTAD, *Dispute Settlement: WTO Safeguard Measures* (United Nations 2003) 3.
49 WTO *Secretariat, Guide to the Uruguay Agreements* (Kluwer Law International 1999), 103. See also Dam (Ch.2 n.105) 99.
50 *Norwegian Restriction on Imports of Certain Textile Products*, BISD 1981, Suppl. 27, 119
51 Picone and Ligustro (n. 118) 307.
52 According to Rodriguez, after 10 years, particularly as a result of the WTO Appellate Body's strict approach to safeguards, the conditions set up in the Safeguard Agreement have been notably hardened. The main examples can be seen in (1) the recovery of some obsolete conditions foreseen in Article XIX such as the requirement to demonstrate 'unforeseen developments'; (2) the so-called RSSS rule in order to evaluate the increase in

The text that is still in force and not subject to negotiations has been deeply analysed by the WTO panellists and members of the Appellate Body. In report after report the provisions of the articles have been clarified in such a restrictive manner that, as noted by Sykes, it is almost impossible to meet the standard set for the use of safeguards.[53]

3.2.2. Countervailing measures

Although subsidies are a widespread practice which was already employed in the mercantilist era, the first international rules were only provided for by Article XVI of GATT in 1974.[54] Before the adoption of the GATT, only domestic rules regulated the use of countervailing measures against subsidies, allowing the importing State the possibility of levying duties on imports of allegedly subsidized goods.

Under the first international GATT rules, Contracting Parties were required to notify other Contracting Parties of their granted or maintained subsidies and cease to grant export subsidies to non-primary goods that result in the export of such products at a price lower than the comparable price charged for like products to buyers in the domestic market ('bi-level' or 'dual price' requirements).[55] More than rules to restrict the use of subsidies, the Article tried to create a framework where States affected by subsidies could hold consultations with the granting State to find friendly solutions where there are diverging interests.[56] Countervailing measures were regulated by a general provision of GATT Article VI dealing with both subsidies and dumping.

imports; (3) the non-attribution requirement within the framework of the assessment of causation; (4) the completeness demanded of the internal investigation in relation to the proceduralization of some substantive conditions; (5) the restriction of the scope of safeguard measures to the parallelism and effective injury attributed to the increase in imports; and (6) the reinforcement of the content and timing of notifications. Pablo Martin Rodriguez, 'Safeguards in the World Trade Organization Ten Years After: A Dissociated State of the Law?' (2007) 41.1 *Journal of World Trade* 189. For an overview on the GATT/WTO cases related to safeguards Working Party Report, *Report on the Withdrawal by the United States of a Tariff Concession under Article XIX of the General Agreement on Tariffs and Trade* (Hatter's Fur); Panel Report, *Norway – Restrictions on Imports of Certain Textile Products*; Panel Report *Chile – Price Band System*; Appellate Body Report, *US – Line Pipe*; Appellate Body Report, *US – Lamb*; Appellate Body Report, *US – Wheat Gluten*; Appellate Body Report, *Korea – Dairy*; Appellate Body Report, *Argentina – Footwear (EC)*.

53 Alan O. Sykes, 'The Safeguards Mess: A Critique of WTO Jurisprudence' (2003) John M. Olin Program in Law and Economics Working Paper No. 187.

54 Triggiani (Ch.2 n.62) 1.

55 One of the main characteristics of the first GATT rules on subsidies was the distinction between primary (any product of farm, forest or fishery, or any mineral) and non-primary products. Developing countries always complained about this distinction that favoured developed countries because allowed subsidies in fields such as agriculture. Picone and Ligustro (n. 118) 235.

56 Richard Rivers and John Greenvald, 'The Negotiation of a Code on Subsidies and Countervailing Measures: Bridging Fundamental Policy Differences' (1979) 11 *Law & Policy International Business* 1447, 1460.

At the conclusion of the Tokyo Round in 1979, a specific Subsidies Code was agreed after years of negotiations delayed by the initial opposition of the United States and the European Communities. The US position was aimed at maintaining its 1930 Tariff Act rules which, by virtue of the grandfather clause, allowed it to levy countervailing measures without showing evidence of injury to its domestic industries. Similarly, the European Communities did not want to commit to any text that could limit its Common Agricultural Policy. One of the main changes in the GATT rules that negotiators achieved during the Tokyo Round was a stringent prohibition against granting of any export subsidies to non-primary products.

The Agreement on Subsidies and Countervailing Measures (SCM Agreement) entered into force in 1995 and applies to subsidies and countervailing duties on (all industrial) goods (the agreement does not apply to services).[57] In its 32 articles, the SCM Agreement defines the meaning of subsidy and provides 'judicial' and unilateral remedies for States seriously prejudiced by the subsidy, whose domestic industry has been injured or whose benefits accruing under the GATT have been nullified or impaired. The so called *'traffic light approach'* of the SCM Agreement divided subsidies into prohibited, actionable and non-actionable subsidies.[58] Under this system, *'red light'* subsidies are prohibited subsidies; *'yellow light'* actionable subsidies, meaning subsidies that are not prohibited but that could be subject to remedies or countervailable where they cause prejudice, injury or impairment or nullification of benefits accruing under the GATT and *'green light'* meaning non-actionable subsidies. This distinction reflects the willingness of negotiators to allow, on the one hand, governments to intervene in the market by subsidizing their industries but, on the other hand, to give Members the possibilities to react where subsidies granted by other Members affect their domestic

57 The SCM Agreement has a 'complex' relationship with the Agreement on Agriculture. Both Agreements include legal provisions that provide explicit or implicit reference to their reciprocal relationship. Article 21.1 of the Agreement on Agriculture, in particular, regulates more broadly the relationship with the other covered agreements relating to the trade in goods (the SCM Agreement is among the Multilateral Trade Agreements in Annex 1A to the WTO Agreement). The mentioned Article provides: 'the provisions of GATT 1994 and of other Multilateral Trade Agreements in Annex 1A to the WTO Agreement shall apply subject to the provisions of this Agreement'. In the *EC – Bananas III* case the Appellate Body stated that Article 21.1 establishes that provisions of the GATT 1994 and of other Multilateral Trade Agreements in Annex 1A apply, 'except to the extent that the Agreement on Agriculture contains specific provisions dealing specifically with the same matter'. Consequently, the interpreter shall find whether the Agreement on Agriculture contains 'specific provisions dealing specifically with the same matter' as the provision of the SCM Agreement which should be compared with. For a deeper analysis on the issue of the relationship between the SCM Agreement and the Agreement on Agriculture see the Appellate Body report, *US – Upland Cotton*, para. 533, the Appellate Body Report, *EC – Bananas III*, para. 155 and the Appellate Body report, *Chile – Price Band System*, para. 186.

58 The non-actionable subsidies provisions are no longer in force after the expiration of the time limit provided by Article 31 of the SCM Agreement in 1999.

industries.[59] In order to counteract subsidies (prohibited and actionable), the SCM Agreement provides two different kinds of remedies: unilateral (track I) and multilateral (track II).

During the Doha Round, negotiations focused mainly on fishery subsidies. On this issue the Ministerial mandate from Hong Kong directed the Negotiating Group on Rules to 'strengthen disciplines on subsidies in the fisheries sector, including through the prohibition of certain forms of fisheries subsidies that contribute to overcapacity and over-fishing' and, as an integral part of the negotiations, to establish 'appropriate and effective special and differential treatment for developing and least-developed Members'.[60] The negotiations were also related to the calculation of the amount of subsidies, the concept of 'export competitiveness' for developing countries and export credit provisions.[61]

3.3. The structure of trade remedies

As described above, the structure of trade remedies is only partially similar to classical forms of self-help. They are triggered by a lawful act that is not in itself sufficient to justify a reaction unless injury is caused.

3.3.1. The act

Differing from traditional forms of self-help, trade remedies are reactions to very narrowly defined acts. In fact, countermeasures, self-defence or retorsion do not clearly describe the act against which they can react. They address any form of aggression, violation of international law or interest, without entering into the details of the act. However, trade remedies can only be adopted to react to specific behaviours.

3.3.1.1. Subsidies

Subsidies are important and widespread instruments of economic policy employed by many governments to pursue domestic and social policies. This form of governmental assistance has a variety of purposes such as fostering production or exports, facilitating the creation and expansion of new industries, creating jobs, etc.[62] On the one hand subsidies improve the conditions of some market agents in

59 For a general overview on the discipline of subsidies see Gustavo Luengo Hernandez de Madrid, *Regulation of Subsidies and State Aids in WTO and EC Law* (Kluwer Law International 2006); Americo Beviglia Zampetti, 'The Uruguay Round Agreement on Subsidies. A Forward-Looking Assessment' (1995) 29.6 *Journal of World Trade* 5; Marc Benitah, *The Law of Subsidies under the GATT/WTO System* (Kluwer Law International 2001); Gary Horlick and Pa Clarke, 'The 1994 WTO Subsidies Agreement' (1994) 17.4 *World Competition* 41.

60 Chairman text Doc. TN/RL/W/236, (December 19, 2008), 85.

61 *Ibid.*

62 The Subsidies code after the Tokyo Round Agreement listed some governmental objectives such as: (a) the elimination of industrial, economic and social disadvantages of specific regions; (b) to facilitate the restructuring, under the socially acceptable

the domestic market. On the other hand, they may distort competition, negatively affecting non-subsidized competitors.

Subsidies have different forms and characteristics. They may be granted to producers or consumers, be specific or general, direct or indirect, have the form of a grant, a 'tax holiday', a loan at a preferential interest rate, etc.[63] The main distinction in international trade rules is between 'domestic' and 'export' subsidies. A domestic subsidy is granted to a recipient for the production of a good regardless of whether the good will be exported or sold in the domestic market.[64] Let's assume for example that the domestic industry of Patria, before receiving a subsidy for the production of good X, sells its product at $10 and cannot compete with foreign X goods imported into Patria's market at $8. In such a case, the domestic industry of Patria would be excluded from the market. If, however, the government of Patria granted a subsidy of $4 to its domestic producer of good X, this product made in Patria would then be sold for less than the imported one and appear more attractive to consumers. In addition to a misallocation of resources into a product whose production would be 'uneconomic but for the subsidy',[65] the subsidy drives competitors out of the market. An export subsidy, on the other hand, is granted to the recipient on the condition that the good be exported. Those subsidies, similar to the 'domestic' ones, misallocate resources, but they lower the price of the good in foreign markets and may distort competition in the market(s) where the subsidized product is exported. The market distortion effect of subsidies prompted governments to find international rules in order to prohibit the granting of subsidies that could negatively affect domestic producers.

Subsidies are difficult to define. Before the entry into force of the SCM Agreement neither the GATT (Articles XVI and VI) nor the Subsidies Code provided a definition of the term 'subsidy'. The lack of clarity and the shortcomings of the Subsidies Code allowed Contracting Parties to adopt their own definition in their domestic norms legitimating frequent recourse to countervailing duties.[66] Internal

conditions, of certain sectors, especially where this has become necessary by reason of changes in trade and economic policies, including international agreements resulting in lower barriers to trade; (c) generally to sustain employment and to encourage re-training and change in employment; (d) to encourage research and development programmes, especially in the field of high-technology industries; (e) the implementation of economic programmes and policies to promote the economic and social development of developing countries; and (f) redeployment of industry in order to avoid congestion and environmental problems. The Agreement on Interpretation and Application of Articles VI, XVI and XXIII of the General Agreement on Tariffs and Trade (hereinafter the 'Subsidies Code') art 11(1).

63 See for example the *US – Tax Incentives* case.

64 Jackson, Davey, and Sykes (Ch.1 n.48) 767.

65 *Ibid.* 768.

66 In the period 1980–86 the US initiated 281 cases, Chile 140, Australia 20, Canada 11, EC 7 and Japan 1. In the same period the States subject to countervailing duties investigations were: Brazil (88), Spain (38), Argentina (32), Mexico (28), Peru (22), France (21), Korea (21), Italy (18), New Zealand (16), Federal Republic of Germany (14), UK (12). According to Stewart, 'the inadequacy of the Subsidies Code to deal with the problem of adverse trade effects of subsidization on imported products can be

rules of the United States defined as 'countervailable subsidies' *benefits* arising from government action, regardless of the nature of that action.[67] On the other hand, many Contracting Parties did not consider that 'every sort of government measure that conferred a benefit could be considered to be a potential subsidy'.[68] During negotiations, whereas the 'Panel on Subsidies' established to prepare works on Article XVI affirmed that it was unnecessary, and in fact impossible, to give a definition to the term,[69] many Parties expressed their view on the need to agree on a specific meaning for the word 'subsidy'.[70] As underlined by scholars,

seen in a sampling of the number and variety of subsidies disputes that arose during the 1980s e.g. the disputes between US and EC mainly on agricultural products, between US and Canada on softwood lumber and between US and Mexico on the preferential price of natural resources for Mexican companies'. Stewart (n. 280) 818.

67 The United States in particular developed a definition which treated as countervailable subsidies 'formal, enforceable' government measures 'which directly led to a discernible benefit being provided'. *Ibid.* 824. See also e.g., the US DOC determination in the 1982 steel cases, set forth in SCM/36, (October 27, 1982). In a dispute between US and Canada the Panel noted that 'the DOC, to determine whether respondents had received subsidies within the meaning of the US CVD law, sought to determine "whether or not respondents have received directly or indirectly an economic benefit"'. Panel Report, *US – Export Restraints*, footnote 157.

68 For example, the European Communities stated that '[w]hile [a] benefit is necessary for a determination of the existence of subsidy, it is not, however, the measure of the subsidy'. Rather, in the view of the European Communities, in order for a subsidy to exist, there needed to be a charge on the public account, from which a benefit flowed to an industry. European Community Paper to the Tokyo Round SCM Committee GATT Doc. G/SCM/35, item A.2, Footnote 159.

69 A 'dissenting opinion' was expressed by certain scholars sustaining that: 'agreeing on what is meant by a subsidy within the meaning of GATT rules is simply the inevitable first step of agreed on rules and disciplines [...] Without the Ariadne thread of an agreed definition, participants nearly always ended up getting lost in the labyrinth of peripheral issues'. Jacque H. J. Bourgeois, 'The GATT Rules for Industrial Subsidies and Countervailing Duties and the New GATT Round – The Weather and the Seeds', in Ernst-Ulrich Petersmann and Mehinard Hilf (eds.), *The New GATT Round of Multilateral Trade Negotiations – Legal and Economic Problems* (Kluwer Law 1991) 228.

70 Canada stated: 'a basic condition for countervailability of a given measure should be the existence of a financial contribution by a government', Framework for Negotiations, Communication from Canada, GATT Doc. MTN.GNG/NG10/W/25 (June 28, 1989); the European Communities: 'subsidies in international trade exist only when a financial charge has been incurred by a government or administrative authority on behalf of a beneficiary', Framework for Negotiations, Communication from the European Communities GATT Doc. MTN.GNG/NG10/W/7 (June 11, 1987); Egypt: 'Only "measures which constitute a charge on the public account or government budget such as grants, concessional loans, loan guarantees" constitute a subsidy', Framework for Negotiations, Communication from Egypt, GATT Doc. MTN.GNG/NG10/W/14 (November 30, 1987); India: 'A financial contribution is a necessary prerequisite', Framework for Negotiations, Communication from India GATT Doc. MTN.GNG/NG10/W/16 (February 1, 1988); Japan: 'A financial contribution by a government [should] be considered as an essential criterion for determining the existence of a subsidy', Framework for Negotiations, Communication from Japan GATT Doc. GNG.NG10/W/8 (August 12, 1987); the Nordic countries: 'Countervailing

'the problem would never be solved by "importing" into the Agreement a definition used by economists that considers a subsidy any benefit granted directly or indirectly from the State to an enterprise'.[71] Too broad a definition would allow WTO Members to legitimate the levying of anti-subsidy measures (*e.g.* countervailing duties) in reaction to any governmental assistance to enterprises thus affecting the entire WTO trade system. On the other hand, too narrow a definition would risk excluding clever governmental practices that subsidize their industries. Despite difficulties and contrary opinions, the Parties agreed on a compromise, among the different positions, on a general[72] definition which considers a subsidy to be a financial contribution made by or on behalf of a State conferring a benefit to (or passed through)[73] the recipient.

The Panel in the *Canada – Aircraft* case stated that the purpose of the SCM Agreement is to provide regulations to '*some* forms of government intervention that distort international trade, [or] have the potential to distort [international trade]' (italics added).[74] Thus, the panel underlined that the application of the SCM Agreement is limited only to 'subsidies' as defined in the Agreement and does not cover every government intervention. The *China – GOES* case involves "Buy America" provisions of the American Recovery and Reinvestment Act of 2009 and also state government procurement laws. Following the economic crisis, many States introduced internal rules aimed at favouring the conclusion of State contracts with domestic entrepreneurs or subsidised national industries. This case demonstrated that these measures can be considered as subsidies by WTO Members, as done by MOFCOM (Ministry of Commerce of the People's Republic of China).[75]

action [should] be made conditional upon a government practice which involves a net transfer of funds from public sources to the recipient', Framework for Negotiations, Communication from the Nordic Countries GATT Doc. GNG.NG10/W/30 (November 27, 1989); Switzerland: 'Actionable subsidies are all measures which result directly or indirectly in a net transfer of funds [...] from public sources to the recipient', Framework for Negotiations, Communication from Switzerland GATT Doc. MTN.GNG/NG10/W/26 (September 13, 1989). The positions of the countries and the problems that emerged during negotiations are resumed in the document GATT Doc. MTN.GNG/NG10/W/3 (March 17, 1987).

71 Jackson, *The World Trading System. Law and Policy* (n. 126) 293.

72 The definition applies in every case the term subsidy is used in the SCM Agreement. Appellate Body Report, *United States – FSC*, para. 93.

73 Article 10 of the SCM Agreement and Article VI:3 of the GATT 1994 require the investigating authorities to conduct a "pass-through" analysis in circumstances where a subsidy is received by the producer of an input product and the imported product subject to the countervailing duty investigation is a different, downstream product manufactured by an unrelated producer operating at arm's length from the recipient of the subsidy. Appellate Body Report, *EC and certain member States – Large Civil Aircraft*, para 773; Appellate Body Report, *US – Upland Cotton*, para. 476

74 Panel Report, *Canada – Aircraft*, para. 9.119.

75 Roberto Soprano, commentary of the 'China – Countervailing and Anti-Dumping Duties on Grain Oriented Flat-Rolled Electrical Steel from the United States' *2013 Italian Yearbook of International Law*.

The first element of a subsidy is a financial contribution and not every form of governmental action can be considered a financial contribution. Article 1.1 restricts to a 'finite list the kinds of government measures that would, if they conferred benefits, constitute subsidies'.[76]

Those financial contributions cover: A government practice that involves a direct transfer of funds (e.g. grants, loans and equity infusion), potential direct transfers of funds or liabilities (e.g. loan guarantees); (ii) government revenue that is otherwise due is foregone or not collected (e.g. fiscal incentives such as tax credits); (iii) a government provides goods or services other than general infrastructure, or purchases goods or there is any form of income or price support in the sense of Article XVI of GATT 1994.[77] The SCM Agreement requires the financial contribution to be granted by governments or public bodies. Without the provision of Article 1.1 (a) (4) it would be possible for a government to circumvent SCM Agreement provisions by using a private entity to carry out one of the functions illustrated above. In order to avoid this possibility, the SCM Agreement extended the application of its rules to any case in which a government

> makes payments to a funding mechanism, or entrusts or directs a private body to carry out one or more of the type of functions illustrated in (i) to (iii) above, which would normally be vested in the government and the practice, in no real sense, differs from practices normally followed by governments.[78]

76 Panel Report, *US – Export Restraints*, para. 8.73.

77 See for example the Appellate Body Reports on *US – Tax Incentives, US – Aircraft* and *EC – Aircraft*.

78 In the *US – Countervailing and Anti-Dumping Measures (China)* the Panel considered that 'We see no reason to consider that the concept that "control" of a company resides with its majority owner, which is uncontested in the private sector, would be inapplicable to government-owned companies. Logically, quite the reverse should be true, given the generalized power of governments over economic affairs within their territories. As such, we consider that, on its own, majority government ownership is clear and highly indicative evidence of government control, and thus of whether an entity is a public body for purposes of the SCM Agreement'. Furthermore, the Panel added that 'We find no legal error, in analysing whether an entity is a public body, in giving primacy to evidence of majority government-ownership. Of course, public body determinations are to be made case-by-case, on the basis of the evidence of record in a given investigation, and the authority's determination must explain its analysis based on the evidence before it, in order for that determination to be reasoned and adequate and thus consistent with the SCM Agreement. We note in this regard that there could be cases (however rare in practice) in which a government-owned entity was completely insulated (e.g., by law) from any government involvement in, or influence over, its operations, such that the entity was not controlled by the government and thus fell outside the scope of the term "public body". In such a situation, it would be the entity and the government in question that would have in their possession the information as to the absence of government control, and in our view it would be incumbent upon them, and certainly it would be in their interest, to bring that information to the attention of the investigating authority'. Panel Report, *US – Countervailing and Anti-Dumping Measures (China)*, VIII.135 and 136.

In order to fulfil all the criteria required by the SCM Agreement to define a subsidy, it is necessary that the financial contribution granted by or 'on behalf of' the State confers a benefit which is a specific and separate element from the financial contribution. In *Brazil – Aircraft*, the Appellate Body indicated that it considers a 'financial contribution' and a 'benefit' as two separate legal elements in Article 1.1 of the SCM Agreement, 'which together determine whether a subsidy *exists*'.[79] As repeated by the jurisprudence of the *Canada – Aircraft* case a financial contribution confers a benefit, 'i.e., an advantage, if it is provided on terms that are more advantageous than those that would have been available to the recipient on the market'.[80]

Another limitation to the application of the SCM Agreement to only some forms of subsidies is provided by Article 2 which specifies that SCM Agreement provisions apply only to 'specific' subsidies. Although specificity is not a substantive element for the definition of subsidy, it is for the application of the norms related to export and actionable subsidies.[81] Under Article 2, a subsidy fulfils the specificity test when it 'is specific to an enterprise or industry or group of enterprises or industries within the jurisdiction of the granting authority'. The distinction is easier in cases where the domestic legislation of a WTO Member explicitly limits access to a subsidy to 'certain enterprises'.[82] In addition, the subsidy can be *de facto* specific. This is when, notwithstanding any appearance of non-specificity resulting from the application of the principles for the *de jure* determination of specificity, there are reasons to believe that the subsidy may be *de facto* specific.[83] The evidence of a *de facto* specificity could be found in the use of a subsidy programme by a limited number of certain enterprises, predominant use by certain enterprises, the granting of disproportionately large amounts of subsidy to certain enterprises, and the manner in which discretion has been exercised by the granting authority in the decision to grant a subsidy.[84] For prohibited subsidies, however, a

79 Appellate Body Report, *Brazil-Aircraft*, para. 156.

80 Appellate Body Report, *Canada – Aircraft*, para. 149.

81 Valeria Di Comite, 'La nozione di sovvenzione nell'OMC alla luce dell'interpretazione offerta dai panels e dall'organo di appello' (2005) 19.2 *Diritto del Commercio Internazionale* 277.

82 An enterprise or industry or group of enterprises or industries. Article 2.1 of the SCM Agreement.

83 The Panel in *US – Carbon Steel (India)* stated that while a *de jure* analysis examines concrete evidence relating to explicit limitations on access, a *de facto* analysis focuses on *indicia* of the allocation or use of a subsidy that support a finding of specificity. The aim of this latter inquiry, by virtue of the fact that it discerns the existence of specificity through *de facto* considerations, and does so notwithstanding any appearance of non-specificity that might arise from a *de jure* analysis, is to identify evidence of allocation or use that provides an investigating authority or panel sufficient assurance as to the existence of specificity. In this way, the second sentence of Article 2.1(c) lists particular factors regarding allocation or use of a subsidy, such as the use of a subsidy programme by either a limited number of, or through predominant use by, certain enterprises, the granting of disproportionately large amounts of subsidy to certain enterprises, or the manner in which discretion has been exercised in the decision to grant a subsidy. Panel Report *US – Carbon Steel (India)*, para. 4.373.

84 Article 2.1(c) of the SCM Agreement.

different regime applies.[85] By explicit provision of Article 2.3 of the SCM Agreement, 'any subsidy falling under the provisions of Article 3 shall be deemed to be specific'.

3.3.1.2. Increased imports

Article 2.1 of the Safeguard Agreement sets forth the requirements that import trends must possess to justify a safeguard. According to that Article, a Member may apply a safeguard measure if it has determined that

> a product is being imported into its territory in such increased quantities, absolute or relative to domestic production, and under such conditions as to cause or threaten to cause serious injury to the domestic industry that produces like or directly competitive products.[86]

Under Article 2.1 of the Safeguard Agreement two requirements shall be fulfilled: 'the first one is a quantitative requirement, while the second is more generally related to the "conditions" under which foreign products come into the territory of the Member seeking to take a safeguard measure'.[87] Article 2.1 of the Safeguard Agreement generally reproduces the provision of Article XIX:1 of the GATT. However, Article XIX:1 requires that the increase in imports occurs as a result of 'unforeseen developments' and 'of the effect of the obligations incurred by a contracting party'.[88] Under Article XIX:1 of the GATT, not all increased imports can be considered as fulfilling the substantive element required by the GATT and the Safeguard Agreement.[89] For example, increased imports after the entry into force of the WTO or other trade agreements are normal and expected

85 Roberto Soprano, 'Doha Reform of WTO Export Credit Provisions in the SCM Agreement: The Perspective of Developing Countries' (2010) 44.3 *Journal of World Trade* 611.

86 According to UNCTAD, Article 2.1 must then be read together with Article 4.2 of the Safeguard Agreement, which sets out the operational requirements for determining whether the conditions identified in Article 2.1 exist. Article 4.2(a) requires in relevant part that: '[i]n the investigation to determine whether increased imports have caused or are threatening to cause serious injury to a domestic industry under the terms of this Agreement, the competent authorities shall evaluate (…) in particular, the rate and amount of the increase in imports of the product concerned in absolute and relative terms, the share of the domestic market taken by increased imports'. The link with Article 4.2(a) also suggests that to be relevant under Article 2.1, import increases must have such characteristics as to cause or threaten to cause serious injury. UNCTAD, *Safeguards* (n. 307) 9–10. See also: Appellate Body Report, *Argentina – Footwear (EC)*, para. 131.

87 *Ibid.* 9.

88 For an analysis on this issue, see Yaji Lee, 'Destabilization of the Discipline on Safeguards? Inherent Problems with the Continuing Application of Article XIX after the Settlement of the Agreement on Safeguards' (2001) 35.6 *Journal of World Trade* 1245.

89 Panel Report, *Argentina – Footwear*, para. 8.161.

consequences of trade liberalization. Accordingly, they cannot be considered as fulfilling the requirement set forth by the GATT and the Safeguard Agreement. The Appellate Body has clarified that only some forms of increased imports, qualified by specific conditions and circumstances, are taken into consideration by the GATT and the Safeguard Agreement. According to UNCTAD, 'its broad language is presumably meant to cover a wide range of unexpected circumstances, which by definition is difficult to anticipate precisely in the abstract'.[90]

A first interpretation of the clause was given by the Working Party in the *US – Hatters' Fur* case where it observed that

> [t]he term 'unforeseen development' should be interpreted to mean developments occurring after the negotiation of the relevant tariff concession which it would not be reasonable to expect that the negotiators of the country making the concession could and should have foreseen at the time when the concession was negotiated.[91]

Some years later, the Appellate Body added that

> [t]he ordinary meaning of the phrase 'as a result of unforeseen developments' requires that the developments which led to a product being imported in such increased quantities and under such conditions as to cause or threaten to cause serious injury to domestic producers must have been 'unexpected'.[92]

The Appellate Body also considered that under Article 2.1 the increase must be 'recent' and 'sudden'.[93] In addition, authorities are required to 'demonstrate' the unforeseen development before taking the measure.[94]

In the *Korea – Dairy* case, the Appellate Body ruled on the meaning of the second requirement i.e. 'as a result of the effect of the obligations incurred by a contracting party under this Agreement, including tariff concessions'. In the Appellate Body's opinion, this means that domestic authorities shall demonstrate, as a matter of fact, that the importing Member has incurred obligations under the GATT 1994, including tariff concessions.[95]

In order to analyse whether there have been 'increased imports', investigating authorities shall select a so-called 'investigation period' (IP) which is a time span prior to the determination when import trends will be studied. In the absence of

90 UNCTAD, *Safeguard* (Ch.3 n.48) 10.

91 Working Party Report, *Report on the Withdrawal by the United States of a Tariff Concession under Article XIX of the General Agreement on Tariffs and Trade, (Hatters' Fur)*, adopted October 1951, para. 9.

92 Appellate Body Report, *Korea – Dairy*, para. 84 and Appellate Body Report, *Argentina-Footwear*, para. 91.

93 Appellate Body Report, *Argentina – Footwear (EC)*, para.131.

94 Appellate Body Report, *US – Lamb*, paras. 72–76.

95 Appellate Body Report, *Korea – Dairy*, para. 84; Appellate Body Report, *Argentina – Footwear (EC)*, para. 91.

any guidelines WTO Members are left free to select a period they deem appropriate. Of course, the choice of the IP could affect the result of the investigation. As UNCTAD remarked, 'the choice of the beginning of the period (the "base year") may be decisive as to whether the determination of "increased imports" over the entire IP will be affirmative or negative'.[96]

Under Article 2.1 of the Safeguard Agreement, domestic authorities can assess the increase in imports either in absolute terms (e.g., an increase by tons or units of imported products)[97] or in its magnitude relative to domestic production of like or directly competitive products.[98] The conjunction 'or' underlines that those conditions are alternative. In sum, in order to meet the 'increased imports' requirement it is sufficient that one form of increase has occurred. According to the Appellate Body, 'the increase in imports must have been recent enough, sudden enough, sharp enough, and significant enough, both quantitatively and qualitatively, to cause or threaten to cause "serious injury"'.[99]

The term 'sharp' underlines that the magnitude of the increase is necessary to determine the 'increased imports'. While the term 'sudden' highlights that the increase must occur over a relatively short time span. With regard to the duration of the increase, the Appellate Body ruled that the increase shall be 'recent' and 'sudden'.[100] In order to assess the increase in imports both the rate and amount (in absolute and relative terms) shall be analysed. As stated by the Appellate Body,[101] investigating authorities have to analyse the trends in imports over the period of investigation, rather than just comparing the situation of imports at the beginning and at the end of the reference period (the so-called 'end points' of the period).[102] It is not by case that, among trade remedies, safeguard measures are the lowest used since 1995.[103]

96 It may be argued that the IP should not go too far backwards, but should rather be the one for which the most recent import data are available. UNCTAD, *Safeguard* (Ch.3 n.48) 12–15.

97 It has been argued that 'for example, it may happen that in an exporting WTO Member, production increases, or simply a larger share of the production, becomes available for export. This may result in a higher quantity of imports into another WTO Member without simultaneously also leading to a relative increase, if the importing Member's domestic production also increases'. *Ibid.*, 12.

98 UNCTAD reported that 'assume for example that in 1999 imports into X amount to 100t and domestic production amounts to 200t. The import-to-domestic-production ratio is therefore 1:2 or 0.5. If in 2000 imports remain 100t, but domestic production falls down to 150t, the ratio is 1:1.5, or 0.66. There will thus have been a 0.16 increase in imports relative to domestic production without, however, one extra import entering the importing Member's territory. Depending on the magnitude of the change in ratio, this type of development may be sufficient to fulfil the 'increased imports' requirement in Article 2.1 of the Safeguard Agreement'. *Ibid.*, 13.

99 The so-called 'RSSS' rule. Appellate Body Report, *Argentina – Footwear (EC)*, para. 131.

100 *Ibid.* para.130.

101 *Ibid.* para. 126.

102 *Ibid.*

103 Statistics are available on the WTO website: www.wto.org..

The Safeguard Agreement lays down substantive requirements that must be fulfilled (and proved by domestic authorities) to adopt a safeguard measure; rules on investigation procedure; conditions relating to the measures taken to prevent or remedy serious injury or threat thereof (to be applied together with Article XIII of the GATT 1994); trade compensation; other general procedural requirements and rules on transparency and multilateral surveillance over the implementation of the agreement by setting up a Committee on Safeguards under the authority of the Council for Trade in Goods. Under the Safeguard Agreement, a WTO member may restrict imports of a given product if its domestic industry is seriously injured by a surge in imports.[104]

3.3.1.3. Dumping

Pursuant to GATT Article VI and the Anti-dumping Agreement, WTO Members might impose anti-dumping measures against dumped imports of a product concerned from targeted countries. They can only impose the measures if the investigating authorities found that the imported product is being 'dumped' and thereby causing injury to the domestic industry that produces the like product.

Although the term dumping may have different meanings, in the GATT/WTO context, it is exclusively used to indicate the practice where a product concerned, of one or more countries, is introduced into the commerce of another country at less than its normal value. Put differently, dumping is when a firm exports a product at an export price which is lower than its normal value (the price of the good in the domestic market). It is a form of price discrimination in which 'goods are sold at a lower price abroad than on the domestic market'.[105] For example, the firm 'Unfair Ltd.' located in Patria sells the good A in its domestic market at $5 but exports it to country Xandia at $2. In order to see whether dumping exists, the normal value of a good shall be compared with its export price. If the export price is lower than the normal value then there is dumping. The rationale of dumping is manifold. A firm can practise dumping to drive competitors out of business and establish a monopoly (predatory dumping), because of over-capacity due to a downturn in demand (cyclical dumping), to gain market share (market expansion dumping), to earn hard currency (state-trading dumping) and by benefiting from an overall strategy which includes both low export pricing and maintaining a closed home market in order to reap monopoly or oligopoly profits (strategic dumping).[106]

104 Article 2 of the Agreement on Safeguard.

105 International Trade Centre, *Business Guide to Trade Remedies in the European Community. Anti-Dumping, Anti-Subsidy and Safeguard Legislation, Practices and Procedures* (International Trade Centre 2004) 24. See also, Francis Snyder, *Regional and Global Regulation of International Trade* (Hart Publishing 2002) 111.

106 UNCTAD, *Handbook on Dispute Settlement, Anti-Dumping Measures* (UNCTAD 2003) 4.

This form of WTO dumping should not be confused with other practices such as *e.g.* exchange rate dumping,[107] social dumping[108] or environmental dumping.[109] In fact, from an etymological point of view, the term 'dumping' refers to the act of disposal. In economic and legal terms dumping is associated with the practice of dumping a currency meaning to manipulate the monetary instrument (competitive devaluation) in order to serve the interests of commercial objectives. This is typically the case of competitive devaluation to incentivise exports. The term dumping is also associated with the practice of producing goods from a country with weak or poorly enforced labour or environmental standards, and thus where the production costs are artificially lower than those of the competitors located in countries with higher standards. Trade in those goods also represents an unfair advantage in international trade. Despite their huge relevance for trade the WTO Anti-dumping Agreement is not supposed to provide remedies for those concerns.[110]

3.3.2. Injury and the injured State

The concept of injury and its role and relevance in the structure of trade remedies differ largely from those of self-help. In fact, while injury is an essential element for the adoption of trade remedies, it has only a limited role for self-help measures. In trade remedies, injury is the evidence of the economic damage caused by the act. It is the proof that the interest of the State that is indirectly protected by the relevant WTO agreements has been affected. It is an essential element in the structure of trade remedies and, as described before, it is the basis of the injury-oriented structure of trade remedies.

107 Nejdet Delener, *Strategic Planning and Multinational Trading Blocs* (Greenwood Publishing Group 1999) 133.

108 Jagdeep Bhandari and Alan O Sykes, *Economic Dimension in International Law Comparative and Empirical Perspectives* (Cambridge University Press 1996) 185; Pitou van Dijck and Gerrit Faber, *Challenges to the New World Trade Organization* (Kluwer Law International 1996) 219; Francesco Francioni, *Environment, Human Rights and International Trade* (Hart Publishing 2001) 299; Hans Werner Sinn, *Social Dumping in the Transformation Process* (CESIFO 2001). See also Roberto Soprano, *L'Accordo Antidumping nel Diritto dell'Organizzazione Mondiale del Commercio* (Giuffrè 2013) 240.

109 Countries with lax environmental policies have lower cost of production and, therefore, an unfair trade advantage that permits them to sell relevant goods at low prices relative to competitors in other countries where regulation is in place. Godfrey Bahiigwa, *Environmental Impacts of Trade Liberalization and Policies for the Sustainable Management of Natural Resources: A Case Study of India's Automobile Sector* (Earthprint 1999) 10. See also, Gary C. Hufbauer and Jeffrey Schott, *North American Free Trade: Issues and Recommendations* (Peterson Institute 1992) 146; Michael Rauscher, *International Trade, Factor Movements, and the Environment* (Oxford University Press 1997) 28; Francis Macmillan, *WTO and the Environment* (Sweet & Maxwell 2001) 12.

110 With reference to exchange rate dumping see also the Ad Note to art. 2 of GATT.

In self-help on the other hand, injury is not an essential element and it is relevant merely for the assessment of reparation. In international law a State is entitled, as an injured State, to invoke the responsibility of another State where

> the obligation breached is owed to: (a) that State individually; or (b) a group of States including that State, or the international community as a whole, and the breach of the obligation: (i) specially affects that State; or (ii) is of such a character as radically to change the position of all the other States to which the obligation is owed with respect to the further performance of the obligation.

Under international law the injured State is the State whose individual right has been denied or impaired by the internationally wrongful act or which has otherwise been particularly affected by that act.[111] This could be a single State or a broader range of States. Furthermore, in some circumstances all States may have such a legal interest. Accordingly, the ICJ in the *Barcelona Traction* case stated that 'all States can be held to have a legal interest' in cases where the internationally wrongful act violates obligations *erga omnes*. In sum, the concept of 'injured State' under international law coincides with the holder of the right which has been violated by the internationally wrongful act. The injured party has to be one to whom an international obligation is owed.[112]

In general international law the meaning of injury is separated from that of damage. Breaches of international law do not always involve material damage. According to Gomaa, 'in some cases the damage be only legal or just moral'.[113] Material damage is not a pre-condition for the determination of the existence of international responsibility.[114] The DARSIWA states that an internationally wrongful act exists as soon as an international obligation is not performed, independently of the existence or non-existence of damage, according to the principle of 'objective responsibility for result'. Put differently: 'material damage is not a constitutive element of an internationally wrongful act nor a requirement of State Responsibility'.[115] The general definition of injury is set out in Article 31 of the

111 *Barcelona Traction, Light and Power Company, Limited*, Second Phase, *I.C.J. Reports* 1970, 3 32 para. 33. See also, James Crawford, *The International Law Commission's Articles on State Responsibility: Introduction, Text, and Commentaries* (Cambridge University Press 2002) 254–260.

112 Mohamed Gomaa, *Suspension or Termination of Treaties on Grounds of Breach* (Martinus Nijhoff Publishers 1996) 65.

113 *Ibid.* 63.

114 For an overview on the relation between damage and responsibility see Bernard Graefrath, 'Responsibility and Damage' (1984) 187 *Recueil des Cours de l'Académie de Droit International de La Haye*; Attila Tanzi, 'Is Damage a Distinct Condition for the Existence of an Internationally Wrongful ACT?', in Maria Spinedi and Bruno Simma (eds.), *United Nations Codifications of State Responsibility* (Oceana 1987) 1; Gaetano Arangio-Ruiz, *Second Report on State Responsibility*, Doc. A/CN.4/425 of 9 June 1989.

115 Ernst-Ulrich Petersmann, *The GATT/WTO Dispute Settlement System* (n. 85) 136.

ILC Articles on State Responsibility stating that 'Injury includes any damage, whether material or moral, caused by the internationally wrongful act of a State'. It is important to note that this principle falls under the Article dealing with reparation and not under those describing primary rules addressing the wrong or the recourse to self-defence or countermeasures. In fact, as mentioned above, injury is not an essential element of an internationally wrongful act nor a pre-requisite for recourse to self-help. There is in general no requirement in international law that a State should have suffered material harm or damage before it can seek reparation for a breach.[116] Wrongfulness focuses on the violation of an international rule *per se* and entitles the injured State to react and seek reparation. The responsibility of the wrongdoer arises directly from the commission of the wrong. Professor Ago argued that damage is not a necessary requirement of international responsibilities and there may be internationally wrongful acts that do not cause injury. The element of injury is included in the violation itself.[117]

The existence of damage under international law is, however, relevant to the assessment of the form and quantum of reparation.[118] If a State suffered an injury caused by an internationally wrongful act, the injured state is entitled to claim reparation. In that respect, in the *Gabčíkovo-Nagymaros Project* case, the ICJ held: 'It is a well-established rule of international law that an injured State is entitled to obtain compensation from the State which has committed an internationally wrongful act for the damage caused by it.'[119] It also stated that 'it is equally well established that an international court or tribunal which has jurisdiction with respect to a claim of State responsibility has, as an aspect of that jurisdiction, the power to award compensation for damage suffered'.[120] The fundamental concept of 'damages' is considered to be reparation for a loss suffered and a judicially ascertained compensation for the wrong.[121] Within the meaning of paragraph 2, 'injury' includes any damage caused by that act. In particular, it includes any material or moral damage deriving from the wrongful act. As noted in the DARSIWA this formulation is intended both as inclusive – covering both material and moral damage as broadly understood, and as limitative – excluding merely abstract concerns or general interests of a State which is individually unaffected by the breach. It is also interesting to note how the term 'material' is interpreted in the context of the DARSIWA. In fact, the adjective refers to the damage to property

116 Draft Articles on Responsibility of States for Internationally Wrongful Acts, with commentaries (2001) 2.2 *Yearbook of the International Law Commission* 92.
117 *Ibid.* 20.
118 *Ibid.* 92.
119 *Gabčíkovo-Nagymaros Project*, p. 81, para. 152.
120 It is a principle of international law that the reparation of a wrong may consist in an indemnity corresponding to the damage which the nationals of the injured State have suffered as a result of the act which is contrary to international law. *Factory at Chorzów*, Germany v Poland, Judgment, Claim for Indemnity, Merits, Judgment No 13, (1928) PCIJ Series A No 17, ICGJ 255 (PCIJ 1928), 13th September 1928, para. 68. See also *Fisheries Jurisdiction* (Federal Republic of Germany v. Iceland), Merits, Judgment, I.C.J. Reports 1974, p. 203–205, paras. 71–76.
121 Opinion in the *Lusitania* Cases, (November 1, 1923), UNRIAA, vol. VII 39.

or other interests of the State and its nationals which is assessable in financial terms. It is used in contrast to 'moral' which is described as the 'individual pain and suffering, loss of loved ones or personal affront associated with an intrusion on one's home or private life'.[122]

The DARSIWA also indirectly addresses the definition and assessment of the damage caused by the wrong. In fact, it held that the scope of the obligation of reparations is delimited by the phrase 'any financially assessable damage'; that is, any damage which is capable of being evaluated in financial terms. Financially assessable damage encompasses both damage suffered by the State itself (to its property or personnel or in respect of expenditures reasonably incurred to remedy or mitigate damage flowing from an internationally wrongful act) as well as damage suffered by nationals, whether persons or companies, on whose behalf the State is making a claim within the framework of diplomatic protection.

The existence of damage and its quantification have been addressed by arbitration tribunals and the rules and principles developed by these bodies in assessing compensation can be seen as manifestations of the general principle stated in Article 36.[123]

The existence of material damage is also not an essential element for a State to seek some form of reparation. In the 'Rainbow Warrior' arbitration, parties initially argued that 'in the theory of international responsibility, damage is necessary to provide a basis for liability to make reparation'.[124] However, they subsequently agreed that:

> unlawful action against non-material interests, such as acts affecting the honour, dignity or prestige of a State, entitle the victim State to receive adequate reparation, even if those acts have not resulted in a pecuniary or material loss for the claimant State.

In the case at stake, the tribunal held that the violation committed by France

> provoked indignation and public outrage in New Zealand and caused a new, additional, non-material damage of a moral, political and legal nature,

122 Draft Articles on Responsibility of States for Internationally Wrongful Acts, with commentaries, 92.

123 *Ibid.* In assessing the existence of damage it is important in all cases to distinguish between unlawful takings and lawful takings. In the former what is due is damages. In the latter it must be compensated. Chittharanjan Amerasinghe, 'Issues of Compensation for the Taking of Alien Property in the Light of Recent Cases and Practice' (1992) 41.1 *International and Comparative Law Quarterly* 22, 37. See also, Irmgard Marboe, *Calculation of Compensation and Damages in International Investment Law* (Oxford University Press 2017).

124 *Case concerning the difference between New Zealand and France concerning the interpretation or application of two agreements concluded on 9 July 1986 between the two States and which related to the problems arising from the Rainbow Warrior Affair*, Decision of 30 April 1990 (Rainbow Warrior) 266–267, paras. 107 and 109.

> resulting from the affront to the dignity and prestige not only of New Zealand as such, but of its highest judicial and executive authorities as well.[125]

According to García Amador, injury can be classified according to the personality of the actual victim.[126] It could be an injury caused to the State (as a body corporate) or to private persons (aliens).[127] The scholar précised that 'according to the traditional concept, the distinction is between an injury caused to the State "directly" through one of its organs or component elements, and an injury caused "indirectly" through its nationals'.[128] As stated by O'Brien, in principle a State 'will only take up the claims of its own nationals or those of companies registered with its own territory'.[129] Each State has its own domestic rules on diplomatic and consular protection which in turn shall comply with the mentioned principles of international law.

When the State acts to takes up the case of an individual, it is asserting its own rights in international law. According to the Permanent Court of International Justice in the *Mavrommatis Palestine Concession* case 'a State is in reality asserting its own rights, its right to ensure, in the person of its subjects, respect for the rules of international law'.[130] Thus the injury to the national became an injury to the nation and thus should be espoused internationally by the injured nation.[131] A State may seek to act on behalf of a company who has been affected by the wrongful act committed by a State. In the *Barcelona Traction* case, the ICJ dealt with the question of the different legal personality of the company and the position of both the company and its shareholders. In that case the ICJ decided that the nationality of the company shall prevail over the nationality of the shareholders apart from in certain specific circumstances. According to O'Brien, 'in respect of the national state of the company, this is normally determined by the place of incorporation of the company, but it can also be determined by where real control is held or where the centre of management exists'.[132]

In trade remedies the concept of injury has a completely different role. It is (the) a fundamental element that legitimates the reaction. The injured State could be seen as the Member whose domestic industry has been affected by dumping, subsidy or increased imports. In such a WTO context, the concept of injury is not related to the violation of a norm but is the economic consequence of a specific act. It is not linked to a legal relationship which has been breached but to the

125 *Ibid.* 266–267, para. 110.

126 Another classification is based on the nature 'moral and political' or 'private' of the injury. Francisco V. García Amador, Louis B. Sohn and Richard R. Baxter, *Recent Codification of the Law of State Responsibility for Injuries to Aliens* (Oceana Publications 1974) 91.

127 *Ibid.*

128 *Ibid.*

129 *Ibid.*

130 *The Mavrommatis Palestine Concession*, Judgment of 30 August 1924, PCIJ, Ser. A, No, 2 12.

131 John O'Brien, *International Law* (Routledge 2001) 371.

132 *Ibid.* 376.

'health' situation of the domestic industry. In trade remedies injury tends to be used as a synonym of damage. Thus, the injured State is the State which has suffered the damage.

The injured State is also the State which has the right to adopt trade remedies. In (almost) all the cases the injured State is the importing country. As unilateral measures they are adopted by the injured State to protect its own rights and interests. However, it could be argued that dumping, subsidies or increased exports from one country to another could negatively affect the domestic industry of a third State. For example, this is the case where private firms located in country A dump their product in country B to which firms of country C also export their products. If dumped exports from country B are at a price lower than those coming from country C, exporters in country C would be worse off because dumped goods would probably be preferred by users or consumers in the importing country. Only the Anti-dumping Agreement contains a provision aimed at addressing this situation by the use of trade remedies.[133] Under Article 14 of the Anti-dumping Agreement, the authorities of the third country may request the importing country to adopt antidumping measures on its behalf. According to that Article, in considering the request of the third country, the authorities of the importing country shall consider the effects of the alleged dumping on the industry concerned, as a whole, in the third country.[134] In this case the importing country would not be the injured State but the decision whether or not to proceed with a case shall rest with it. However, this option is regulated by stricter rules. Where the importing country decides to take action, it has to seek the approval of the Council for Trade in Goods.

In the trade remedy field, the State is only considered as injured where the producers affected are located in its territory, regardless of the nationality of the companies. Domestic industry is composed of producers of a product like or similar to that under investigation and who are based within domestic boundaries. Thus, for example, a Chinese company based in Europe (not related to exporters) can be considered as part of the domestic European industry during an anti-dumping investigation. Yet, it could also lodge a complaint under European rules.

The obligation for the investigating authority to prove the existence of the injury also means that the fact that a State is injured cannot be determined implicitly from the evidence of a violation of international law but shall be demonstrated through a specific (economic) analysis. Accordingly, a State cannot be considered injured by the simple fact that imports have been subsidized, dumped or have suddenly increased. In order to be considered 'injured' that State must prove the existence of injury. The Trade Remedies agreement allows for the possibility of imposing measures only in cases where investigating authorities prove

133 A similar situation may also happen in case of the granting of a subsidy. However, remedies contained in Articles 4 and 7 of the SCM Agreement are multilateral remedies. Thus, they are not unilateral and do not fit in the definition of trade remedies.

134 In addition, Article 14.3 of the Anti-dumping Agreement sets forth that 'the injury shall not be assessed in relation only to the effect of the alleged dumping on the industry's exports to the importing country or even on the industry's total exports'.

that dumping, subsidies or a surge in imports cause or threaten to cause injury, or materially delayed the creation of the *domestic industry* of the importing member.[135]

More important, for the purpose of this study, is the definition of injury that is a substantive element in trade remedies investigations[136] and represents the economic 'damage' suffered by the domestic industry of the importing country. The WTO rules require that injury be based on positive evidence and that investigating authorities conduct an objective examination of listed factors.

The first element requires that the evidence on which the existence of injury is based be affirmative, objective, verifiable and credible.[137] This permits an investigating authority making an injury determination 'to base its determination on all relevant reasoning and facts before it'.[138] The second element obliges an investigating authority to conform to the general principle of fairness and good faith during the assessment phase of injury.[139] Put differently, the principle imposes an obligation on States to conduct injury investigations in an unbiased manner without favouring any party interested in the investigation. This principle ensures even-handedness in the assessment of injury and avoids investigating authorities conducting investigations in a way that is likely to determine that the domestic industry is suffering injury.

The injury mentioned in the WTO agreements is not just any kind of 'prejudice' which could be due to the impact of lower price imports on the domestic industry. They require States to examine specific factors which could show whether or not the domestic injury is suffering from the dumping, subsidy or surge in imports.[140]

The WTO agreements require States to source evidence of injury from the volume of the dumped or subsidized imports and their effect on prices in the domestic market for like products, and the consequent impact of these imports on domestic producers of such products.[141] The examination of the impact of the dumped imports on the domestic industry concerned shall include an evaluation of all relevant economic factors and indices having a bearing on the state of the industry, including actual and potential decline in sales, profits, output, market share, productivity, return on investments, or utilization of capacity; factors affecting domestic prices; the magnitude of the margin of dumping; actual and potential negative effects on cash flow, inventories, employment, wages, growth,

135 For the purposes of the Anti-dumping Agreement, the term 'domestic industry' shall be interpreted as referring to the domestic producers as a whole of the like products or to those of them whose collective output of the products constitutes a major proportion of the total domestic production of those products. Article 4.1 of the Anti-dumping Agreement.
136 Appellate Body Report, *Thailand – H-Beams*, para. 106.
137 Appellate Body Report, *US – Hot Rolled Steel*, para. 192.
138 Appellate Body Report, *Thailand – H-Beams*, para. 111.
139 Appellate Body Report, *US – Hot Rolled Steel*, para. 193.
140 Appellate Body Report, *Thailand – H-Beams*, para. 111.
141 Article 3.1 of the Anti-dumping Agreement.

ability to raise capital or investments.[142] The list, of course, is not exhaustive and investigating authorities may find evidence of injury by analysing other factors which are not listed in Article 3.4 of the Anti-dumping Agreement.

Despite the limited attention given by the legislator to this matter, the jurisprudence has helped to clarify the aim of the analysis and in particular to limit the discretion of the authorities in assessing and taking a decision on the existence of injury. In examining the nature of Article 15.1 of the SCM Agreement, the Panel in *EC – Countervailing Measures* on DRAM Chips recognized that positive evidence and objective examination is an overarching provision informing the other obligations contained in Article 15 of the SCM Agreement. *Mutatis mutandis* similar could be said of the Safeguard Agreement and the Anti-dumping Agreement.

During investigations, authorities are requested to examine the trend of the economic factors and indices which have a bearing on the state of the industry described above. It is often the case that not all the factors and indices show a negative trend. It may be possible that market share and profitability are decreasing while employment records do not follow a similar trend.

It is therefore necessary to analyse all the data and information on the injury factors before taking a decision on the existence (or not) of injury. In that respect, both the SCM Agreement and Anti-dumping Agreement contain a sentence specifying that, 'nor can one or several of these factors necessarily give decisive guidance'. In addition, considering that the period of injury analysis usually goes back to 3 or 5 years from the initiation of the investigation it is possible that the variation in the data is not always negative but varies depending on the benchmark chosen. It is therefore necessary to counter the 'cherry picking' analysis, based on which authorities may pick the data that show the trend and parameters that could more easily justify the existence of injury. In that regard, the Panel in *Argentina – Poultry* considered that

> to the extent that a Member failed to conduct a proper 'examination of the impact of dumped imports' for the purpose of Article 3.4, that Member also failed to conduct an 'objective examination of … the consequent impact of the imports' within the meaning of Article 3.1(b).[143]

When the Appellate Body in *US – Hot-Rolled Steel* analysed the concept of 'objective assessment' as compared with 'positive evidence', it stressed that the latter is concerned with the investigating process itself as opposed to the facts justifying the injury determination. In its words,

> the term 'objective examination' aims at a different aspect of the investigating authorities' determination. While the term 'positive evidence' focuses on the facts underpinning and justifying the injury determination, the term 'objective

142 Article 3.4 of the Anti-dumping Agreement.
143 Panel Report, *Argentina – Poultry*, para. 7.325.

> examination' is concerned with the investigative process itself. The word 'examination' relates, in our view, to the way in which the evidence is gathered, inquired into, and subsequently evaluated; that is, it relates to the conduct of the investigation generally. The word 'objective', which qualifies the word 'examination', indicates essentially that the 'examination' process must conform to the dictates of the basic principles of good faith and fundamental fairness.[144]

In short, an 'objective examination' requires that the domestic industry, and the effects of dumped imports, be investigated in an unbiased manner, without favouring the interests of any interested party, or group of interested parties, in the investigation. The duty of the investigating authorities to conduct an 'objective examination' recognizes that the determination will be influenced by the objectivity, or any lack thereof, of the investigative process.[145]

The Appellate Body in *Mexico – Anti-Dumping Duties on Rice* reinforced its statement by stressing that an injury analysis can only be considered as 'objective' 'if it is based on data which provide an accurate and unbiased picture of what it is that one is examining'. If an injury analysis is based on selective use of the information gathered (in that case by selecting a period of investigation which allegedly represented the period of highest import penetration) the investigating authority has not provided an 'accurate and unbiased picture.'[146] Similarly the Panel in *EC – Fasteners (China)* considered that 'to conduct an objective examination based on positive evidence investigating authorities shall consider the injury factors in relation to an industry in a consistent manner.'[147] In that case for example, the authorities relied on information coming from the whole industry for analysing certain factors while for others they relied only on those coming from sampled producers.

Another risk comes from the possibility of limiting the analysis to certain factors that could more easily provide evidence of injury. In *US – Hot-Rolled Steel*, the Appellate Body explained that

> an important aspect of the 'objective examination' required by Article 3.1 is further elaborated in Article 3.4 as an obligation to 'examin[e] the impact of the dumped imports on the domestic industry' through 'an evaluation of all

144 The Appellate Body stressed that 'in this respect, we recall that panels are under a similar duty, under Article 11 of the DSU, to make an "objective assessment of the matter [...] including an objective assessment of the facts". In our Report in EC Measures Concerning Meat and Meat Products (Hormones), we indicated that the obligation to make an "objective assessment" includes an obligation to act in "good faith", respecting "fundamental fairness"' (Appellate Body Report, *EC – Hormones*, para. 133)

145 Appellate Body Report, *US – Hot-Rolled Steel*, para. 193.

146 Appellate Body Report, *Mexico – Rice*, para. 181.

147 Panel Report, *EC – Fasteners (China)*, para. 7.390.

> relevant economic factors and indices having a bearing on the state of the industry'.[148]

The definition of injury in the context of trade remedies is of utmost importance because, as described in the previous chapter, trade remedies are a particular form of State reaction in which the damage element plays a central role in the justification of their use. Therefore, the objective examination provided for by the legislation should be considered as a central element in any investigation.

3.3.3. Causality

Causality is the relationship between a cause and its effects. While it is a fundamental element of any trade remedies investigation, it is a concept that has only limited relevance for traditional forms of self-help.[149] As previously described, in State responsibility the effects that are caused by the wrongful act are not relevant to triggering the responsibility of a State. In fact, any self-help measure can be taken irrelevant of any effect caused by the wrongful act. It is the violation of the norm or, in the case of retorsion, the unfriendly act that triggers the possibility for the injured State to react. In classical forms of self-help, the emphasis is placed on the notion of wrongfulness and its independence from primary rules in explaining the absence of causal analysis from the determination of a breach.[150]Any consideration on causality is therefore not relevant for the responsibility of the wrongdoer, but for the calculation of the reparation of the damage suffered by the injured State. As pointed out by Honoré,

> causation in law addresses the need to define the harm for which compensation is to be paid in a tort action. This means that the damage must amount in law to injury, and must be of a sort which it is the policy of the legal system to compensate, and must be adequately delimited.[151]

In 1953 Cheng stated that the principle of integral reparation should be analysed in conjunction with that of 'proximate or effective causality' that is valid in international law. Accordingly, the duty to make reparation extends only to those damages which are legally regarded as the consequences of an unlawful act. They are damages 'that would normally flow from such an act, or which a reasonable

148 Appellate Body Report, *US – Hot-Rolled Steel*, para. 194.
149 Eagleton stated that 'writers have devoted but little attention to the measure of damages in international law'. Clyde Eagleton, 'Measure of Damages in International Law' (1929) 39.1 *The Yale Law Journal* 39, 52.
150 Leon Castellanos-Jankiewicz, 'Causation and International State Responsibility' (2012) ACIL Research Paper No 2012–07, 19.
151 Anthony Honoré, 'Causational and Remoteness of Damage', in Andre Tunc (ed.), *International Encyclopedia of Comparative Law* (Mohr 1983) also cited in Leon Castellanos-Jankiewicz, 'Causation and International State Responsibility' (Ch.3 n.150) 5.

man in the position of the wrongdoer at the time would have foreseen as likely to result, as well as all intended damages'.[152]

Despite the fact that trade remedies should not be perceived as reparation but as a form of *autotutele*, the element of causation in the context of reparation contains guiding principles for trade remedies. Article 31 Paragraph 2 of the DARSIWA addresses the issue of the causal link between the internationally wrongful act and the injury. In fact, it is only the '[i]njury … caused by the internationally wrongful act of a State' that entitles a State to seek full reparation. In the commentary of the DARSIWA, the ILC analysed how the wording included in the paragraph is used to make clear that the subject matter of reparation is 'the injury resulting from and ascribable to the wrongful act, rather than any and all consequences flowing from an internationally wrongful act'.[153]

In international law, different terms have been used to describe the relationship that should be found between the wrongful act and the injury. The ILC noted that, international law or tribunals may refer to damages 'attributable to [the wrongful] act as a proximate cause',[154] or to injury which is 'too indirect, remote, and uncertain to be appraised', or to 'any direct loss, damage including environmental damage and the depletion of natural resources, or injury to foreign Governments, nationals and corporations as a result of the wrongful act'.[155] It should

152 Cheng, *General Principle of Law as Applied by International Courts and Tribunals* (Stevens and Sons 1953) 253 cited in Sergey Ripinsky and Kevin Williams, *Damages in International Investment Law* (BIICL 2008) 136.

153 Draft Articles on Responsibility of States for Internationally Wrongful Acts, with commentaries, 92.

154 Where the loss is far removed in causal sequence from the act complained of, it is not competent for this tribunal to seek to unravel a tangled network of causes and of effects, or follow, through a baffling labyrinth of confused thought, numerous disconnected and collateral chains, in order to link Germany with a particular loss. All indirect losses are covered, provided only that in legal contemplation Germany's act was the efficient and proximate cause and source from which they flowed. The simple test to be applied in all cases is: has an American national proven a loss suffered by him, susceptible of being measured with reasonable exactness by pecuniary standards, and is that loss attributable to Germany's act as a proximate cause? United States-German Mixed Claims Commission, Administrative Decision No. II, UNRIAA, vol. VII, 23, at 30 (1923).

155 In the commentary, the ILC quoted the Security Council resolution 687 (1991) of 3 April 1991, para. 16. This was 'a resolution adopted with reference to Chapter VII of the Charter of the United Nations, but it is expressed to reflect Iraq's liability "under international law … as a result of its unlawful invasion and occupation of Kuwait". UNCC and its Governing Council have provided some guidance on the interpretation of the requirements of directness and causation under paragraph 16. Recommendations made by the panel of Commissioners concerning individual claims for serious personal injury or death (category 'B' claims), report of 14 April 1994 (S/AC.26/1994/1), approved by the Governing Council in its decision 20 of 26 May 1994 (S/AC.26/Dec.20 (1994)); Report and recommendations made by the panel of Commissioners appointed to review the Well Blowout Control Claim (the 'WBC claim'), of 15 November 1996 (S/AC.26/1996/5/Annex), paras. 66–86, approved by the Governing Council in its decision 40 of 17 December 1996 (S/AC.26/Dec.40 (1996))'.

also be considered that proving causality between the wrongful act and injury also implies the exclusion of that injury which has not been caused by the wrong. According to the ILC, Article 31 embodies the notion of a 'sufficient' causal link which is 'not too remote'. Therefore, the injury should be a consequence of the wrongful act and it is not necessary to add any particular qualifying phrase. The exclusion of injury that is too 'remote' or 'consequential' to be the subject of reparation is a necessary corollary of injury. Practice of international law suggests that the criterion of 'directness' may be used, or 'foreseeability'[156] or 'proximity'.[157] As summarized by Castellanos-Jankiewicz the ILC analysis of the causal link involves an assessment of the sufficiency and proximity i.e. to find a 'sufficient' causal link that is 'not too remote'.[158] With reference to the first criterion, injury must 'flow from the wrongful conduct as a matter of course and in natural sequence'. In this sense, the scholar suggests that it is an objective standard, but can also have subjective connotations, such as the due diligence exercised by the wrongdoer. The second criterion, the proximity requirement, needs a direct relationship to be established between wrongful conduct and injury 'to prevent infinite regress towards irrelevant facts and acts'. This would avoid the seeking of redress for damages considered too remote from a wrongful act.[159]

However, the ILC has argued that, depending on the case under analysis, the requirement of a causal link is not necessarily the same in relation to every breach of an international obligation. Assessing the remoteness of the damage 'is not a part of the law which can be satisfactorily solved by search for a single verbal formula'.[160] This should be dealt with by primary rules. Similar conclusions were drawn by Professor Brownlie who recognized that the nature of the duty and the breach described in the primary rules may better describe the approach to the question of damages.[161]

Castellanos-Jankiewicz also describes two other requirements that are relevant for the analysis: directness and proximity. In the opinion of the scholar, direct causation requires a 'clear and unbroken link' between the act and the injury

156 In *Amco vs Indonesia*, the Tribunal stated that as 'far as international law is concerned, it is clear that damages are due for the harm caused by the wrongful act'. It also said that 'the loss must be attributable to the wrongful act and foreseeable'. *Amco vs Indonesia*, Award on the Merits of 31 May 1990, 89 ILR 368 para 172.

157 Security Council resolution 687 (1991), para. 16 and the 'Naulilaa' *Portuguese Colonies* case (Naulilaa incident), UNRIAA, vol. II (Sales No. 1949.V.1), p. 1011, at p. 1031. Cited in the ILC commentary.

158 NAFTA art 1116 and 1117 stated that investor may claim loss or damages 'by reason of, or arising out of [...] a breach of section ...'. In interpreting causality in a NAFTA context, in the *S. D. Myers vs Canada* case, *arbitrators* ruled that 'damages may only be awarded to the extent that there is a sufficient causal link between the breach of a specific NAFTA provision and the loss sustained by the investor. [T]he harm must not be too remote or that the breach [...] must be the proximate cause of the harm'. Second Partial of 21 October 2002, para 140.

159 Leon Castellanos-Jankiewicz (Ch.3 n.150) 46.

160 *Ibid.*

161 Ian Brownlie, *Principles of Public International Law* (Oxford University Press, sixth ed., 2003) 446.

arising therefrom. It is not relevant for the purpose of the analysis whether 'parallel or concurrent causes contributed to the damage. By analysing directness alongside sufficiency, it only matters that the act was an effective cause of the damage'.[162] Under the proximate causation test, the duty to make reparation would extend only to those damages 'which are legally regarded as the consequences of an unlawful act'. More precisely, he describes these as damages which would normally flow from such an act, or which a reasonable man in the position of the wrongdoer at the time would have foreseen as likely to result, as well as all intended damages.[163]

The assessment of causality in trade remedies includes a positive and negative test.[164] First of all, in order to impose antidumping, countervailing or safeguard measures the relevant agreements require that a causal link between the dumping, subsidy and increased imports and injury exists and can be proved. Authorities need to prove that a link of causality exists between the act and injury. They need to prove that there is a link between the cause and effect. In other words that injury is caused by the dumped, subsidized or increased imports. In the context of safeguard investigations,[165] it has been held that the aim of the causal link requirement is to demonstrate that a *genuine* and *substantial* relationship of cause (increased imports) and effect (serious injury) between these two elements exists.[166]

The verification of the existence of a causal link should be based on the examination of all relevant evidence before the investigating authorities. This requires the analysis of the evaluation of import volumes and prices and their impact on the domestic industry.[167] In trade remedies, this is often proven by demonstrating a correlation in time between the act and injury. By analysing the economic conditions of the domestic industry and the import trends in a given period, authorities should determine whether the act is causing injury.[168] In more practical terms, authorities should demonstrate the relationship between the injury factors and the trend of (dumped, subsidized or increased) import volumes and prices. Where there are several injury factors to be analysed, it is possible that only some of them will show a link with the act. The weight and assessment of the factors is left to the discretion of the investigating authority. In an antidumping investigation it may be

162 Leon Castellanos-Jankiewicz (Ch.3 n.150) 48 and 49.
163 *Ibid.* 52 and 53.
164 For an overview of the test in antidumping in the European Union see Van Bael and Bellis (n. 273) 331.
165 In the opinion of Messerlin and Fridh, the causality determination standard is flawed. Patrick A. Messerlin and Hilda Fridh, 'The Agreement on Safeguards: Proposals for Change in the Light of the EC Steel Safeguards' (2006) 40.4, *Journal of World Trade* 713, 726.
166 Appellate Body Report, *United States – Wheat Gluten Safeguard*, para. 96.
167 Judith Czako, Johann Human and Jorge Miranda, *A Handbook on Anti-Dumping Investigations* (Cambridge University Press 2003) 297–302.
168 There is no prescribed methodology as to how a non-attribution analysis is to be conducted. Panel Report, *China – Cellulose Pulp*, para. 7.159.

possible, for example, to exclude causality when an increase in imports was smaller than the drop in market share or sales by the domestic industry.

As a part of the investigation process, the causality assessment is also subject to the principle of conducting unbiased and objective investigations.[169] This principle entails an obligation to conduct the investigation in an unbiased manner to prevent authorities from favouring the interests of certain parties over those of other parties. The behaviour of the authority should be even-handed. The authorities should be led by objectivity and any lack thereof in the examination phase would be a breach of such a principle.[170] Additionally, the authorities are under an obligation to prove the existence of a causal link and therefore need evidence collected and verified during the investigation.

In addition to proving the causal link, the trade remedies agreements also contain a 'non-attribution requirement'.[171] This requires that the investigating authority examine any known factors other than dumped, subsidized and increased imports which could cause injury to the domestic industry.[172] This is of foremost importance to ensuring the non-arbitrariness of the investigations. It ensures that other injurious factors are excluded from the determination of the injury for the purposes of the investigations. It ensures that injury caused by dumping, subsidies and increased imports are evaluated separately and that other factors injurious to domestic industry are distinguished and not attributed to dumped imports. The Anti-dumping Agreement and in parallel the SCM Agreement, do not require that dumping is the principal cause of injury, but do require the evaluation of other known factors which could negatively affect domestic industry. The negative test has been introduced to deal with the possibility that

169 Panel Report, *Mexico – Steel Pipes and Tubes*, para. 7.351.

170 Panel Report, *EC – Bed Linen* (21.5 – India) para. 114.

171 Noting that the non-attribution requirement had been addressed by the Appellate Body in several recent cases in the context of Article 3.5 of the Anti-dumping Agreement, the Panel in *US – DRAMs* considered that, while the requirement had not been considered in cases involving the SCM Agreement, the identical wording of the relevant provisions called for the same approach: 'The non-attribution requirement in anti-dumping investigations has been addressed by the Appellate Body in several recent cases. Although it has not been specifically considered in a countervailing duty case, given that the relevant provisions in the two Agreements are identical, and in light of the "need for the consistent resolution of disputes arising from anti-dumping and countervailing duty measures," [set out in the Ministerial Declaration on Dispute Settlement Pursuant to the Agreement on Implementation of Article VI of the General Agreement on Tariffs and Trade 1994 or Part V of the Agreement on Subsidies and Countervailing Measures] it is clear to us that the requirement is the same in the context of both anti-dumping and countervailing duty investigations.' Panel Report, *US – Countervailing Duty Investigation on DRAMs*, para. 7. 351. See also the Panel Report in *Mexico – Olive Oil*, para. 7.298.

172 The illustrative list of Article 3.5 of the Anti-dumping Agreement includes: the volume and prices of imports not sold at dumping prices, contraction in demand or changes in the patterns of consumption, trade-restrictive practices of and competition between the foreign and domestic producers, developments in technology and the export performance and productivity of the domestic industry.

different factors would cause injury to the domestic industry at the same time. While it need not be demonstrated that the act is the sole or principal cause of the injury, it is necessary to examine separately the effects of the dumped, subsidized or increased imports on the domestic industry.

This generally prohibits the attribution to dumping of the injury suffered by the domestic industry for other reasons. In the view of the Panel,

> an investigating authority must make a better effort to quantify the impact of other known factors, relative to subsidized imports, preferably using elementary economic constructs or models. At the very least, the non-attribution language of Article 15.5 requires from an investigating authority a satisfactory explanation of the nature and extent of the injurious effects of the other factors, as distinguished from the injurious effects of the subsidized imports.[173]

The non-attribution language in the second sentence of Article 4.2(b) means that

> the effects of increased imports, as separated and distinguished from the effects of other factors, must be examined to determine whether the effects of those imports establish a 'genuine and substantial relationship of cause and effect' between the increased imports and serious injury.[174]

In practice it is not so easy to separate and distinguish all injurious effects which could affect domestic industry. Different factors can be interrelated and produce combined effects. In this respect, the Appellate Body précised that: Although this process may not be easy, this is precisely what is envisaged by the non-attribution language. If the injurious effects of the dumped imports and the other known factors remain lumped together and indistinguishable, there is simply no means of knowing whether injury ascribed to dumped imports was, in reality, caused by other factors. In fact, the causal link analysis imposes on the investigating authority the obligation to undertake the process of assessing appropriately, and separating and distinguishing, the injurious effects of dumped imports from those of other known causal factors.[175] The Appellate Body stated that in a situation where

173 Panel Report, *EC – Countervailing Measures on DRAM Chips*, paras. 7.404–7.405.

174 Appellate Body Report, *US – Lamb*, para. 168. See also *China – Autos (US)*: 'in our view, MOFCOM's discussion of the purportedly limited impact of apparent consumption does not follow from the evidence on the record before it, and does not present a reasoned evaluation of that evidence. MOFCOM confined its assessment to two indicators, production and sales, in finding that trends in apparent consumption did not cause injury to the domestic industry. However, a decline in apparent consumption will normally lead to decreased sales, increased inventories, and possibly lower prices, with resulting negative consequences for the state of the domestic industry. Yet, MOFCOM did not address any of these elements, in determining that the decline in apparent consumption was immaterial to its causation analysis'. Panel Report, *China – Autos (US)*, para. 7.349.

175 Appellate Body Report, *US – Hot-Rolled Steel*, para. 228.

several factors are causing injury 'at the same time', a final determination about the injurious effects caused by increased imports can only be made if

> the injurious effects caused by all the different causal factors are distinguished and separated. Otherwise, any conclusion based exclusively on an assessment of only one of the causal factors – increased imports – rests on an uncertain foundation, because it assumes that the other causal factors are not causing the injury which has been ascribed to increased imports.[176]

The Appellate Body further pointed out that

> the non-attribution language in Article 4.2(b) precludes such an assumption and, instead, requires that the competent authorities assess appropriately the injurious effects of the other factors, so that those effects may be disentangled from the injurious effects of the increased imports. In this way, the final determination rests, properly, on the genuine and substantial relationship of cause and effect between increased imports and serious injury.[177]

According to Sykes, the interpretation by the Appellate Body of the non-attribution obligation imposes on national authorities the duty to take 'the analytical step of identifying the other factors causing injury, and then assigning to those other factors the injury attributable to them, so as to ensure that such injury is not erroneously attributed to increased imports'.[178] This would ensure that other causal factors[179] are not included in the assessment of the injury ascribed to increased imports.[180]

Investigating authorities are thus obliged to separate and distinguish the effects of 'other factors' from those of increased imports. Furthermore, they have to identify: '[t]he nature and extent of the injurious effects of the known factors' as well as 'a satisfactory explanation of the nature and extent of the injurious effects of the other factors, as distinguished from the injurious effects of the increased imports'.[181] In the Appellate Body's opinion,

> [t]o fulfil the requirement of Article 4.2(b), last sentence, the competent authorities must establish explicitly, through a reasoned and adequate explanation, that injury caused by factors other than increased imports is not attributed to increased imports. This explanation must be clear and

176 Appellate Body Report, *US – Lamb*, para. 179.

177 *Ibid.*

178 Alan O. Sykes, 'The Fundamental Deficiencies of the Agreement on Safeguards: A Reply to Professor Lee', (2006) 40 *Journal of World Trade* 979, 984.

179 Appellate Body Report, *US – Lamb*, para. 185.

180 In Sykes's opinion, the 'non-attribution' exercise required by Appellate Body precedent is often logically impossible to perform. Sykes (Ch.3 n.178) 985.

181 Appellate Body Report, *US – Line Pipe*, para. 213.

unambiguous. It must not merely imply or suggest an explanation. It must be a straightforward explanation in express terms.[182]

In practice, in cases where the domestic authorities verify that 'other factors' are causing injury to the domestic industry, they also have to assess the injurious effects of these other factors and adequately describe how they did not attribute to the injury caused by the acts, the injurious effects of other factors.[183] In sum, 'they cannot only state that a given "other factor" hurts the domestic industry, they must evaluate it and estimate how it may evolve or disappear'.[184]

Drawing from the work of the DSB, certain Member States are also trying to find amendments to the causality matter to ensure that trade remedies are not used as a remedy for injuries caused by other factors. The 'FAN group of countries that support amendment of the Anti-dumping Agreement aimed at limiting the abuse of anti-dumping, criticized the current non-attribution test which has been accused of allowing States to adopt measures even in cases where 'other factors' are the real cause of injury. In that respect, the FAN considered that the current provision deserves further elaboration and proposed to introduce new rules aimed at excluding the possibility of adopting antidumping measures in cases where dumped imports merely 'contributed' to material injury. Moreover, a causal link should be deemed proven only in cases where there is a *substantial* causal relationship between dumped imports and injury.[185]

182 *Ibid.*, para. 217.

183 The Panel in the *China – HP-SSST (Japan)* observed that 'MOFCOM sought to comply with the non-attribution requirement contained in Article 3.5 of the Anti-Dumping Agreement by considering whether certain other factors broke the causal link between dumped imports and material injury to the domestic industry it had found, stating that such methodology provides an appropriate basis for ensuring non-attribution'. The Panel also observed that, 'before it becomes relevant or necessary for an investigating authority to separate and distinguish the injury caused by other factors from the injury caused by subject imports, the investigating authority must first properly establish that the dumped imports have caused material injury, and the "nature and extent" of the injury caused by subject imports and the injury caused by the other factor(s)'. Recalling its prior conclusion that MOFCOM had failed properly to establish the causal link between dumped imports and material injury to the domestic industry, the Panel held that 'MOFCOM could not have meaningfully assessed whether or not injury caused by other factors was sufficient to break that wrongly-determined causal link'. The Panel therefore considered that it was not necessary to address every aspect of the parties' non-attribution arguments in detail. Appellate Body Report, *China – HP-SSST (Japan)*, para. 5.279. See also Appellate Body Report, *US – Hot-Rolled Steel*, para. 226.

184 Appellate Body Report, *US – Lamb*, para. 185.

185 In 2003, China proposed to clarify Article 3.5 in order to ensure that a causal link could only be established when the dumped import is the 'substantial reason' for the injury to the domestic industry. In that regard, Australia specifically asked a question whether the use of the 'substantial cause' standard would undermine the scope of the antidumping. China however asserted that Article 3.5 of the Anti-dumping Agreement, as it stands, fails to provide a methodology of defining the causal relationship between dumping and injury. WTO Negotiating Group on Rules, Proposal of the

It is not the first time that States have tried to insert an adjective with the intention of raising the bar of causality. As described before, other examples of public international law demonstrate that the desire to find a 'magic word' that could solve the matter of causality is not merely confined to the WTO. It is also true that the insertion of an adjective would limit the discretion of the authorities and also give guiding elements for interpretation and analysis to the DSB. In the negotiation of the AD Code 1967 certain Members requested that anti-dumping measures should be applied only if dumping was the principal cause of injury. A few decades later, China pushed for a reform by which anti-dumping measures could only be taken when the dumped imports are the *major* cause of the injury.[186]

The distinction between the injury caused by dumped imports from that caused by other factors is almost entirely made in qualitative and not quantitative terms. This limitation by Member States in their approach is triggered by the fact that the quantitative assessment envisaged by many Member States during Doha Round negotiations is 'easier said than done'. Even the FAN proposal recognized the difficulty in distinguishing and calculating the injurious effects of dumped imports from the injurious effect of other known factors. Accordingly, the FAN group stated that: '[i]t might be difficult, in most cases, to quantify precisely the degree to which dumped imports have contributed to the injury being experienced by the domestic industry relative to the effects of other factors'. Based on that statement they proposed that such a separation could be based on 'qualitative information or less than perfect quantitative information or estimates based on such information'.

Some authors also suggest the use of econometric analysis in the causality test. This form of computer-based analysis tries to quantify 'the degree to which dumped imports have affected factors such as domestic prices, revenues and industry production levels as compared to other potential causes of injury'.[187] Therefore, it may be used to understand whether there is a sufficient causal link between dumped, subsidized or increased imports and the injury suffered by the domestic industry. To counter the request of the FAN, the United States, one of the few countries adopting econometric analysis in trade remedies investigations, submitted two documents during Doha Round negotiations trying to clarify that authorities shall not quantify the effects of other factors during the investigations.[188]

People's Republic of China on the Negotiation on Antidumping, TN/RL/W/66 (March 6, 2003) and WTO Negotiating Group on Rules, Submission from the People's Republic of China, Replies to the Questions and Comments of the WTO Members Concerning the Proposal of China, TN/RL/W/94 (May 5, 2003).

186 Article 3 of the AD Code 1967.

187 Czako, Hunman and Miranda (n. 426) 355–356.

188 Communication from the United States, Identification of Additional Issues under the Anti-Dumping and Subsidies Agreements, TN/RL/W/98 (May 6, 2003) and Communication from the United States, Causation (Anti-dumping Agreement Article 3.5; SCM Agreement Article 15.5), TN/RL/GEN/59 (July 13, 2005).

The divergent approach of the two groups, FAN against the United States,[189] led the Chairman to propose a new text in which delegations continue to hold widely diverging views on issues relating to causation of injury. Although there seems to be a shared view that authorities should carefully consider the effects of factors other than dumped imports, and ensure they are not attributed to dumped imports, there are substantial gaps regarding the degree of precision that can or should be required.[190]

As underlined by the Chairman's text, despite the agreement among countries on the need to ameliorate the causality assessment in trade remedies, there are diverging opinions on the methodology to be used. In particular, countries agree on the necessity to isolate and not to attribute injury caused by other factors to the injury caused by dumping and subsidized imports. However, it is very difficult in practice to suggest concrete methodologies to quantify the effects of the other factors. Not even econometric analysis seemed to be a recommended approach. On the one hand, there is a need to limit the discretion of the authorities who could use the loopholes of the rules to misuse trade remedies. On the other hand, the qualitative vs. quantitative debate is probably too abstract and would be difficult to find a solution to in practice. However, when considering trade remedies, the causality assessment is of vital importance for distinguishing measures adopted with protectionist intents from reactions of injured states. Therefore, the assessment of the causality by authorities should place more attention on describing in a qualitative manner the attribution and non-attribution test, in order to give interested parties the possibility of submitting rebuttals and authorities themselves the possibility of complying with the obligation to conduct unbiased and objective investigations.

3.4. Trade remedies principle

3.4.1. Non-mandatory

Like all unilateral measures and 'species' of self-help the application of trade remedies is not mandatory or automatic. Measures of self-help are rights given to States and not obligations to enforce. The violation of an international norm only gives the offended party a right, if it so wishes, to adopt adequate measures of retaliation.[191] For example, in 1986 when Libya launched missiles against a U.S. Military Base in Sicily, the missiles fell into the Italian territorial sea and thus

189 Negotiating Group on Rules, Hong Kong, China; Japan; Korea; Norway; Switzerland; and the Separate Customs Territory of Taiwan, Penghu, Kinmen and Matsu, TN/RL/W/233 (March 12, 2008). Negotiating Group on Rules, Working Document from the Chairman, TN/RL/W/232 (May 28, 2008). Negotiating Group on Rules, New Draft Consolidated Chair Texts for AD and SCM Agreements, TN/RL/W/236 (December 19, 2008).

190 Negotiating Group on Rules, Communication from the Chairman, Agreement on the Implementation of Article VI of the General Agreement on Tariffs and Trade, TN/RL/W/254 (April 11, 2011).

191 In relation to the principle *inadimplenti non est adimplendum*, see generally Gerald Fitzmaurice, 'Second Report on the Law of Treaties', *Yearbook of the International Law Commission*, Vol. II, 1957, 53.

violated Italy's right to sovereignty under international law. Accordingly, Italy was the injured State entitled to adopt measures against Libya. However, Italy decided not to adopt any retaliatory measures against Libya.[192]

The non-mandatory principle in the use of trade remedies is also contained in relevant WTO agreements. Under WTO law, once the national authority of the importing member has conducted an investigation and found evidence of the essential elements, that authority is not obliged by WTO law to adopt remedies. Such a Member can decide not to adopt any measures or can further analyse whether or not there is a need to adopt such remedies. The analysis of the necessity to impose trade remedies is generally left to political and economic considerations. Every Member can decide to take, or not to take, remedies based on its assessment of national interest and relations with other states. Despite the technical nature of trade remedies they are very often subject to political pressure that could derive from domestic producers asking for protection or, for example, indirect pressure of foreign governments whose firms and interests would be affected by the decision of the importing State.

Certain WTO Members have adopted internal legislation that includes a 'national interest test' so as to give stakeholders the possibility to be heard by the authorities and to give the investigating authority the possibility of hearing all the different interests and to weigh them up. For example, the European Union adopted a Union interest test that is a further condition which must be met during the investigations. Under EU laws, the Commission (investigating authority in the EU) shall determine whether the Union interest calls for intervention.[193] In accordance with domestic regulations, the Commission shall make an evaluation of all the various economic interests taken as a whole, including the interests of the domestic industry, users and consumers. In other words, it has to collect the information received by interested parties and evaluate whether or not the imposition of the measures is in conflict with the interest of the EU. During such a phase of the investigation, emphasis is placed on the need to give special consideration to the need to eliminate the trade distorting effects of injurious dumping or subsidization and to restore effective competition.

The usefulness of the community interest test in the EU investigation has been debated. The community test has mainly been criticized because it is considered to be 'EU producers oriented'. The manner in which the national test is written would make the interests of the producers prevail over those of the exporters or importers. Certain scholars considered that it only played a minor role in the decisions not to adopt trade measures.[194] The interest test is also faced with the issue of fully reflecting the interest of the Union. In the last decade, many more domestic firms outsourced their production into other countries for import into

192 Giuliano, Scovazzi and Treves (Ch.1 n.12) 444.

193 Articles 21 of the EC Regulation 384/96 and 31 of the EC Regulation 2026/97.

194 Van Bael and Bellis (Ch.3 n.14) 295 and Adinda Sinnaeve, 'The "Community Interest Test" in Anti-dumping Investigations: Time for Reform?' (2007) 4.2 *Global Trade and Customs Journal* 157.

the EU. Furthermore, the Union interest test has been limited to economic interests and excludes an evaluation of possible social, developmental and environmental concerns. The European Community had imposed anti-dumping measures on energy saving bulbs and solar panels produced in China. The impediment for consumers to find cheaper Chinese bulbs in the market did not only contrast with environmental policies of the EU but did not fully reflect the global interests of reducing energy and protecting the environment.[195] In addition, trade remedies on developing countries' exports may deeply affect the economy in the exporting countries and contrast with other EU or international developmental policies.

The EU is no longer the sole WTO Member to adopt an interest test. Following a revision of its domestic anti-dumping legislation, Brazil also introduced an interest test into its national legislation.[196] The test requires the involvement of certain ministries that are called on to express their opinion on the adoption of the measures. Other countries such as Australia, New Zealand and South Africa have legislation which grants their Ministers responsible for trade remedies the power to exercise discretion on the application (or not) of the duties. India and China formally mention domestic public interest rules but no evidence of real application has been found in practice. The United States has not introduced a similar provision for a public interest test into its national legislation.[197]

It could also be argued that the interest test should become part of WTO rules. In this way all countries would be required to make a further evaluation of the necessity of adopting trade remedies. The introduction of a mandatory industry test would help investigating authorities to understand whether or not they should adopt trade remedies. On the other hand, a defender of a pure technical approach towards trade remedies may argue that such an opportunity will open the door to politicization and thus affect their predictability and use by the domestic industry. In that case, lobbying activities may prevail over the evidence of the existence of elements essential to triggering the reaction of the injured States. However, as the interest of a State is composed by the different interests of all the stakeholders, the test will simply give a further opportunity to the State to review the whole country interest before the adoption of the measures. Moreover, a national test could be extended beyond purely economic considerations and could also include environmental, social and developmental concerns. Such an approach would contribute to

195 See also the cases *Canada – Renewable Energy* and *India – Solar Cells.*

196 Resolution CAMEX 13/2012, which creates the Technical Group for Evaluation of Public Interest (GTIP) with the purpose of analysing the suspension, alteration and non-application of provisory and definitive anti-dumping measures in light of the public interest; which is under the coordination of the Secretariat for International Affairs of the Ministry of Finance (Safeguard Agreement) (Resolution CAMEX No. 30/2016). Resolution CAMEX No. 29/2017 regulates the procedure before the GTIP.

197 Independent evaluation of trade defence instruments carried out for the European Commission in 2012 available at http://trade.ec.europa.eu/doclib/press/index.cfm?id=786 (accessed 2 January 2018).

reducing potential 'externalities' of the adoption of trade remedies and improve consistency with other domestic and international policies.

3.4.2. Specificity

International law does not require that countermeasures assume the same form as the action which caused the internationally unlawful act.[198] It does not require that the violation be the same or similar to that made by the wrongdoing State.[199] Nor does international law oblige states to react with specific means to the violation of their rights. In the self-defence context, international law does not require States to respond to the aggression by the use of specific arms and weapons. Similarly, countermeasures are not based on *lex talionis* and therefore for a violation of primary rules there are no specific reactions that are described in secondary norms. The choice of the means of reaction is left to the injured State though limited by international law.[200]For example, for forms of self-help other than self-defence the use of force is prohibited. In addition, they cannot violate basic obligations of international law such as those protecting fundamental human rights, of a humanitarian character and norms of *ius cogens*, or impair diplomatic inviolability.[201]

Similarly, trade remedies cannot violate those norms. Furthermore, in anti-dumping and countervailing measures, the imposing State cannot raise tariffs, adopt quota, import bans or other forms of unilateral measures. The WTO legal system imposes strict limits on States, *rectius* imposes that anti-dumping and countervailing measures can only have the form of duties or undertakings.[202] This matter has been addressed by the DSB in the *US-Antidumping Act 1916* case. The mentioned Act contained other measures to counteract dumping such as fines or imprisonment or the recovery of treble damages. The panel and the Appellate Body found those measures to be inconsistent with WTO anti-dumping rules.[203] The latter considered that Article VI of the GATT 1994 and the Anti-dumping

198 Angelo Sereni, *Diritto internazionale III* (Giuffré, 1962) 1559.
199 It shall be noted by contrast that countermeasures can be taken against violations of provisions embodying obligations imposed by international law independently of the treaty. Gomaa (Ch.3 n.11)132.
200 For example, the prohibition of the use or threat of force for countermeasure, the use of nuclear weapons in self-defence, the suspension or termination of the treaty violated in the case *inadimplenti non est adimplendum*, etc.
201 *United States Diplomatic and Consular Staff in Teheran, Judgment*, I.C.J. Reports 1980, paras 84–86.
202 Article VI and, in particular, Article VI:2, read in conjunction with the Anti-dumping Agreement, limit the permissible responses to dumping to 'definitive anti-dumping duties, provisional measures and price undertakings'. Appellate Body Report, *US – 1916 Act*, para. 137; Appellate Body Report, *US – Offset Act (Byrd Amendment)*, para. 265 and Appellate Body Report, *US – Customs Bond Directive*, para. 206.
203 Panel Report, *US – Anti-Dumping Act of 1916* (Complainant: European Communities), para. 6.204 and Appellate Body Report, *US – Anti-Dumping Act of 1916*, para. 138.

Agreement apply to 'specific action against dumping'. More precisely, Article VI:2 of GATT, read in conjunction with the Anti-dumping Agreement, limits the permissible responses to dumping to definitive anti-dumping duties, provisional measures and price undertakings. Therefore, the United States 1916 Act providing for 'specific action against dumping' in the form of civil and criminal proceedings and penalties was found to be inconsistent with Article VI:2 and the Anti-dumping Agreement.[204]

In reference to safeguard, the WTO system allows the imposing State to choose the form which can best achieve the purpose of eliminating the serious injury suffered. It can be a duty or a quota but the Safeguard Agreement sets forth that it cannot be a voluntary export restraint, orderly market arrangements, export moderation, export-price or import-price monitoring system, export or import surveillance, compulsory import cartels and discretionary export or import licensing schemes, or other similar measures.[205] In addition, an implicit limit could be found in Article 5 of the Safeguard Agreement. That Article sets forth that a Member shall apply safeguard measures only to the extent necessary to prevent or remedy serious injury and to facilitate adjustments. By setting the purpose of the measures, the Safeguard Agreement implicitly restricts the range of measures to those which, by their nature, could be aimed at remedying injury and facilitating adjustments. Thus, measures which are not aimed at addressing those purposes cannot be considered compliant with Article 5 of the Safeguard Agreement.

Anti-dumping and countervailing measures shall also be specific, in the sense that they shall be applied only against countries and firms that have received the subsidy or practised dumping. This means that a Member cannot levy anti-dumping and countervailing measures on all the imports coming from a country without assessing their dumped or subsidized imports. Leaving aside safeguards, anti-dumping and countervailing measures must only be applied on goods exported from countries and by firms whose exports have been found to be subsidized or dumped. Thus, it is not possible to impose measures on all exporters of a specific product so as to apply a hidden protectionist barrier to trade.

The Safeguard Agreement provides a different discipline. Under Article 2.2 of that agreement, safeguard measures shall be applied to imports 'irrespective of their source'. While anti-dumping and countervailing measures 'discriminate' among firms, the application of safeguards follows a 'most-favoured-nation' basis.[206] According to UNCTAD, 'this is a major guiding principle of the

204 Appellate Body Report, *US – Anti-Dumping Act of 1916*, para. 137.

205 Article 11.1(b) of the Safeguard Agreement and footnotes 3 and 4 thereof.

206 All the Agreements contain specific rules for the application of measures on imports from developing countries. Anti-dumping and SCM Agreement contain norms on special and differential treatment for developing countries (article 27); the Anti-dumping Agreement requests Member to explore constructive remedies before applying duties which could affect the essential interest of developing country Members (article 15). In the Safeguard Agreement the WTO Members are obliged not to apply trade remedies to imports from developing countries if below certain thresholds (article 9).

Safeguard Agreement and indeed a fundamental achievement compared to Article XIX of the GATT'.[207] An issue may arise on whether a Member can exclude from a safeguard measure the products imported from its partners in a Free Trade Area (FTA) or a Customs Union (CU). Under article XXIV of the GATT 1994, Members are allowed to depart from GATT provisions (and in particular from the MFN clause) by establishing a CU or FTA which facilitates deeper economic integration between the members of a FTA or a CU under certain conditions. The question is whether or not a Member may derogate from Safeguard Agreement Article 2.2 and thus exclude its FTA or CU partners from the imposition of the measure.[208]The Appellate Body held, by reversing the panel's finding, that Members are not allowed to make such a departure though it did not explicitly rule on the issue.[209] Furthermore, as described in Chapter 2, the principle of non-discrimination contained in Article 2.1 of the Safeguard Agreement embodies the 'parallelism' requirement. Thus, under that principle the scope of a safeguard measure must correspond to the scope of imports which were investigated and in respect of which the requirements for the imposition of safeguard measures ('increased imports', 'serious injury' or threat thereof, and 'causation') were established.[210] According to the parallelism requirement, if a Member assesses the requirements for the imposition of a safeguard measure by considering the imports from Members A, B and C (all Members exporting the product under investigation) the imposing Member, by excluding Member A (or B or C) from the imposition of the safeguard measure, would not respect the parallelism between scope of imports investigated and the scope of imports subjected to the measure. The Appellate Body has considered that if a WTO Member has imposed a measure after conducting an investigation on imports from all sources, it is also required under Article 2.2 of the Safeguard Agreement to apply such measure to all sources (including partners in a FTA).[211]

3.4.3. Reversibility and temporary limits

Similar to other forms of self-help, trade remedies are reversible.[212] In general international law this characteristic allows for the possibility that 'future legal relations between victim state and responsible state can be restored'.[213]

207 UNCTAD, *Safeguard* (n. 307) 35.

208 As noted by UNCTAD, 'the issue is further complicated by the fact that Article XXIV only refers to GATT rules (thus, in principle, it does not cover derogations from other WTO provisions, such as Article 2.2 of the Safeguard Agreement)'. UNCTAD, *Safeguard* (Ch.3 n.48) 35.

209 Appellate Body Report, *US – Line Pipe*, para. 263, point (f).

210 Appellate Body Report, *Argentina – Footwear (EC)*, para. 111 and Appellate Body report, *US – Line Pipe*, para. 197.

211 Appellate Body Report, *Argentina – Footwear (EC)*, para. 112

212 *Gabčíkovo-Nagymaros Project* (Hungary vs. Slovakia), Judgment, I.C.J. *Reports 1997*, 57, para. 87.

213 White and Abbas (n. 175) 512. In the *Gabčíkovo-Nagymaros* case the ICJ stated that the purpose of the countermeasures is to induce the wrongdoing State to comply with its

Under trade remedies legislation, the imposition of duties, undertakings or quota can be timely and suddenly withdrawn where it is considered necessary or when the conditions which justify their imposition have disappeared. This can be done upon request of the interested parties or *ex officio* through a review of the measures imposed. During the time the measure is in force the investigating authorities shall review the need for the continued imposition of the measures.[214] Thus, in cases where they find that the measures are no longer warranted they shall be terminated or withdrawn immediately. In addition, in cases where panels or the Appellate Body find that measures applied are not in compliance with WTO Agreements they shall be withdrawn or modified such that they comply with the rulings and indirectly with WTO rules.

Measures shall be limited in time. Measures of self-help must be halted when their purpose has been achieved.[215] Accordingly, trade remedies shall remain in force as long as and to the extent necessary to counteract the act which is causing injury, or in case of safeguard, only for such a period of time necessary to prevent or remedy serious injury and to facilitate adjustments. They shall terminate as soon as the cause of injury or the injury itself disappear. Anti-dumping and countervailing measures shall last 5 years from their imposition or the latest review, while safeguards cannot exceed 4 years.

A problem may arise for reviews. The reviews permit the extension of measures in force for a further 5 years. At the time of elapsing of reviewed measures, the investigating authority may conduct another review and impose measures for more years and so on. This risks measures remaining in force for many years and transforms 'limited' measures into permanent import barriers. This risk is aggravated by the fact that during the reviews the scope of investigation is not to prove the existence of dumping/subsidy, injury and causal link, but that the expiry of duty would be likely to lead to continuation or recurrence of dumping/subsidization and injury. This means that it is possible to extend measures even in the case where no imports occur in the imposing country but the investigating authorities

obligations under international law, and that measures must be reversible. *Gabčíkovo-Nagymaros*, Judgement, paras. 56–57. According to Crawford the 'international community has moved away from the classical terminology of reprisals and towards the notion of countermeasures as temporary, reversible steps'. James Crawford, 'The Relationship between Sanctions and Countermeasures', in Vera Gowlland-Debbas (ed.), *United Nations Sanctions and International Law* (Kluwer Law International 2001) 66.

214 Articles 11.2 of the Anti-dumping Agreement and 7.4 of the Safeguard Agreement. It is important to underline that for safeguards, the duty to review the situation is only when the duration of the measure exceeds 3 years.

215 The ICJ in the Military and Paramilitary Activities in and Against Nicaragua hold that the US activities were not proportionate because 'the reaction of United States in the context of what is regarded as self-defence was continued long after the period in which any presumed armed conflict by Nicaragua could reasonably be contemplated'. *Military and Paramilitary Activities in and Against Nicaragua*, 122, para. 237. According to Cassese, the act of retorsion 'should be discontinued as soon as the unfair, unfriendly, or wrong behaviour to which is intended to react ceases'. Antonio Cassese, *International Law* (Oxford University Press 2001) 244.

determine the likelihood of recurrence of dumping/subsidization or injury. In the Safeguard Agreement the WTO rules impose on the authorities the obligation to determine (by using the same methods) whether the measures continue to be necessary to prevent or remedy injury and facilitate adjustments. The Safeguard Agreement introduces a temporary limit to safeguard measures. They cannot exceed, in total, a period of 8 years.[216] Furthermore, once the measure has terminated no safeguard measures can be applied again to the import of the product which has been subject to a measure for a period of time equal to that during which such a measure had been previously applied.[217]

This is probably due to the emergency nature of safeguard measures which, as stated by the heading of Article XIX of the GATT, cannot be imposed for a long period time and to the fact that such measures are less economically justifiable and apply indiscriminately to all the imports of a product. Although anti-dumping and countervailing measures do not have the emergency nature of safeguard, their potential misuse should be strictly limited by rules. In line with the comparison conducted so far and in order to improve current discipline, it is the opinion of the author that an explicit temporary limit should be introduced in the Anti-dumping Agreement and SCM Agreement. These WTO agreements shall limit the imposition of measures up to the end of the first review (maximum 10 years). Furthermore, after this period a new investigation shall be conducted in order to see whether dumping/subsidy, injury and causal link exist.

As stated before, the imposition of anti-dumping or countervailing measures for too long a period, and in particular the manner in which the review is conducted, risks giving investigating authorities the power to adopt excessively long-lasting trade barriers which undermine the benefit of free trade. The introduction of a temporary limit would balance the trade-off between, on the one hand, the necessity to counter injurious dumping and subsidies and on the other hand the need to avoid the possibility of using trade remedies with protectionist intents.

3.4.4. Consultation before adoption

Under general international law, the injured State, before adopting countermeasures, shall demand that the responsible State comply with its international obligations. The injured State shall call upon the wrongdoing State to meet its obligations and notify the State of its intentions and offer to negotiate.[218] Moreover, in cases where the responsible State has ceased to commit the wrongful act, and the dispute has been submitted to a tribunal with binding authority, the countermeasures must be suspended.[219] According to Cassese, the aim of negotiations is either to settle the

216 Article 7.2 of the Safeguard Agreement.

217 Provided that the period of non-application is at least 2 years. Article 7.5 of the Safeguard Agreement.

218 Crawford, *Draft Articles* (n. 370) 292–293.

219 Article 52 of the DARSIWA.

dispute or agree upon another means of settlement. He also stressed that this requirement follows from the general principle of peaceful settlement of disputes.[220]

Such obligations are not found in all trade remedies. Although the Anti-dumping Agreement imposes an obligation to notify the parties concerned, such notifications have different purposes. They are aimed at informing parties concerned of the initiation or conclusion of the investigations thereby giving them the opportunity to submit documents or other information that parties consider relevant for the investigations. They are aimed more at ensuring due process during investigation than a possible mutually agreed solution. However, the SCM Agreement and the Safeguard Agreement do contain a duty to consult. Under Article 13 of the SCM Agreement, after the initiation of an investigation Members concerned shall be invited for consultation with the aim of clarifying the situation and arriving at a mutually agreed solution. Article 13.2 of the SCM Agreement explicitly requires that the Member which initiates investigations affords a reasonable opportunity to continue consultations throughout the period of investigation. The duty to consult introduced by the SCM Agreement underlines the similarity between countermeasures and countervailing measures.

The Safeguard Agreement also contains a duty to consult. Under Article 12.3 of the Safeguard Agreement the Member proposing to apply or extend safeguard measures shall provide adequate opportunity for prior consultations with those Members with a substantial interest as exporter of the product concerned. The purpose of those consultations shall be *inter alia* to review the information on which the decision is based (about the evidence of injury caused by increased imports, date of imposition, duration, timetable for progressive liberalization),[221] to exchange views on the measures to reach an understanding on the maintenance of the level of concession. The structure of the norm seems to suggest that Members shall consult with a view to achieving the abovementioned purposes. However, the term '*inter alia*' allows Members to use consultations to find a mutually agreed solution which of course cannot include voluntary export restraints or other '*grey area*' measures prohibited by Article 11.1 (b) of the Safeguard Agreement.

In line with other trade remedies, classic forms of self-help and with the general principle of the 'reaction of the injured States' it could be interesting to explore a possibility of introducing a duty to consult in the Anti-dumping Agreement. According to this norm, before starting an investigation or review, parties involved, in particular those allegedly dumping, and national States shall be invited for consultations in order to find a possible mutually agreed solution. Parties involved in the case will engage in consultations *bona fide* with the aim of finding a satisfactory reciprocal solution in compliance with WTO law. The consultation will contribute to clarifying the situation and the position of the parties and, in the case of agreement, reduce the costs of investigation.

220 Antonio Cassese, *International Law* (Ch.2 n.46) 235.

221 In case of extension of the measures, evidence that the industry concerned is adjusting. Article 12.2 of the Safeguard Agreement.

3.4.5. Non-reparation

Trade remedies do not give rise to a right of reparation.[222] In the *Chorzow Factory* case in 1928, the Permanent Court of International Justice held that

> it is a general conception of law that every violation of an engagement involves an obligation to make reparation [...] a principle of international law that the reparation of a wrong may consist in an indemnity corresponding to the damage which the nationals of the injured state have suffered as a result of the act which is contrary to international law.[223]

The duties collected by the customs authorities of the importing State cannot be considered as forms of reparation for the injury suffered by the domestic industry. This principle has been précised by the WTO jurisprudence in the *US – Continued Dumping and Subsidy Offset Act* case. Under the United States' law, the American firms which were injured by dumped or subsidized imports were eligible to receive offsetting payments from the custom authorities. Those payments were financed by anti-dumping and countervailing duties paid to the United States' customs. According to the Appellate Body, the Act effects a transfer of financial resources from the producers/exporters of dumped or subsidized goods to their domestic competitors.[224] The recipients of the offset payments could use the money received to bolster their competitive position *vis-à-vis* their competitors, including the foreign competitors subject to anti-dumping or countervailing duties.[225] Thus, foreign producers/exporters had an incentive not to engage in the practice of exporting dumped or subsidized products or to terminate such practices. The Appellate Body found that the Act 'has an adverse bearing on, and, more specifically, is designed and structured so that it dissuades the practice of dumping or the practice of subsidization, and creates an incentive to terminate such practices'.[226]

222 Under article 34–37 of the DARSIWA, 'full reparation for the injury caused by the internationally wrongful act shall take the form of restitution, compensation and satisfaction, either singly or in combination, in accordance with the provisions of this chapter'. The text further defines the obligation of compensation by which the State responsible for an internationally wrongful act is under an obligation to compensate for the damage caused thereby, insofar as such damage is not made good by restitution. The compensation shall cover any financially assessable damage including loss of profits insofar as it is established and satisfaction under which The State responsible for an internationally wrongful act is under an obligation to give satisfaction for the injury caused by that act insofar as it cannot be made good by restitution or compensation. Satisfaction may consist in an acknowledgement of the breach, an expression of regret, a formal apology or another appropriate modality. Satisfaction shall not be out of proportion to the injury and may not take a form humiliating to the responsible State.

223 *Case Concerning the Factory at Chorzow*, Permanent Court of International Justice, Collection of Judgments, Series A, 29.

224 Appellate Body report, *US – Continued Dumping and Subsidy Offset Act*, para. 255.

225 *Ibid.*

226 *Ibid.* para. 256.

3.4.6. Pre-emptive use of trade remedies

Another important issue is the use of pre-emptive trade remedies. The use of pre-emptive measures of self-help, and in particular self-defence, has been highly debated in international law. Is it possible under international law to have recourse to self-defence before the commission of the wrongful act?

The pre-emptive theory has been invoked by States (Israel and United States) to justify armed attack against States which have not yet attacked Israel and the United States but which in their opinion were going to do it. Those were the cases of the destruction of atomic reactor Osiraq in Iraq by the Israeli army and the justification of the attack on Iraq by United States. In relation to the Israeli-Iraq case, the Security Council of the UN strongly condemned the attack as being in violation of the UN Charter and international norms of conduct.[227]

Pre-emptive self-defence entitles a State to use armed force unilaterally, and in the absence of prior international authorization, in order to halt 'an incipient development that is not yet operational or directly threatening, but that, if permitted to mature, could be seen by the potential pre-emptor as susceptible to neutralization only at a higher and possibly unacceptable cost to itself'.[228] However, as remarked by Reisman and Armstrong, pre-emptive self-defence differs from anticipatory self-defence because in the latter the threat is palpable and imminent. Thus, according to the scholars,

> anticipatory self-defense (which was, in our view, not in the contemplation of the drafters of the Charter, though claimed by many to have been grafted thereon by subsequent practice) is at least akin to the armed attack requirement of Charter Article 51, because there may be palpable evidence of an imminent attack. A claim for pre-emptive self-defense can point only to a possibility among a range of other possibilities, a contingency.[229]

In sum, it seems to emerge that neither pre-emptive nor anticipatory self-defence are considered lawful under international law.

The use of pre-emptive force is not admissible because under Article 51 of the UN Charter a State can only have recourse to self-defence where a previous armed attack against the State has been committed. Thus, the reaction of the State is admissible only in cases where a previous unlawful act i.e. armed attack has been committed. Put differently, the State cannot use force against another State before it has been attacked by that State.

In order to have recourse to self-defence the *'fait generateur'* of the international responsibility under classical international law, the wrongful act and in the specific case of self-defence the armed attack, must already have been made. By analogy, this principle could be applied to other forms of self-help. Accordingly, a

227 Security Council Resolution N. 487 of 19 June 1981.

228 Michael Reisman and Andrea Armstrong, 'The Past and Future of the Claim of Pre-emptive Self-Defense' (2006) 100 *American Journal of International Law* 526.

229 *Ibid.*

countermeasure cannot be applied in the absence of an unlawful act against the victim State or an act of retorsion before the commission of an unlawful or unfriendly act.[230]

WTO trade remedies do not follow this principle. As mentioned before the *fait déclencheur* of trade remedies is a combination of an act and the *injury* caused by that act and suffered by the injured State. Accordingly, in the absence of evidence of injury an investigating authority cannot impose trade remedies. However, the definition of injury in the Anti-dumping Agreement, SCM Agreement and Safeguard Agreement also includes the *threat* of injury.[231] By definition, a threat refers to a future act which has not yet been undertaken and is based on speculative knowledge about the future. In sum, in the trade remedy field a WTO Member State is allowed to adopt a measure of reaction before, and in the absence, of injury.

This wide possibility to react against injurious practices is counterbalanced by certain limits that are imposed on investigating authorities. In fact, Article 3.7 of the Anti-dumping Agreement establishes that

> a determination of a threat of material injury shall be based on facts and not merely on allegation, conjecture and remote possibility. The change in circumstances which would create a situation in which the dumping would cause injury must be clearly foreseen and imminent.

In sum, investigating authorities are required to make an evaluation of future events that would occur in the absence of anti-dumping measures.

In order to avoid possible abuses, the Appellate Body in the *Mexico – Corn Syrup* case précised that

> in determining the existence of a threat of material injury, the investigating authorities will necessarily have to make assumptions relating to 'the occurrence of future events' since such future events 'can never be definitively proven by facts'. Notwithstanding this intrinsic uncertainty, a 'proper establishment' of facts in a determination of threat of material injury must be based on events that, although they have not yet occurred, must be 'clearly foreseen and imminent' [...].[232]

230 In relation to the *inadimplenti non est adimplendum principle*, Gomaa stated that 'it is not preventive or preemptive. It cannot be exercised in anticipation of a future breach. Article 60 presumes that breach has already taken place'. See Gomaa (n. 371) 119 and 123.

231 The Anti-dumping Agreement and SCM Agreement contain also provisions related to the *material retardation*.

232 Appellate Body Report, *Mexico – Corn Syrup* (Art 21.5), para 85. With relation to the Safeguard Agreement, it has been argued that: 'in making a determination of a threat of serious injury the competent authorities need to demonstrate, on the basis of facts rather than conjecture, that serious injury is highly likely to occur in the very near future, unless protective action is taken. In our view, this specific inquiry involves not only an assessment of historical and existing facts but also involves making fact-based

Furthermore Article 3.8 of the Anti-dumping Agreement and 15.8 of the SCM Agreement require the investigating authorities to consider and decide, with special care, the imposition of anti-dumping measures when the investigations involve the determination of a threat of material injury. Although the Anti-dumping Agreement and SCM Agreement do not give any further guidance on the meaning of the term 'special care' the Panel in *US – Coated Paper (Indonesia)* clarified that this term imposes on authorities a 'high degree of attention' in threat of injury determinations.[233] Van den Bossche pointed out that, 'it is clear that the provision cautions against the "automatic" imposition of measures in such cases'.[234] In addition, the material retardation clause is a quite anomalous (but rarely used) form of injury included in footnotes 9 and 45 respectively of the Anti-dumping and SCM Agreements. Basically, there is the possibility for a Member to adopt anti-dumping measures to 'protect' a domestic industry which does not yet exist but is going to be built. In the absence of explanations by the Anti-dumping Agreement, some guidance can be derived from the 1967 Code which indicates that facts must be based on convincing evidence that such a new industry is forthcoming.[235]

The adoption of trade remedies merely on the basis of threat of injury has not been a common practice for the United States and China[236] and was never used by the European Commission before the anti-dumping case on seamless pipes and tubes in 2009.[237] In a few circumstances the Commission denied the existence of threat of injury because material injury was not clearly foreseeable or imminent.[238] In other cases measures have been adopted on the basis of both material injury and threat thereof.

projections concerning future developments in the domestic industry's condition'. Panel Report, *Ukraine – Passengers Cars*, para. 7.232. The phrase 'clearly imminent' indicates that, as a matter of fact, it must be manifest that the domestic industry is on the brink of suffering serious injury. Appellate Body Report, *US – Lamb*, para. 125.

233 The Panel in *US – Coated Paper (Indonesia)* made the following observations on this matter: 'First, the ordinary meaning of the "special care" language implies an obligation on Members to apply a high degree of attention in threat of injury determinations. Second, [...] Articles 3.7 and 15.7, which immediately precede Articles 3.8 and 15.8, provide the most relevant context for the interpretation of Articles 3.8 and 15.8, and this context suggests that the "special care" requirement relates to the obligations set out in those preceding provisions'. Panel Report *US – Coated Paper (Indonesia)*, para. 7.346

234 Van den Bossche (Ch.1 n.50) 532.

235 For example, business plans at an advanced state.

236 Xiaochen Wu, *Antidumping Law and Practice of China* (Wolters Kluwer 2009) 84.

237 As reported by Stanbrook and Bentley, in one case the initiation was based upon threat of injury. However, on investigation, the Community Authorities concluded there was no evidence to support even a threat of injury (OJ C84, 2.4.85, p.5; OJ L202, 25.7.86, 43). Clive Stanbrook and Philip Bentley, *Dumping and Subsidies – The Law and Procedures Governing the Imposition of Anti-dumping and Countervailing Duties in the European Community* (Kluwer Law International 1996) 123.

238 Regulations imposing anti-dumping measures on Refined Antimony Trioxide from the People's Republic of China (OJ L176, 9.7.94, 41) and Paint Brushes from the People's Republic of China (OJ L127,25.5.93, 5).

In the abovementioned case the European Commission did not find evidence of injury and went on further to analyse whether there was threat of injury. It examined the listed factors (although did not find evidence of threat of injury in all of them) and other possible indicators of the threat of material injury such as market share and the 'environment' in which Chinese companies operate in periods of crisis. In reference to the latter, the EU Commission stated that 'in a situation of worldwide economic crisis, it is likely that the Chinese government be tempted to further intervene to support these companies [...]'.[239] Although this is not the only relevant factor on which the decision on the imposition of the anti-dumping measures has been taken, it raises deep concerns about speculative determination of threat of injury. As we have described in Chapter 2, the determination of the material injury shall be based on facts and not merely on allegation, conjecture or remote possibility. This shall impose limits on investigating authorities as the analysis is made of future events and the threat refers to something that has not occurred yet. Article 3.7 of the Anti-dumping Agreement cautions that change in circumstances which would create a situation in which the dumping would cause injury must be clearly *foreseen* and *imminent*. This is another limit explicitly aimed at limiting the room for manoeuvre of investigating authorities.

The adoption of measures on the basis of the mere threat of injury risks creating an unhealthy precedent and leads domestic producers to believe that the European Union is willing to consider anti-dumping complaints even on the basis of the mere threat of injury. There is a risk of creating domino effects in other countries and possible retaliatory measures.[240]The issue necessitates a deep evaluation during the Doha Round. This requires a further analysis of the trade-off between, on the one hand, the need to have pre-emptive and prompt instruments to tackle, in advance, the effects of injurious practices and, on the other hand, the risk of granting to investigating authorities a large and discretionary power in the use of trade defence instruments. In other words, the possibility to adopt pre-emptive measures could be seen as a rapid means of preventing the negative effects of an unfair practice from spreading across domestic industry. The possibility to resort to the threat of injury gives domestic producers the possibility of being protected before the damage is done. Due to the fact that investigations usually last between 12 and 15 months somebody could argue that prevention is better than cure. However, this would give the possibility to domestic authorities to adopt trade restrictive measures on the basis of future events which might never take place. To grant WTO Members wide discretion in levying anti-dumping duties risks undermining benefits of trade liberalization or the use of non-protectionist measures as trade remedies for protectionist intents. According to Stanbrook and Bentley, if abused, the criterion of threat of material injury could be used for pure

239 Commission Regulation (EC) No 289/2009 of 7 April 2009 imposing a provisional anti-dumping duty on imports of certain seamless pipes and tubes of iron or steel originating in the People's Republic of China (OJ L94, 8.4.2009, recital 125).

240 Roberto Soprano, 'The Threat of Material Injury in Antidumping Investigations: A Threat to Free Trade' (2010) 11.1 *Journal of World Investment and Trade* 67.

protectionism.[241] Opponents of anti-dumping affirm that giving relief for threats or likelihood of injury involves speculation, not hard facts, and should not be available as a second resort when the effort to prove actual injury has been unsuccessful.[242] The risk of using antidumping measures for protectionist purposes is not remote. It is probably not coincidence that the first use of anti-dumping measures by the EC on the mere threat of injury took place during the financial crisis. Accordingly, and in line with the reasoning described before in reference to other measures of self-help, trade remedies agreements should be amended in order to eliminate the possibility of adopting measures on the basis of the mere threat of injury. No measures shall be imposed before the damage (injury) can be proved by evidence based on real facts and not on foreseeable future events.

3.4.7. Proportionality

Like other forms of self-help, trade remedies must respect proportionality requirements. According to Cannizzaro, the principle of proportionality ensures the equilibrium between the protection of the legal order breached and the social control over the reaction.[243] It also 'represents a key element for controlling the exercise of the decentralised power conferred to States to individually react to internationally wrongful acts'.[244] Proportionality is recognized as a customary principle of international law and limits the reaction of the victim State by avoiding, as stated by Newton, that 'if someone punches you in the nose, you [...] burn their house down'.[245]

241 Stanbrook and Bentley (Ch.3 n.237) 123.

242 Lowenfeld, *International Economic Law* (n. 285) 268.

243 Enzo Cannizzaro, *Il principio della proporzionalità nell'ordinamento internazionale* (Giuffré 2000) 359. Bardonnet distinguished the 'proportionalité qualitative, de nature subjective, entre la violation et la reponse comme entre l'action et le but visé et la proportionnalité quantitative, en quelque sorte mathématique, qui fournirait une base objective à l'équité. Cette dernière, [...], n'est cependant qu'une circonstance pertinente. En revanche, la proportionnalité qualitative, [...] est généralement reconnue comme une règle bien établie de droit international [...]'. Rene-Jean Dupuy, *Le développement du rôle du conseil de sécurité* (Martinus Nijhoff Publishers 1993) 135. The centrality of proportionality in international law 'results both from proportionality's impressive historical and cultural pedigree and from the underdeveloped state of a global legal system still quite reliant on mutuality of obligation, reciprocity, and self-enforcement. In this, international law is hardly unique. Underdeveloped legal systems almost inevitably generate a notion of self-enforcement and then develop the principle of proportionality to keep countermeasures from spiraling out of control'. Thomas M. Franck, 'On Proportionality of Countermeasures in International Law' (2008) 102 *American Journal of International Law* 763.

244 Enzo Cannizzaro, 'The Role of Proportionality in the Law of International Countermeasures' (2001) 12.5 *European Journal of International Law* 916.

245 Quoted in Lionel Beehner, 'Israel and the Doctrine of Proportionality', Council on Foreign Relations, 13 July 2006, available at http://www.cfr.org/publication/11115/israel_and_the_doctrine_of_proportionality.html (last accessed 02/01/2018). Proportionality is also a principle related to self-defence in the domestic system of

Quoting the Shorter Oxford English Dictionary on Historical Principles, Mitchell précised that 'the ordinary meaning of "proportionality" is the "quality, character, or fact of being proportional", which in turn is defined as "corresponding in degree, size, amount, etc."'.[246] It is the antonym of 'disproportionate' and synonym of 'commensurate'. Proportionality does not mean 'this for that', that would be symmetry, proportionality involves the balance of the relationships between two things. Thus it requires determining what should be proportioned to what. Furthermore, proportionality implies measuring. It measures the extent of something in respect to something else, the ratio between two elements. So, firstly it is important to understand which elements shall be compared and then find parameters for the evaluation of the proportionality.

The principle of proportionality is used in many fields of international law, *inter alia*, in relation to measures of self-help.[247] It is not possible to use the same definition of the concept of proportionality for all the different forms of self-help.[248] It depends greatly on the context in which it is used, the purpose of the (re)action and many other aspects. Thus, the evaluation of the proportionality of a measure has to be made on a case by case basis and in relation to the type of measure taken. Proportionality is a substantial requirement, the violation of which will result in an internationally wrongful act.

many countries, e.g., Article 34 of Canadian criminal code on self-defence against unprovoked assault: '(1) Every who is unlawfully assaulted without having provoked the assault is justified in repelling force by force if the force he uses is not intended to cause death or grievous bodily harm and is no more than is necessary to enable him to defend himself. (2) Everyone who is unlawfully assaulted and who causes death or grievous bodily harm in repelling the assault is justified if (a) he causes it under reasonable apprehension of death or grievous bodily harm from the violence with which the assault was originally made or with which the assailant pursues his purposes; and (b) he believes, on reasonable grounds, that he cannot otherwise preserve himself from death or grievous bodily harm'; the Article 122–7 of the French criminal code 'a person is not criminally liable if confronted with a present or imminent danger to himself, another person or property, he performs an act necessary to ensure the safety of the person or property, except where the means used are disproportionate to the seriousness of the threat'; the Article 52 of the Italian criminal code under which the defence shall be proportionate to the offence: 'non è punibile chi ha commesso il fatto, per esservi stato costretto dalla necessità di difendere un diritto proprio od altrui contro il pericolo attuale di una offesa ingiusta, sempre che la difesa sia proporzionata all'offesa'.

246 Andrew D. Mitchell, 'Proportionality and Remedies' (Ch.2 n.60) 985.

247 Proportionality is also used in the law of the sea context (in allocating shares of territorial seas between coastal states, exclusive economic zones and oceanic and subsoil resources) and international criminal law where it ensures that sentence is not disproportionate to the international crime. *Award in the arbitration regarding the delimitation of the maritime boundary between Guyana and Suriname*, Award of 17 September 2007, R.I.A.A. vol. XXX, 2007 para. 392 and *Continental Shelf* (Libya v. Malta), Judgments, I.C.J. Reports, 1985, 56, para. 78 and *Prosecutor v. Galić*, No. IT-98-29-A, p204–05, paras. 6–7 (Nov. 30, 2006).

248 Under article 51 of the DARSIWA, countermeasures must be commensurate with the injury suffered, taking into account the gravity of the internationally wrongful act and the rights in question.

In the law of countermeasures, the Special Rapporteur Crawford considered that proportionality, as codified in Article 51 of the DARSIWA is relevant in determining 'what countermeasures may be applied and their degree of intensity [and] provides a measure of assurance inasmuch as disproportionate countermeasures could give rise to responsibility on the part of the State taking such measures'.[249] According to Cannizzaro, the concept of proportionality in the law of countermeasures can be analysed in light of the unlawful act; its effects (proportionality in relation to the damages suffered by the injured State), and the purpose of the countermeasure.[250] When assessing the proportionality of countermeasure in relation to the first criterion, the type, size and measure of the wrongful act should be considered. In 1928 the Arbitral Tribunal in the *Naulilaa* case held that:

> even if one were to admit that the law of nations does not require that the reprisal should be approximately in keeping with the offence, one should certainly consider an excessive and therefore unlawful reprisals out of all proportion to the act motivating them.[251]

However, as stated before, countermeasures do not have to be '"reciprocal" in the sense of being limited to suspension of the performance of the same or a closely related obligation'.[252] In those circumstances a countermeasure would only be proportionate to the wrongful act if it violates the same or a similar obligation. This *lex talionis* is not required in the law of countermeasure.[253]

A similar view in relation to self-defence is expressed by Kirgis who stated that 'the intensity of the use of force must be about the same as the intensity defended against'.[254] The scholar focused mainly on the intensity, a quality, of the wrongful act as a benchmark for the comparison with the reaction. Yet, in relation to the *inadimplenti non est adimplendi* rule, Article 60 of the VCLT read together with paragraph 3 thereof, seems to prohibit disproportionate recourse to it. By

249 Crawford, Draft Article (Ch.2 n.11) 294.

250 Cannizzaro, *Il principio della proporzionalità* (Ch.3 n.243) 369.

251 Responsibility of Germany for damage caused in the Portuguese colonies in the south of Africa, R.I.A.A. Vol. II, p.1013, 1928, at 1028.

252 Anthony Aust, *Handbook of International Law* (Cambridge University Press 2005) 426.

253 For example, the Old Testament's injunction 'life for life, eye for eye, tooth for tooth, hand for hand, foot for foot, burning for burning, wound for wound, stripe for stripe' and the Holy Quran similar injunction 'Life for life, eye for eye, nose for nose, ear for ear, tooth for tooth, and wounds equal for equal'. Respectively in Exodus 21:23–25 and the Holy Quran 5:45. See, Thomas Franck, 'On Proportionality of Countermeasures in International Law' (2008) 102.4 *American Journal of International Law* 715.

254 Frederic Kirgis, 'Some Proportionality Issues Raised by Israel's Use of Armed Force in Lebanon, available at http://www.asil.org/insights/2006/08/insights060817.html (accessed 05 January 2018).

précising the definition of the material breach the article removes the possibility for a State to invoke it as a ground for the suspension or termination of the treaty in case of a violation of minor intensity. As stated by Gomaa, 'the grounds for the application of Article 60 laid down in paragraph 3 are grave enough as to render termination or suspension not a disproportionate response'.[255] In sum, also in those circumstances, the proportionality of the reaction of the State is evaluated in respect of the gravity of the unlawful act. Furthermore, the reaction of the victim State is proportioned to the unlawful act only if it consists of the suspension or termination of the treaty in which the breached obligation is included.

Proportionality can also be assessed in light of the effects of the wrongful act meaning in relation to the damages suffered by the injured State.[256] The 'value' of

255 Gomaa (n. 371) 121. According to Harris, support for the view that only a material, as opposed to any, breach justifies the termination or suspension of a treaty under the law of treaties is found in the Tacna-Arica Arbitration. By Art.3 of the 1883 Treaty of Ancon between Chile and Peru it was provided that the Peruvian provinces of Tacna and Arica, sovereignty over which was sought by both parties, were to remain in the possession of Chile, which had obtained possession of them by armed force, for 10 years and that after that time a plebiscite would be held to determine their future. In 1922, after the parties had been unable to agree upon arrangements for the plebiscite, the question whether the plebiscite had still to be held was referred to arbitration. Peru alleged, inter-alia, that Chile by preventing the performance of Article 3 has discharged Peru from her obligations thereunder, and hence that a plebiscite should not now be held and that Chile should be regarded as a trespasser in the territory now in question since the year 1894. Chile had prevented the holding of the plebiscite as envisaged in Art.3, Peru argued, by her policy of 'Chileanization' of the provinces by the introduction of Chilean nationals and by measures discriminating against Peruvians. The Arbitrator (President Coolidge, US) rejected this argument on the facts: The Arbitrator is far from approving the course of Chilean administration and condoning the acts committed against Peruvians to which reference has been made, but finds no reason to conclude that a fair plebiscite in the present circumstances cannot be held under proper conditions or that a plebiscite should not be had. It is manifest that if abuses of administration could have the effect of terminating such an agreement, it would be necessary to establish such serious conditions as the consequence of administrative wrongs as would operate to frustrate the purpose of the agreement, and, in the opinion of the Arbitrator, a situation of such gravity has not been shown. *Chile v. Peru* (1925) 2 R.I.A A. 921, also quoted in David J. Harris, *Cases and Materials on International Law* (Sweet and Maxwell, sixth edition, 2004) 862.

256 A particularly clear example comes from the appreciation by France of the lawfulness of the action undertaken by Israel in Gaza in 1955: 'Il n'y a pas de commune mesure, ni en droit ni en fait, entre les actes de maraudage, de pillage, ou d'attaque armée, commis par quelques individus isolés, au travers de la ligne de démarcation – même si ces actes bénéficient d'une complicité tacite de la part d'autorités égyptiennes subalternes – et une action collective de représailles, telle que celle qui a été déclenchée dans la nuit du 28 février 1955 … Il n'y a pas de commune mesure entre le quatre Israéliens tués au cours de ces incidents de frontière, du novembre 1954 à février 1955, et les 38 victimes égyptiennes faites par l'attaque israélienne sur Gaza' (in SCOR 749). See the position of the United States regarding the Israeli attack on Tiberiade, in 1955: 'Israel's deed is so out of proportion to the provocation that it cannot be accurately described as a retaliatory raid' (SCOR 710, para. 58), and on the

the breach calculated on the harm suffered by the victim State would be the benchmark for evaluating the proportionality of the retaliation.[257] The injury suffered is the degree of gravity of the effects of the wrongful act and seems to refer to the quantifiable damage or, as stated by Hoogh, to 'any economically assessable damage'. Thus, the damage done to the victim State must be compared with the actual or potential damage for the author State.[258]

This quantitative equivalence was confirmed in the *Naulilaa* case where the Arbitral Tribunal held that 'le mal causé par le second des actes doit être proportionné au mal causé par le premier'[259] and in 1978 in the *Air Services Agreement* case where the Tribunal held that: 'it is generally agreed that all countermeasures must, in the first instance, have some degree of equivalence with the alleged breach: this is a well-known rule [...]'[260] and in the *Gabčíkovo-Nagymaros Project* case where 'in the view of the Court, an important consideration is that the effects of a countermeasure must be commensurate with the injury suffered'.[261] According to Sicilianos, this criterion is 'le plus fiable, puisque tangible et donc plus facilement

Beirut Airport in 1968: 'In magnitude it is entirely disproportionate to the act that preceded it. It is disproportionate in two ways: first, on the degree of destruction involved; and secondly, in a more fundamental way, in the difference between the acts of two individual terrorists and those of a sizeable military force operating openly and directly under governmental orders' (SCOR 1460, para. 73). The response was qualified as fully proportional by Israel, in consideration of the risk involved and of the dissuasive aim of the action (in SCOR 1461, para. 121). Cannizzaro, 'The Role of Proportionality' (Ch.3 n.244) 907 footnote 56.

257 Cannizzaro reported as example the dispute which arose in 1941 between the United States and Italy concerning the lawfulness of a measure of confiscation of some Italian merchant ships. Italy affirmed that 'if the vessels were confiscated Italy might confiscate American property of equivalent value'. *Ibid.* footnote 52.

258 Andre De Hoogh, *Obligations Erga Omnes and International Crimes: A Theoretical Inquiry into the Implementation and Enforcement of the International Responsibility of States* (Martinus Nijhoff Publishers 1996) 267.

259 *Responsibility of Germany for damage caused in the Portuguese colonies in the south of Africa*, R.I.A.A. Vol. II, 1928 (*Naulilaa case*), Portugal v. Germany, Special Arbitral Tribunal, p. 1028.

260 The tribunal held that: '[it] thinks that it will not suffice, in the present case, to compare the losses suffered by Pan Am on account of the suspension of the projected services with the losses which the French companies would have suffered as a result of the countermeasures; it will also be necessary to take into account the importance of the positions of principle which were taken when the French authorities prohibited changes of gauge in third countries. If the importance of the issue is viewed within the framework of the general air transport policy adopted by the United States Government and implemented by the conclusion of a large number of international agreements with countries other than France, the measures taken by the United States do not appear to be clearly disproportionate when compared to those taken by France. Neither Party has provided the tribunal with evidence that would be sufficient to affirm or reject the existence of proportionality in these terms and the Tribunal must be satisfied with a very approximative appreciation'. Air Service Agreement of 27 March 1946 (United States v. France), R.I.I.A, vol. XVIII, 1978, 444 para. 83.

261 *Gabčíkovo-Nagymaros Project*, cit., para. 85, 56.

quantifiable'.[262]Article 49 of a previous draft of the DARSIWA which had a negative formulation embodied both of the criteria analysed so far: 'countermeasure shall not be out of proportion to the degree of gravity of the internationally wrongful act and the effects thereof on the injured State'.[263] However, according to some scholars, 'most of the practice collected requires that acts taken in reprisals be proportionate to the original violation. Only a few pieces of practice specify that proportionality must be observed with regard to the damage suffered'.[264]

Two other criteria that shall be taken into account in assessing proportionality under Article 51 of the DARSIWA are: 'the gravity of the wrongful act and the rights in question'. This was also remarked on by the ICJ in the *Gabčíkovo-Nagymaros* case where the Tribunal held that the reaction shall be commensurate to the injury suffered 'taking account of the rights in question'[265] and in the *Air Service* case in which the Arbitrators held that 'in the Tribunal's view, it is essential, in a dispute between States, to take into account not only the injuries suffered by the companies concerned but also the importance of the questions of principle arising from the alleged breach'.[266] Accordingly, Crawford underlines that

> considering the need to ensure that the adoption of countermeasures does not lead to inequitable results, proportionality must be assessed taking into account not only the purely 'quantitative' element of the injured suffered, but also 'qualitative' factors such as the importance of the interest protected by the rule infringed and the seriousness of the breach.

The former, according to Crawford, 'has a broad meaning and includes not only the effect of a wrongful act on the injured State but also on the rights of the responsible State'.[267]

262 Sicilianos and Forlati Picchio (Ch.3 n.16) 75.

263 On the negative formulation of the proportionality, Sicilianos and Forlati Picchio (n. 175) 73–76; Omer Y. Elagab, 'The Place of Non-Forcible Counter-Measures in Contemporary International Law', in Ian Brownlie, Guy Goodwin-Gill, Stefan Talmon and Robert Jennings (eds.), *The Reality of International Law: Essays in Honour of Ian Brownlie* (Oxford University Press 1999) 131.

264 Jean-Marie Henckaerts and Louise Doswald-Beck, *Customary International Humanitarian Law: Rules* (Cambridge University Press 2005) 518.

265 *Gabčíkovo-Nagymaros Project*, 56, para. 85.

266 *Air Service Agreement of 27 March 1946*, 444 para. 83.

267 Crawford, Draft Article (Ch.3 n.11) 296. According to Sicilianos, 'en effet, s'en tenir uniquement au préjudice subi constituerait une approche purement quantitative de la proportionnalité, qui ne refléterait pas les éléments qualitatifs pris en compte par les Etats lorsqu'ils adoptent des contre-mesures. Ajuter la gravité du fait illicite – que l'on trouve également dans l'article 60 de la Convention de Vienne sur le droit des traités- et les "droits en cause" constitue une approche plus modulée qui permettra d'apprécier la proportionnalité des contre-mesures en fonction de l'importance des intérêts juridiques atteints par la violation. On distinguera alors entre l'Etat lésé, atteint dans ses droits subjectifs, et les autres Etats affectés par la violation dont seul sera atteint

The purpose of the measure is another criterion to take into consideration in the assessment of proportionality. Depending on the desired end of the reaction a measure can be considered proportionate or disproportionate. A measure could be seen to have the purpose of restoring the violated right. For example, Ziccardi Capaldo underlines that the principle of proportionality in self-defence means that

> the degree of use of force in self-defence must be commensurate with the end to be achieved – the restoration of the rights violated as the result of an armed attack. This means that force must be 'strictly necessary' in any situation and 'directed' at the removal of the violation and the restoration of the violated rights.[268]

Although not specifically included in the criteria for assessing proportionality under Article 51 of the DARSIWA the proportionality of the countermeasure shall also be commensurate with the aim thereof: *i.e.* to induce the State which is responsible for the internationally wrongful act to comply with its obligations. According to Crawford,

> in some respects proportionality is linked to the requirement of purpose specified in article 49: a clearly disproportionate measure may well be judged not to have been necessary to induce the responsible State to comply with its obligations but to have had a punitive aim and to fall outside the purpose of countermeasures enunciated in article 49.[269]

Thus, when the aim of the response is that of inducing the wrongdoer to reverse the course of its action and abide by its obligation on the basis of its appropriateness and reasonableness to the aim pursued by the reacting State, proportionality would be understood through the relation between the aim and means of the action of self-redress.[270]

For normative countermeasures which, according to Cannizzaro, are aimed at 'reproducing, at a different level, the legal balance altered by the breach' proportionality has to be assessed by 'the capacity of the response to attain a legal

l'intérêt juridique à voir le droit international respecté lui-même'. Sicilianos and Forlati Picchio (Ch.2 n.50) 76.

268 Ziccardi Capaldo, 'Providing a Right of Self-Defence' (Ch.2 n.93) 103.

269 Crawford (Ch.3 n.11) 296. The chairman of the meeting of the International Law Commission experienced some difficulties if the principle of proportionality was construed in terms of balance with the injury suffered or the gravity of the wrongful act. 'As countermeasures were authorized to induce the wrongdoers to comply with their obligations proportionality shall be relevant to that purpose, so proportional to the minimum degree of measures necessary to induce compliance'. 2649th meeting, Tuesday, 1 August 2000, State responsibility, *Yearbook of the International Law Commission*, Vol. I, 2000, para 56.

270 Cannizzaro, 'The Role of Proportionality' (Ch.3 n.244) 891.

equivalence between breach and response'.[271] For some scholars, reprisals are retributive in nature[272] and thus proportionality should be measured by a test of equivalence between the injurious effects, respectively, of the breach and the response. In cases where countermeasures are acts of constraint, the proportionality shall be measured between the injurious consequences of the response and those of the wrongful act. For executive countermeasures which are aimed at directly securing the implementation of the breached obligation, without the co-operation of the wrongdoer, the victim State 'may substitute the wrongdoer in the performance of the breached obligation, or produce by itself, through the breach of a different rule, the beneficial effect expected from its performance'.[273]

In conclusion, different and various criteria exist in order to assess the proportionality of a measure. They cannot be used in an exclusive manner *i.e.* where the use of a criterion shall exclude the use of another, but they are all useful tools to evaluate on a case by case basis whether the reaction of the State has been proportionate. According to Hoogh, an important remark is that

> any element inherent in the wrongful act must of necessity be evaluated in relation to the same element contained in the measures adopted. Thus damage done to the injured State by reason of the wrongful act must in first instance be compared to the damage done to the author State by way of countermeasure(s). Similarly the importance of the rule under which an author State has breached its obligation should be put against the importance of the rule(s) affected by the countermeasure(s). And if one takes into account the seriousness of the wrongful acts, then the seriousness of the countermeasures must also be evaluated. Only when an element is not at the same time inherent in both parts, wrongful act and countermeasure, should one compare unequal elements.[274]

3.4.7.1. Proportionality in the WTO context

Proportionality plays an important role in the field of international economic law. According to Hilf, the principle of proportionality is one of the more basic principles underlying the multilateral trading system and its basic idea, *i.e.* the due balancing of competing rights, is reflected several times in WTO agreements.[275] The term 'proportionality' does not appear explicitly in the WTO covered

271 Cannizzaro also notes that in the case where 'the breached rule presents a bilateral structure: such as when the obligations of one party are counterbalanced by the performance of reciprocal or related obligations by the other party [t]he concept of proportionality tends to overlap with that of reciprocity'. *Ibid.* 900.

272 Giuliani, Scovazzi and Treves (n. 12) 441.

273 Cannizzaro, 'The Role of Proportionality' (Ch.3 n.250) 911.

274 De Hoogh (n. 517) 266.

275 Mehinard Hilf, 'Power, Rules and Principles: Which Orientation for WTO/GATT Law?' (2001) 111.4 *Journal of International Economic Law* 120–121. See also, Axel Desmedt, 'Proportionality in WTO Law' (2001) 4 *Journal of International Economic Law* 441.

agreements though it is implicitly included in the DSU and also in the SCM Agreement, the Anti-dumping Agreement and the Safeguard Agreement.[276] As described above, when a WTO Member fails to bring the measure found to be inconsistent with WTO law by the panel and/or the Appellate Body within WTO law, as a last resort, the complainant may suspend the application of concession or other WTO obligations *vis-à-vis* the other Member.[277] According to Mitchell, in retaliatory actions under the WTO dispute settlement system, similarly to Article 60 of the DARSIWA, proportionality 'has qualitative and quantitative requirements'.[278] As a general principle, the qualitative requirement means the complaining party must first seek to suspend concessions or other obligations with respect to the same sector(s) as that in which the panel or Appellate Body has found a violation or other nullification or impairment.[279] This general principle privileges symmetry in the retaliation and 'spring from the same rationale as lex talionis'.[280] In the case where the complaining party considers that

> it is not practicable or effective to suspend concessions or other obligations with respect to the same sector(s), the mentioned article allows a State to cross-sector retaliate and thus suspend concessions or other obligations in other sectors under the same agreement.[281]

When a party considers that it is not practicable or effective to suspend concessions or other obligations with respect to other sectors under the same agreement, and that the circumstances are serious enough, it may have recourse to cross-agreement retaliation by seeking 'to suspend concessions or other obligations under

276 Bryan Mercurio, 'Why Compensation Cannot Replace Trade Retaliation in the WTO Dispute Settlement Understanding' (2009) 8.2. *World Trade Review* 315–338; Arwel Davies, 'Reviewing Dispute Settlement at The World Trade Organization: A Time to Reconsider the Role/s of Compensation' (2006) 5.1 *World Trade Review* 31; Thomas Sebastian, 'World Trade Organization Remedies and the Assessment of Proportionality: Equivalence and Appropriateness' (2007) 48 *Harvard International Law Journal* 337.

277 On WTO retaliation and cross retaliation see, Steve Charnovitz, 'The WTO Problematic "Last Resort" Against Noncompliance' (2007) 57.4 *Aussenwirtschaft* 407; Thomas Jurgensen, 'Crime and Punishment: Retaliation under the World Trade Organization Dispute Settlement System' (2005) 39 *Journal of World Trade* 327; Holger Spamann, 'The Myth of "Rebalancing" Retaliation in WTO Dispute Settlement Practice' (2006) 9.1 *Journal of International Economic Law* 31; Cherise Valles and Brenan McGivern, 'The Right to Retaliate under the WTO Agreement – The Sequencing Problem' (2000) 34.2 *Journal of World Trade* 63 and Joost Pauwelyn, 'Enforcement and Countermeasures in the WTO: Rules Are Rules: Toward a More Collective Approach'(2000) 94 *American Journal of International Law* 335.

278 Mitchell, 'Proportionality and Remedies in WTO Dispute' (Ch.2 n.60) 994.

279 Article 22.3 (a) of the DSU.

280 Mitchell, 'Proportionality and Remedies in WTO Dispute' (Ch.2 n.60) 994.

281 Article 22.3 (b) of the DSU.

another covered agreement'.[282] This is of foremost importance for developing and least developing Members. As noted by Spadano,

> in order to be effective as a tool to induce compliance, the threat of retaliation of course has to be credible. A serious concern among developing countries is that effective retaliatory measures are not available to countries with little economic power.[283]

This ensures that David may induce Goliath to comply with WTO rules. The other quantitative requirement imposes on Members that 'the level of the suspension of concessions or other obligations authorized by the DSB shall be equivalent to the level of the nullification or impairment'.[284] The term nullification or impairment is imported from Article XXIII of the GATT which sets out that if any Contracting Party should consider that any benefit accruing to it, directly or indirectly, under this Agreement is being nullified or impaired, it may have recourse to the WTO Dispute Settlement Mechanism. In broad terms, in this context proportionality is assessed by reference to the harm suffered by the complaining Member and not by taking into account the gravity of the violation or the rights. However, as remarked by Anderson,

> it needs to be recognized that ensuring equivalence between the damage and the retaliation in terms of the gross value of trade between the respondent and the complainant does not mean that retaliation has the same economic welfare effect on the respondent as the initial damage is having on the complainant.[285]

As remarked by Arbitrators in the *US – Byrd Amendment*, 'it is not completely clear what role is to be played by the suspension of obligations in the DSU'.[286] According to Palmeter and Alexandrov its aim 'is not to induce compliance but to maintain the balance of reciprocal trade concessions negotiated in the WTO Agreements'.[287] Similarly Lawrence stated that: 'while WTO remedies achieve several goals simultaneously, the goal achieved most precisely is maintaining reciprocity'.[288] Charnovitz instead considers that this form of retaliation 'is conceived

282 Article 22.3 (c) of the DSU.

283 Lucas E.F.A. Spadano, 'Cross-Agreement Retaliation in the WTO Dispute Settlement System: An Important Enforcement Mechanism for Developing Countries' (2008) 7.3 *World Trade Review* 512.

284 Article 22.4 of the DSU.

285 Kim Anderson, 'Peculiarities of Retaliation in WTO Dispute Settlement' (2002) 1.2 *World Trade Review* 127.

286 Decision by arbitrators (Article 22.6), *US – Byrd Amendment*, para. 6.4.

287 Palmeter and Alexandrov, 'Inducing Compliance in WTO Dispute Settlement' (Ch.2 n.60) 647.

288 Robert Lawrence, *Crimes and Punishments? Retaliation under the WTO* (Institute for International Economics 2003) 47

primarily as a sanction, while the rebalancing idea retains vestigial influence'.[289] In Mitchell's opinion it is intended to induce compliance even if it cannot be disproportionate to the harm caused even if a greater penalty would be required to induce compliance.[290] Yet, according to Schwartz and Sykes, 'in the parlance of contract theory, the objective is to deter inefficient breaches but to encourage efficient breaches'. The scholars considered that WTO retaliation should put the complaining Member in the position in which it would have been if the 'condemned' Member had complied with WTO law. This means that retaliation should provide the complaining Member with 'expectation damages'.[291]

In the absence of a clear provision stating the purpose of those countermeasures, some arbitrators stated that the aim of suspending concessions suggests that

> this purpose does not mean that the DSB should grant authorization to suspend concessions beyond what is equivalent to the level of nullification or impairment. In our view, there is nothing in Article 22.1 of the DSU, let

289 Steve Charnovitz, 'Rethinking WTO Trade Sanctions' (2001) 95 *American Journal of International Law* 611.

290 According to the scholar, 'in my view, the suspension of concessions is intended to induce compliance. This is consistent with Article 22.8 of the DSU, which states that the suspension of concessions is a temporary measure available only until the inconsistent measure has been removed. It is also consistent with Article 3.2 of the DSU, which indicates that, "[i]n the absence of a mutually agreed solution, the first objective of the dispute settlement mechanism is usually to secure the withdrawal of the [inconsistent] measures". It is true that this purpose is somewhat at odds with the fact that, pursuant to Article 22.4 of the DSU, the DSB cannot authorize suspension of concessions beyond the level of nullification or impairment. However, this reflects a strikingly similar approach to the ILC Articles. In both cases, the purpose of the penalty is said to be to induce compliance, but the penalty itself must not be disproportionate to the harm caused, even if a greater penalty would be required to induce compliance. This contradiction seems no worse under WTO law than under international law, and it seems to flow from the WTO provisions themselves rather than any faulty interpretation in dispute settlement'. Mitchell, 'Proportionality' (n. 185) 998–999.

291 Mitchell argued that: 'Sykes and Schwartz are fully aware of these difficulties and therefore they do not actually argue that the concerned exporters can be compensated as a result of retaliation. Instead, they focus on those who hold political office rather than traders or industry interests. Most importantly, they evaluate injury to these actors in terms of political support rather than financial harm or loss of overall welfare. Sykes and Schwartz argue that the politicians of a given WTO Member are compensated by retaliation because they gain political support from domestic constituents in return for the increased protection that they can deliver to these constituents through retaliation. And the theory of public choice suggests that the metric of welfare for each signatory to a trade agreement will not be money, but instead will be the political welfare (votes, campaign contributions, graft, as the case may be) of its political officials'. Warren Schwartz and Alan O. Sykes, 'The Economic Structure of Renegotiation and Dispute Resolution in the World Trade Organization' (2002) 179.31 *Journal of Legal Studies* 181–83 also quoted in Mitchell, 'Proportionality' (n. 185) 998.

alone in paragraphs 2 and 7 of article 22 that could be read as a justification for countermeasures of a punitive nature.[292]

In the *US – Byrd Amendment* the arbitrators stated that the equivalence requirement 'seems to imply that suspension of concessions or other obligations is only a means of obtaining some form of temporary compensation'.[293] However, in the decision of the arbitrators in the *US-Offset Act*, it was held that inducing compliance is one of several possible purposes.[294]

The purpose of countermeasures taken under the SCM Agreement necessitates a different analysis. In the case of specific remedies contained in the SCM Agreement a distinction in the requirement of proportionality shall be drawn between countermeasures taken on grounds of Article 4 or 7 thereof, dealing respectively with prohibited and actionable subsidies. Where the retaliation is taken on grounds of Article 4 (against prohibited subsidies), countermeasures shall be *appropriate* meaning *not disproportionate.* [295] According to Franck, 'several arbitration panels have given substance to the double-negative term "not disproportionate" thereby casting light on its logical concomitant, the principle of proportionality'.[296] In reference to actionable subsidies, the proportionality requirement is specified in a positive manner. Article 7.9 of the SCM provides that the countermeasures must be commensurate with the degree and nature of the adverse effects caused by the subsidy. This requirement is quite similar to that of Article 22 of the DSU. The differences between manners of referring to the principle of proportionality by the DSU and by Article 4 of the SCM Agreement have been examined by arbitral panels. In the *EC – Banana* case the arbitrators compared the standard of 'appropriateness' of Article 4 of the SCM Agreement with the DSU standard of 'equivalence,' and concluded that 'the ordinary meaning of "equivalent" implies a higher degree of correspondence, identity or stricter balance between the level of the proposed suspension and the level of nullification or impairment'.[297] Thus, the Article 4 of the SCM Agreement proportionality requirement standard is to be interpreted less strictly than the standard set forth by the DSU. The latter standard has been analysed by arbitrators in one of the

292 Decisions by the Arbitrators (Article 22.6), *EC – Bananas, III* (US), para. 6.3. See also, *Brazil – Aircraft*, para. 3.55; *EC – Hormones*, para. 40; *US-1916 Act*, paras. 5.5–5.8; *EC – Bananas (Ecuador)*, para. 76.

293 Decision by the Arbitrators (Article 22.6), *US – Byrd Amendment*, para. 6.3. See also the *US – Gambling* case where arbitrators stated: 'the purpose of suspension of concessions or other obligations under the covered agreements [...] is to "induce compliance"'. Decision by the Arbitrators (Article 22.6), *US – Gambling*, para. 2.7.

294 Decisions by Arbitrators (Article 22.6), *US – Offset Act (Brazil)*, paras. 3.73–3.74 and 6.2–6.4.

295 Art. 4.10 and 4.11 of the SCM Agreement.

296 For example, Decision by the Arbitrator (Article 22.6), *Canada – Aircraft Credits and Guarantees*, paras. 3.9, 3.11 and 3.38.

297 Decision by the Arbitrators (Article 22.6), *EC – Bananas*, para. 7.1, This interpretation has been confirmed and followed also by the Decision by the Arbitrators (Article 22.6), *EC – Hormones*, paras. 20, 36 and 38.

disputes on aircraft between Canada and Brazil.[298] In that circumstance, the arbitrators allowed Canada to adopt countermeasures against Brazil 'to the full value of the latter's subsidies for global sales of Brazilian airplanes, rather than limiting the countermeasures to an amount strictly equivalent to the actual loss sustained by Canada'.[299] Arbitrators considered that the object of the 'appropriateness' standard is not limited to the compensation of the complaining State for losses suffered but is also aimed at inducing the withdrawal of the offending subsidy.[300] Accordingly, a countermeasure may be deemed to be 'appropriate' as long as it is 'not disproportionate,' meaning that proportionality should not be merely assessed in reference to the harm caused by the prohibited subsidy to the complaining State but shall also take into account the inducement effect on the subsidizing country of withdrawing the prohibited subsidy.[301] In sum, by stating that 'a countermeasure is "appropriate" *inter alia* if it *effectively* induces compliance'[302] the arbitrators allowed the possibility for a Member to impose countermeasures at whatever level may be deemed appropriate to induce the withdrawal of the prohibited subsidy,[303] even in the case where they impose a burden higher than that 'equivalent' to the harm suffered and set the proportionality standard at the amount necessary to induce the compliance of the Member with a legal obligation.[304] This reasoning was also confirmed by the arbitrators in the *US – FSC* case, where they suggested that proportionality of the countermeasures should be assessed by

> taking into account the legal status of the wrongful act and the manner in which the breach of that obligation has upset the balance of rights and obligations as between Members. It is from that perspective that the judgement as to whether countermeasures are disproportionate is to be made.[305]

According to the arbitrators, in the SCM Agreement Article 4.10 'appropriate countermeasures' must not be 'limited in its meaning to "equivalence" or correspondence (or some synonym) with the "trade impact" on the complaining Member'.[306]

These limitations on WTO countermeasures are important for a variety of reasons. According to Franck,

> first, they determine the dimensions of any ensuing retaliation and, therefore, are of considerable practical significance for WTO Members in making

298 Decision by the Arbitrators (Article 22.6), *Brazil – Aircraft*.
299 Franck (n. 502) 745.
300 Decision by the Arbitrators (Article 22.6), *Brazil – Aircraft*, paras. 3.44–45
301 *Ibid*. para. 3.54
302 *Ibid*. para. 3.44.
303 *Ibid*. para. 3.45.
304 *Ibid*., para. 3.51.
305 Decision of the Arbitrator (Article 22.6), *US – FSC*, para 5.24.
306 *Ibid*., para. 5.30.

> decisions about whether to comply with their obligations and whether to seek to enforce their rights. Second, these limitations are important because they shed light on broad theoretical questions about the nature of WTO rights and obligations.[307]

Proportionality is also relevant for trade remedies. The WTO system limits the extent of such forms of unilateral reactions. Anti-dumping and countervailing measures cannot exceed, respectively, the margin of dumping and the amount of subsidy. Thus, as remarked by Mitchell, 'the ceiling on the amount of penalty [...] is therefore set by the undesirable act even if the injury caused by that act is higher'.[308] The calculation of dumping margins is relatively easy and made by assessing the difference between export price and the normal value. The calculation of the amount of subsidy is more complicated and usually made by calculating the benefit of the recipient. For example, in the case where the subsidy has the form of a grant at interest rates lower than market rates the amount of the subsidy would be the difference between them; if it is the purchase of goods by the State the amount of subsidy would be the difference between the normal/market price payable for the goods and the price paid by the public authority, etc...

An issue on the respect of the proportionality requirement in antidumping investigations arises where the domestic authority uses the so-called *zeroing* method in assessing margins of dumping.[309] Generally speaking, *zeroing* is a method used during the phase of calculation of dumping margins by which an authority excludes from the calculation of the overall margin of dumping all the single negative margins. The result of this comparison (the margin of dumping) may be positive when the export price is lower than the normal value, or negative when the export price is the same or higher than the normal value. In order to calculate the overall margin of dumping for the product alleged to have been dumped, the domestic authority will sum all the single margins of dumping assessed. However, if the domestic authority will use *zeroing* (in this case called simple zeroing) it will exclude from the calculation all the negative single margins of dumping and thus calculate the overall margin of dumping only on the positive single margins. As a result, the margin of dumping and thus the ceiling of the anti-dumping duty would be higher than would have been the case if *zeroing* had not

307 Sebastian (Ch.3 n.276) 338.
308 Mitchell, 'Proportionality' (Ch.2 n.60) 996.
309 Soprano, 'La rilevanza' 411; Edwin Vermulst, 'The 10 Major Problems With the Anti-Dumping Instrument in the European Community' (2005) 39.1 *Journal of World Trade* 107; Picone and Ligustro (n. 118) 262; Folkert Graafsma, 'Recent WTO Jurisprudence in the Field of Anti-dumping' (2001) 28.3 *Legal Issues of Economic Integration* 338; Edwin Vermulst, 'WTO Dispute Settlement with Respect to Trade Contingency Measures Selected Issues' (2001) 35.2 *Journal of World Trade* 218; Jong B. Kim, 'Fair Price Comparison in the WTO Anti Dumping Agreement – Recent WTO Panel Decision against the "Zeroing Method"' (2002) 36.1 *Journal of World Trade* 52; Aluisio de Lima Campos, 'Nineteen Proposals to Curb Abuse in Antidumping and Countervailing Duty Proceedings' 2005 39.2 *Journal of World Trade* 250.

taken place.[310] By using *zeroing* in antidumping investigations domestic authorities may find a higher margin of dumping or assess a margin of dumping which would even be non-existent in the absence of zeroing. Thus, *zeroing* allows the domestic authority to impose a measure higher than the real margin of dumping or even in the absence of dumping. It is clear that this contrasts *inter alia* with the proportionality requirement of article 9.3.[311]

Accordingly, the principle of general international law could be used to support the amendment of the Anti-dumping Agreement so as to include a new provision which would eliminate the possibility of using *zeroing* during original or review investigations and in relation to any methodology for calculating dumping margins. The prohibition of *zeroing* is supported by a large number of States in the Doha Round though criticized by the United States that kept using it during investigations. The reason, as explained before, is simple: *zeroing* facilitates the finding of the existence of dumping by the domestic authority and thus responds better to the needs of influential lobbies for protection from foreign competitors. The elimination of *zeroing* from the Anti-dumping Agreement would contribute to reducing the possibility of using antidumping for protectionist purposes.

Safeguards are different and do not follow a similar approach to the Anti-dumping Agreement and SCM Agreement *i.e.* by linking the proportionality of the reaction to the undesirable fact, (the increase in imports). Under GATT

310 The Model zeroing is instead applied in connection with the W-W method. The investigating authority identifies the sales of sub-products in the importing country considered 'comparable', and will include such sales in an 'averaging group'. An averaging group consists of merchandise that is identical or virtually identical in all physical characteristics. The weighted-average-to-weighted-average comparison between normal value and export price is made within each averaging group. The amount by which normal value exceeds export price is considered to be the dumping margin. If export price exceeds normal value (the margin is negative), the dumping margin for that averaging group is considered to be zero. The margin of dumping for the overall product is calculated by combining the averaging group results. The total of the dumped amounts (excluding the negative amounts or treating them as zero) is expressed as a percentage of the total export prices (including all averaging groups). See also Appellate Body Report *US – Washing Machines*, 6.9 for the prohibition of the zeroing in the W-T methodology.

311 The use of zeroing (simple and model) has been condemned several times by the DSU. See the reports of the Panel and the Appellate Body in *EC – Bed Linen; US – Stainless Steel Plate in Coils and Stainless Steel Sheet and Streep from Korea; EC – Antidumping Duties on Malleable Cast Iron Pipe Tube or Pipe Fittings from Brazil; US – Softwood Lumber; US – Softwood Lumber (art. 21.5); US – 'Zeroing'; US – Measures Relating to Zeroing and Sunset Reviews; US – Anti-Dumping Measure on Shrimp from Ecuador; US – Measures Relating to Shrimps from Thailand; US – Final Anti-Dumping Measures On Stainless Steel from Mexico; US – Washing Machines*. The FAN group in the Doha Round submitted a document requesting the amendment of the Anti-dumping Agreement so as to prohibit the use of zeroing during the calculation of dumping margins TN/RL/W/113 and TN/RL/W/26, TN/RL/W/66, WT/RL/W/83. On the relation between zeroing and proportionality see also, Andrew Mitchell, *Legal Principles in WTO Disputes* (Cambridge University Press 2008) 231.

Article XIX:1 (b) the contracting party suffering serious injury is free to adopt measures to the extent and for such a time as may be necessary to prevent or remedy such injury. According to Article 5 of the Safeguard Agreement a Member can impose safeguard measures only to the extent, and for such time, as may be necessary to prevent or remedy serious injury and to facilitate adjustments. Thus, the measures can go beyond the simple remedy of serious injury so as to include the facilitation of adjustments.[312] Cottier and other scholars noted that the locution 'to the extent necessary' covers both the elements of suitability and the least-trade restrictiveness. In their opinion

> the measure has to be necessary "to prevent or remedy", in other words, to correct or preclude serious injury to the importing country that produces like or competing products. The test, subject to more detailed provision on quantitative restrictions, is comparable to criteria applicable under Article XX GATT, and which relate to the principle of proportionality in similar ways.[313]

The difference between proportionality requirements between trade remedies is mainly due to their different purposes. Safeguard measures are directed to prevent or remedy injury and facilitate adjustments while anti-dumping and countervailing measures are directed to offset and prevent dumping and the subsidy bestowed respectively.[314] Accordingly, each agreement links the proportionality of the reaction to the purpose to be achieved by the measure.

However, for the sake of coherence, the purpose of all trade remedies should be the elimination of injury. As explained in the second chapter of this book, the main element which justifies the imposition of trade remedies is the injury caused by the specific act. The elimination of injury is the real justification for trade remedies. If the imposition of the measure by the injured State eliminates injury, there is no need to halt the subsidy, the dumping or the increased imports. In the absence of injury, dumping, increased imports and subsidies are not counter actionable and furthermore welcomed. Trade remedies are not reactions against a wrong but against the injury suffered regardless of the lawfulness of the act. Thus, the real objective of such measures is to remedy the injury suffered. The aim is not the protection of a market but the elimination of the harm. In the case where the measure would reach higher than the harm, the use of such measures would go beyond their real intent. Having the elimination of the injury as the objective,

312 Mitchell criticized the Appellate Body for the 'improper' use of the principle of proportionality and the term countermeasures in relation to safeguard. He believes that the invocation of the proportionality principle in the context of ATC safeguard was unnecessary and inappropriate. Due to the absence of culpability, also the use of the term 'countermeasures' and the link with art. 51 of the DRAFHVD were meaningless. Mitchell, 'Proportionality' (Ch.2 n.60) 1004–1008.

313 Thomas Cottier, Roberto Echandi, Rafael Leal-Arcas, Rachel Liechti, Tetyana Payosova and Charlotte Sieber-Gasser, 'The Principle of Proportionality in International Law', NCTR Working Paper No 2012/38 (December 2012), 19.

314 Article VI:2 and VI:3 of the GATT and footnote 36 of the SCM Agreement.

measures would better reproduce the legal and economic rationale of trade remedies. Accordingly, the proportionality of the reaction should be commensurate with the injury suffered and not any other benchmark.[315]

Trade remedies cannot have punitive intents nor induce the wrongdoer into compliance.[316] It makes no sense to pursue the objective of inducing somebody into compliance when this is not bound by any rules. None of the trade remedies rules prohibits the granting of actionable subsidies, practising dumping or increasing exports. Thus, a measure which is directed to eliminate such practices is meaningless. In reference to punitive intent, there is no reason to punish somebody who did not contravene any obligations. Trade remedies are neither executive measures nor directed to enforce international law.[317] They are directed at eliminating the injury suffered by the domestic industry of the importing State. Accordingly, trade remedies should be proportioned to the injury suffered and not to the undesirable fact (dumping or subsidy). As suggested by many, the introduction of a lesser duty rule would produce even better results. By assessing the measures using as a benchmark the lowest between the margin of dumping/subsidy and the margin of injury, the agreements would reduce the risk of applying very high barriers to imports. The introduction of a WTO mandatory lesser duty rule, not only on imports from developing countries, would contribute to the purpose of lowering the risk of trade remedies being used for protectionist purposes.

315 In that respect, it is interesting to note that the purpose of the multilateral remedy of Article 7.8 is to remove the adverse effect (or to withdraw the subsidy).

316 In the *US – Cotton Yarn* case, the Appellate Body excluded punitive damages by WTO and stated that 'Our view is supported further by the rules of general international law on state responsibility, which require that countermeasures in response to breaches by states of their international obligations be commensurate with the injury suffered. In the same vein, we note that Article 22.4 of the DSU stipulates that the suspension of concessions shall be equivalent to the level of nullification or impairment. This provision of the DSU has been interpreted consistently as not justifying punitive damages. These two examples illustrate the consequences of breaches by states of their international obligations, whereas a safeguard action is merely a remedy to WTO-consistent "fair trade" activity. It would be absurd if the breach of an international obligation were sanctioned by proportionate countermeasures, while, in the absence of such breach, a WTO Member would be subject to a disproportionate and, hence, "punitive", attribution of serious damage not wholly caused by its exports. In our view, such an exorbitant derogation from the principle of proportionality in respect of the attribution of serious damage could be justified only if the drafters of the ATC had expressly provided for it, which is not the case'. Appellate Body Report, *US – Cotton Yarn*, para. 120.

317 Countervailing measures against prohibited subsidies may be seen as to be executive measures.

Final remarks

The main purpose of GATT and WTO rules is to avoid the use of protectionist measures and ensure markets remain open. This is premised mainly on economic theories under which the lower the number of trade barriers used, the greater the growth in trade flows which spread potential economic and social effects across the world. Accordingly, the preamble of the WTO Agreement lists amongst its objectives raising standards of living and ensuring full employment, and a large and steadily growing volume of real income and effective demand and expanding the production of, and trade, in goods and services.

As for the last two objectives described above, for about 60 years tariffs have fallen and there has been international trade growth of around 5 per cent per year since 1947, which has made some countries 'richer'. However, the extent to which these rules contribute to ameliorating the living conditions of world inhabitants depends on the point of view through which reality is filtered. It could be argued that free trade and globalization helped countries to grow, helped get millions of people out of poverty and improved living standards for mankind when compared with 50 years ago. It could also be argued that cooperation and dispute settlement mechanisms have contributed to maintaining peaceful relationships amongst countries. On the other hand, it is difficult to deny that billions of people live under the poverty line or are undernourished,[1] that the benefits of trade are unevenly distributed between developed and developing countries and that growth of trade has not been accompanied by a growth in social, human and environmental standards.[2]

The WTO is part of the design to liberalize world trade. It is a first step towards better regulation of international trade and trade related concerns, aimed at lifting millions of people out of poverty in a sustainable manner. Although the basic principles of these rules were written just after World War II they have never been entirely adopted in practice. States are too reluctant to completely abandon custom and external trade policy instruments which may be of vital importance for their industries. Trade barriers impede the spreading of the benefits of free trade.

1 FAO, The State of Food and Agriculture, Doc. C 2009/2, 18 November 2009.
2 UN General Assembly, UN Millennium Declaration, resolution adopted on 8 September 2004.

The history of the WTO is of foremost importance to understanding States' behaviour in regulating international trade. From a 'wild west' situation where only bi/plurilateral treaties disciplined international trade, we currently have a body of rules which goes from non-discrimination in trade in goods and services to technical and sanitary measures through intellectual properties and towards investments and competition. Round after round, States agreed new rules which limited their sovereignty in the use of trade instruments other than tariffs. The policy space of States has gradually been restricted by limits imposed by WTO rules. This is part of a strategy aimed at removing obstacles to the liberalization of trade which are mainly found in the hidden actions taken by States to protect their industries. Trade remedies are amongst them. The increase in their use went hand in hand with the enactment of specific rules which limited the use of custom duties which were the main instruments used by States to regulate imports into their territories. Since the entry into force of the basic Articles VI and XIX of the GATT, the WTO is now endowed with more detailed rules on anti-dumping, anti-subsidy and safeguard measures.

Practice and theories around these instruments suggest that they need to be amended in order to avoid their possible trade distortive use. In line with this, WTO Members met and (at the time of writing) are still meeting in Geneva to find an agreement on new trade rules. In Doha, representatives of 154 Members started a Round which has been called the 'Development Round'. Thus, at least in theory, the negotiating round should be aimed at promoting the economic development and alleviation of poverty for the major parts of developing countries which are WTO Members. Hot topics are the regulation of agriculture and market access for services. These issues basically pitch developed countries against developing countries. The latter criticize the former for not being willing to leave services companies to access their market and the former criticize the latter for the protection and support that farmers and food industries receive. This is evidence of the different comparative advantages between developed and developing countries. While developed countries have modern technologies and have invested in particular in the service sectors, developing countries produce mainly agricultural goods. However, this is also evidence that some economic theories do not work so well in practice. Developed countries should allow agricultural goods to penetrate their markets and developing countries should allow American and British companies to supply services in their territories. This is not exactly what happens in practice and agriculture, which contributes about 2 per cent to the GDP of the 30 OECD countries, receives more than $280 billion annually.[3] On the other hand, developing countries are reluctant to reduce their limitation to access to services because they are afraid that their domestic firms will not be competitive.

3 OECD, The Doha Development Round of trade negotiations: understanding the issues, available at: http://www.oecd.org/tad/agricultural-trade/thedohadevelopmentroundoftradenegotiationsunderstandingtheissues.htm (last accessed 03 January 2018).

What the Doha Round has put into evidence is the strength and power of developing countries. The Doha Round is underlining the fact that current rules were written in a period where Europe and the US were the only powerful actors in the world trade scenario and so reflect the interests of developed countries. The difficulties in reaching the final Doha agreement underline a fundamental difference with previous trade rounds. Fast-growing developing countries such as Brazil, South Africa, China[4] and India or Russia[5] have become new key players in the world trading system. General or tailor-made groups among developing countries have also demonstrated their capacities and abilities to form alliances to achieve common purposes. This demonstrates that it is no longer possible for developed countries to reach an agreement and then impose it on other WTO Members.

In trade remedies negotiations, the general intent is to clarify existing provisions and indirectly reduce the possibility of using them as protectionist measures. Technical amendments being proposed are aimed at eliminating their possible distortive use. In relation to anti-dumping agreement, this is of foremost importance not only for developing countries but also for developed countries. Historical trends have shown that measures have mainly been adopted by developed countries and on imports from developing countries. They used anti-dumping to protect sensitive industries (chemicals, textile and steel in particular) from low cost foreign competition. However, recent trends confirm that developing countries have adopted many more anti-dumping measures on products including those coming from developed countries. Turkey, India, Argentina, Brazil, Colombia, Ukraine, China, Chile, Indonesia and South Africa have increased their measures in recent years. This raised the interest of developed States as the space left by WTO rules to use and abuse trade remedies could be used by developed as well as developing countries. Furthermore, the application of measures by developed countries on other developed countries' exports (in particular for the use of zeroing by the United States on imports from EC and Japan) generated friction among members.

Outsourcing has also played an important role in negotiations. Many industries which decided to outsource their production, in particular to China, are now involved in investigations and subject to duties. Furthermore, outsourced firms are always large or medium size enterprises with huge influential power over politicians. This is the case, for example, of the protest of outsourced European bulb producers in China on whose products an anti-dumping duty has been levied; European producers of footwear in China, etc... Taking into account the interests of national outsourced enterprises became a source of concern for developed countries' negotiators.

4 Paolo Farah, 'Five Years of China WTO Membership: EU and US Perspectives About China's Compliance With Transparency Commitments and the Transitional Review Mechanism' (2006) 33.3 *Legal Issues of Economic Integration* 263.

5 Kim Van der Borght, 'Accession of the Russian Federation to the World Trade Organization: A New Player Joins the Trade Game' (2015) 40.3 *Review of Central and East European Law* 321.

By examining subsidy negotiations, it is clear that the concern is not purely economic but also directed at sustainability, including discussions about biofuels and fishery issues. This does not only involve amending existing rules but deciding whether or not the WTO approach to sustainable development shall be improved. The WTO is not an agency for development, neither a UN agency to support developing countries, but it is often called upon to deal with non-trade concerns and has a huge impact on developmental, environmental and more in general, sustainability policies. The Doha Round is questioning how the WTO can play a positive role on these issues without overstepping (or by enlarging) the bounds of its trade-related mandate. In the regulation of biofuels and fisheries the new rules should include the preservation of the environment and sustainable development. Economic interests behind these issues, and the relevance of the impact on the WTO itself, contribute to slow negotiations.

In addition, the financial crisis has challenged Doha negotiations and showed the real willingness of negotiators to make real progress toward free trade. International trade has been a victim of the crisis which has engulfed the world. We have seen the collapses of banks, the slump of stock prices and there has been an unprecedented decline in economic activity. As in all periods of crisis, States are willing to adopt protectionist measures though they proclaim not to do so. Since the end of 2008, many States have engaged in behaviours different to the speeches of their politicians. In November 2008, G20 leaders declared that they would refrain from raising new barriers to investment or to trade in goods and services, imposing new export restrictions, or implementing WTO inconsistent measures to stimulate exports. While heads of States and governments and ministers of economy were promising that they would not resort to protectionism we have seen the adoption of different measures which hide protectionism. 'Buy National' acts and proclamations, export restrictions, additional pre-shipment inspections, customs clearance, including stricter customs valuation procedures, surges in the imposition of trade remedies worldwide, the large and uncontrolled use of export credit instruments, reduction of transparency in domestic procurement, a deep and particular interest in environmental trade related measures such as carbon taxes which, though they deserve high consideration and need solid evaluation, seem to hide protectionist intents.

These are the new forms by which protectionism takes place. No longer duties and bans on imports but indirect instruments which support domestic producers. In periods of crisis sirens of protectionism sing louder and it is difficult for politicians not to listen to proclamatory sing-songs of entrepreneurs about possible falls in employment and production. At the same time, trade would be an important tool for lifting the world out of this crisis. States are aware that protectionist measures would hurt the economy and hamper the recovery and that protectionist measures could be followed by retaliatory actions. Current protectionism also involves trade remedies as they still represent useful instruments in periods of crisis. Reforming trade remedies in such a way that their use shall be limited to specific circumstances of reaction of injured States would contribute to keeping the market open, also in periods of crisis.

The limits on the use of trade remedies and their amendments should be seen in the light of their broader legal context. As international players have got closer, unilateral actions and in particular unilateral reactions have been replaced by multilateral efforts and dispute settlement mechanisms. Unilateral measures could alter the equilibrium of modern society and spread domino effects worldwide. The creation of peaceful and judicial means of dispute settlement in international law, and in particular the WTO DSU in the trade field, reflects the progress in the international legal system to contribute to reducing unilateral reactions and forms of self-help. However, some forms of unilateralism still exist. These exceptions to the general approach are strictly limited and regulated by international law.

Self-help includes different measures such as self-defence, countermeasures and retorsion which, though they have different characteristics, share a common matrix. What links all the forms of self-help in international law is the fact that they are unilateral reactions of States to preserve their rights and interests. This book analysed whether trade remedies could be considered as particular forms of self-help in international law. This study considered trade remedies to be a unique group although there are many differences between them. Trade remedies could be deemed to address different problems and to have different goals. However, they share a similar structure: *i.e.* all trade remedies address a specific action that causes injury to the domestic industry of the importing State and which gives the right to the importing country to adopt trade restrictive measures. This is due to the fact they are aimed at counteracting a practice which is injurious to domestic industries.

In this study, trade remedies have been defined as *particular* forms of self-help which allow WTO Members to react against specific injurious practices regardless of the quality of the author (public or private firms) and the lawfulness of the action. They constitute an attempt to redress an injurious act by a Members State's own action rather than through WTO multilateral (quasi) judicial process. They are not (or at least should not be) aimed at allowing the complaining domestic industry to improve its economic situation and market position but to restore fair and normal competition in the market. Neither punitive nor protectionist intent should be found in trade remedies.

The fact that trade remedies could be considered as particular measures of self-help underlines the fact that international law changes in order to offer new responses to the new challenges of international society. It could be argued that using traditional concepts to understand modern and particular aspects of WTO law could be meaningless. WTO law could be considered as *sui generis* law and not to fit in among the measures of self-help. International economic law is modifying international law in such a particular way that it is not possible to interpret it by using instruments and theories which are developed in different contexts and situations. However, classical international law furnishes the key to interpreting trade remedies. The concept of self-help is evolving and its evolution includes such reactions which differ from classic forms of self-help. International law evolves and, as in many other fields of law, its evolution reflects change in society and political and philosophical theories. From Westphalian Peace to the

XXI century, through World and Cold wars, the decolonization process and globalization, historical events have had a strong impact on the international community and its rules. At the same time positivism, realism and neorealism, naturalism and other schools of thought have had leading roles in the development of international law. According to Cassese, every legal system is subject to constant change because the law shall continuously adapt to new realities.[6]

This raises an important question on the effects of the modern system over the old one. Does the new system prevail and delete the old one? The answer is negative. The modern and old systems are strictly interlinked and do not preclude each other. The modern system, more than prevailing over the old, completes and fulfils the shortcomings of the old and improves and adapts it to the needs and challenges of the modern international community. As underlined by Director-General Lamy, the WTO is both a product and a vehicle of this evolution. The WTO does not only comply with general international law but adapts it to the realities of international trade.[7]

This book underlined how the reciprocal influence that WTO and public international law have on each other may contribute to their development. Trade remedies offer an opportunity to analyse the fragmentation of international law and understand its evolution and progress. WTO law is definitely a new experience for international law. Although bilateral or plurilateral treaties on trade have existed for centuries, such a detailed and articulated group of multilateral norms are quite modern and evolves more quickly than other aspects of international law. International economic law which also includes WTO law is developing fast, led by progress in international trade and the growing of the international economy. In order to face the challenges of the new reality the international community has enacted and built rules and institutions. In doing so international economic law followed the imprinting influence provided by international law. Leaving aside the doctrinal debate on whether the WTO should be considered as a *self-contained* regime, the relations between international law and WTO law are very strict and the latter reflects the former in the manner in which it copes with new issues. According to classical theories, international law is the system of norms which regulate relations between States which were the only subjects of international law.

Although many authors recognize that international law is still primarily geared towards the international community of States,[8] other authors recognize that new actors such as international organizations, NGOs, private firms and individuals have been recognized as subjects of international law or as having a significant role in international relations. Thus, international law is no longer confined to the regulation of inter-State relations but is called upon to cope with many other issues which involve relations with or between non-State actors.

6 Antonio Cassese, *Il diritto internazionale nel mondo contemporaneo* (Il Mulino 1984) 39.

7 Lamy (Ch.1 n.100) 970–973.

8 Malanczuck (Ch.1 n.76) 3.

This evolution of society and the growing importance of private individuals and firms in international relations push the community to adopt new instruments and rules. Traditional international law could be considered as an ineffective instrument to cope with new challenges. Thus, as international society has become more and more complex and international law covers varieties of transnational concerns, its development has increased specializations in its particular sectors in order to find specific solutions.[9] In these sub-groups of norms, the specific law reflects international law. The creation of international rules on anti-dumping, antisubsidy and safeguards are examples of the limiting and disciplining of unilateral reactions of States by international law. Trade remedies should not be considered as *sui generis* rules out of the concept of self-help. This study on their normative structure of 'reaction of injured states' lead to the conclusion that they could be included among the measures of self-help.

The analysis conducted has also offered a different point of view from which to reflect upon the possible amendments of several aspects of trade remedies with the aim of eliminating their possible protectionist use and enacting new rules which better reflect their role of reactions of injured States. The research and definition of the legal nature of trade remedies is of utmost importance for the amendment of current agreements. By defining trade remedies as particular forms of self-help, it is possible to analyse current WTO agreements from a different perspective. The comparison with other measures of self-help underlines that particular aspects of the current Anti-dumping Agreement, SCM Agreement and Safeguard Agreement (*e.g.* the possibility to adopt measures on the basis of the mere threat of injury, the rules on the calculation of the amount of the measure, the practice of zeroing, the scope of reviews, the duty to consult, etc.) could provide WTO Members with instruments that look more like protectionist measures than reactions for the injury suffered. Reforming trade remedies in such a way as to reduce the possibility of creating unnecessary or disproportionate barriers to trade is important in order to guarantee the effective functioning of free trade.

In conclusion, if we consider trade remedies as reactions of injured States, the relative agreements shall be amended in such a way which would impede or at least restrict their potential use as protectionist measures and thus preserve the benefit of trade liberalization.

9 According to Schachter, it is no longer possible for a 'generalist' to cope with the volume and complexity of the various branches of international law. Increasingly, the professional international lawyer, whether practitioner or scholar, is a specialist in a particular branch of the law and each branch develops its own complicated and often arcane doctrine. Schachter (Ch.2 n.53) 1.

Bibliography

A.

Roberto Ago, 'Le delit international' (1939) 68 *Recueil des Cours de l'Académie de Droit International de La Haye*

Stanimir Alexandrov, *Self-Defense Against the Use of Force in International Law* (Kluwer Law International 1966)

Chittharanjan Amerasinghe, 'Issues of Compensation for the Taking of Alien Property in the Light of Recent Cases and Practice' (1992) 41. 1 *International and Comparative Law Quarterly* 22

Kim Anderson, 'Peculiarities of Retaliation in WTO Dispute Settlement' (2002) 1. 2 *World Trade Review* 127

Dionisio Anzilotti, *Corso di diritto internazionale III* (Athenaeum 1928) 155

Gaetano Arangio Ruiz, *Gli enti soggetti dell'ordinamento internazionale* (Giuffrè 1951)

Gaetano Arangio-Ruiz, *Second Report on State Responsibility*, Doc. A/CN.4/425 of 9 June 1989

Clive Archer, *International Organizations* (Routledge 2001)

Marc Auboin, 'Fulfilling the Marrakesh Mandate on Coherence: Ten Years of Cooperation between the WTO, IMF and World Bank', Discussion paper 13

Hans Aufricht, *The International Monetary Fund: Legal Bases, Structure, Functions* (Stevens and Sons 1964)

Anthony Aust, *Handbook of International Law* (Cambridge University Press 2005)

B.

Godfrey Bahiigwa, *Environmental Impacts of Trade Liberalization and Policies for the Sustainable Management of Natural Resources: A Case Study of India's Automobile Sector* (Earthprint 1999)

Paul Bairoch, *Economics and World History: Myths and Paradoxes* (University of Chicago Press 1993)

John Barcelo, 'The Status of WTO Rules in U.S. Law', Cornell Law School Research Paper No. 06–004, 2006

Lorand Bartels, 'The Separation of Powers in the WTO: How to Avoid Judicial Activism', (2004) 53. 4 *International and Comparative Law Quarterly* 861

Jens Bartelson, *A Genealogy of Sovereignty* (Cambridge University Press, 1995)

David Bederman, 'Counterintuiting Countermeasures' (2002) 96 *American Journal of International Law* 817

Mohammed Bedjaoui, *International Law: Achievements and Prospects* (Martinus Nijhoff Publishers 1991)

Lionel Beehner, 'Israel and the Doctrine of Proportionality', Council on Foreign Relations, 13 July 2006

Christine Bell, 'Peace Agreements: Their Nature and Legal Status' (2006) 100 *American Journal of International Law* 384

Marc Benitah, *The Law of Subsidies under the GATT/WTO System* (Kluwer Law International 2001)

Judson Osterhoudt Berkey, 'The European Court of Justice and Direct Effect for the GATT: A Question Worth Revisiting' (2000) 9. 4 *European Journal of International Law* 626

Americo Beviglia Zampetti, 'The Uruguay Round Agreement on Subsidies. A Forward-Looking Assessment' (1995) 29. 6 *Journal of World Trade* 5

Jadeshi Bhagwati, *Protectionism* (MIT Press 1988)

Jagdish N. Bhagwati, *In Defense of Globalization* (Oxford University Press 2007)

Raj Bhala, 'Assessing the Modern Era of International Trade' (1998) 21. 4 *Fordham International Law Journal* 1647

Jagdeep Bhandari and Alan O. Sykes, *Economic Dimension in International Law Comparative and Empirical Perspectives* (Cambridge University Press 1996)

Dominique Blanchard, 'Les effets des rapports de l'organe de règlement des différends de l'OMC – A la lumière du règlement (CE) 1515/2001 du Conseil de l'Union européenne' (2003) 464 *Revue du Marché Commun et de l'Union Européenne* 42

Mara Blue Jeffords, 'Turning the Protestor into a Partner for Development: The Need for Effective Consultation between the WTO and NGOs' (2003) 28 *Brooklyn Journal of International Law* 937

Gabriella Blum, 'Bilateralism, Multilateralism, and the Architecture of International Law' (2008) 49. 2 *Harvard International Law Journal* 356

Laurence Boisson de Chazournes, *Les contre-mesures en droit international économique* (Pedone 1992)

Ralf Boscheck, 'The Governance of Global Market Relations: The Case of Substituting Antitrust for Antidumping' (2001) 24. 1 *World Competition* 41

Nerina Boschiero, 'Stato e sovranità nel diritto internazionale', in Bruno Montanari (ed.), *L'Europa e la cultura del postmoderno* (Luiss edizioni 2001)

James Boughton and Sarwar Lateef, *Fifty Years After Bretton Woods: The Future of the IMF and the World Bank* (International Monetary Fund and World Bank 1994).

Jacque H.J. Bourgeois, 'The GATT Rules for Industrial Subsidies and Countervailing Duties and the New GATT Round- The Weather and the Seeds', in Ernst-Ulrich Petersmann and Mehinard Hilf (eds.), *The New GATT Round of Multilateral Trade Negotiations – Legal and Economic Problems* (Kluwer Law 1991)

Dereck W. Bowett, 'Reprisals Involving Recourse to Armed Force' (1972) 66. 1 *American Journal of International Law* 3

Dereck W. Bowett, *Self Defence in International Law* (Manchester University Press 1958)

Derek W. Bowett, *The Law of International Institutions* (Sweet and Maxwell 1982)

Jeremy Brecher and Tim Costello, *Contro il capitale globale: strategie di resistenza* (Feltrinelli 2002)

Andrew Brown and Robert Stern, 'Issues of Fairness in International Trade Agreements', discussion paper No. 554 (18 September 2016)

Gordon Brown, *The Change We Choose: Speeches 2007–2009* (Random House 2011)

Ian Brownlie, *Principles of Public International Law* (Oxford University Press, 6th ed., 2003)

Ian Brownlie, *The Rule of Law in International Affairs: International Law at the Fiftieth Anniversary of the United Nations* (Martinus Nijhoff Publishers 1998)

Gary Burtless, *Globaphobia: Confronting Fears about Open Trade* (Brookings Institution Press 1998)

C.

Philippe Cahier, *Le problème de la responsabilité pour risque en droit international, Les Relations internationals dans un monde en mutation* (Sijthoff 1977)

Eric Canal Forgues, *L'institution de la conciliation dans le cadre du GATT: Contribution à l'étude de la structuration d'un mecanisme de règlement des differends* (Bruylant 1993)

Enzo Cannizzaro, 'The Role of Proportionality in the Law of International Countermeasures' (2001) 12. 5 *European Journal of International Law* 916

Enzo Cannizzaro, *Il principio della proporzionalità nell'ordinamento internazionale* (Giuffrè 2000)

Antonio Cassese, *International Law in a Divided World* (Clarendon Press 1986)

Antonio Cassese, *Il diritto internazionale nel mondo contemporaneo* (Il Mulino 1984)

Antonio Cassese, *International Law* (Oxford University Press 2001)

Sabino Cassese, *Oltre lo Stato* (Editori Laterza 2006)

Leon Castellanos-Jankiewicz, 'Causation and International State Responsibility' (2012) ACIL Research Paper No 2012–2007

Franz Cede, 'Historical Introduction' in Franz Cede and Lilly Sucharipa-Behrmann (eds.), *The United Nations: Law and Practice* (Martinus Nijhoff Publishers 2001) 4

Bradnee Chambers, 'International Trade Law and the Kyoto Protocol: Potential Incompatibilities', in Bradnee Chambers (ed.), *Inter-linkages: The Kyoto Protocol and the International Trade and Investment Regimes* (United Nations University Press 2001) 87

Steve Charnovitz, 'The WTO Problematic 'Last Resort' Against Noncompliance' (2007) 57. 4 *Aussenwirtschaft* 407

Steve Charnovitz, 'Rethinking WTO Trade Sanctions' (2001) 95 *American Journal of International Law* 611

Steve Charnovitz, 'Should the Teeth be Pulled? An Analysis of WTO Sanctions', in Daniel Kennedy and James Southwick (eds.), *The Political Economy of International Trade Law: Essays in Honor of Robert E. Hudec* (Cambridge University Press 2002)

Steve Charnovitz, 'Judicial Independence in the World Trade Organization', in Laurence Boisson de Chazournes, Cesare Romano and Ruth Mackenzie (eds.), *International Organizations and International Dispute Settlement: Trends and Prospects* (Transnational Publishers 2002)

Sungjoon Cho, 'A Quest for WTO's Legitimacy' (2005) 4 *World Trade Review* 391

Nupur Chowdhury, 'The (Absence of) Direct Effect of WTO Law – Current Developments within the Indian Legal System', in Claudio Dordi (ed.), *The Absence of Direct Effect of WTO in the EC and in Other Countries* (Giappichelli 2010)

William Clayton, *GATT: An Analysis and Appraisal of the General Agreement on Tariffs and Trade* (US Council of the International Chamber of Commerce 1995) 36

Ronald Coase, *The Firm, the Market and the Law* (The University of Chicago Press 1960 reprinted in 1988)

Clause A. Colliard, *Institutions des relations internationales* (Dalloz 1985)

John Collier and Vaughan Lowe, *The Settlement of Disputes in International Law* (Oxford University Press 1999)

Benedetto Conforti, *The Law and Practice of the United Nations* (Martinus Nijhoff Publishers 2005)

Benedetto Conforti, *Diritto Internazionale* (Editoriale Scientifica 2002)

Benedetto Conforti, *International Law and the Role of Domestic Legal Systems* (Martinus Nijhoff Publishers 1993)

Richard N. Cooper, 'Trade Policy as Foreign Policy', in Robert M. Stern (ed.), *US Trade Policy in a Changing World Economy* (MIT Press 1987)

Thomas Cottier, 'A Theory of Direct Effect in Global Law', in Armin Von Bogdandy, Petros Mavroidis and Yves Mény (eds.), *European Integration and International Coordination, Studies in Transnational Economic Law in Honour of Claus-Dieter Ehlermann* (Kluwer Law International 2002)

Thomas Cottier and Krista Nadakavukaren Schefer, 'The Relationship between World Trade Organization Law, National and Regional Law' (1998) 1. 1 *Journal of International Economic Law* 83

Thomas Cottier and Matthias Oesch, 'WTO Law, Precedents and Legal Change' (2001) 3. 1 *Turku Law Journal* 27

Thomas Cottier and Matthias Oesch, *International Trade Regulation Law and Policy in the WTO, the European Union and Switzerland: Cases Materials and Comments* (Stämpfli Publishers 2005)

Thomas Cottier, Roberto Echandi, Rafael Leal-Arcas, Rachel Liechti, Tetyana Payosova and Charlotte Sieber-Gasser, 'The Principle of Proportionality in International Law', NCTR Working Paper No 2012/38 (December 2012)

James Crawford, *The International Law Commission's Articles on State Responsibility: Introduction, Text, and Commentaries* (Cambridge University Press 2002)

James Crawford, 'The Relationship between Sanctions and Countermeasures', in Vera Gowlland-Debbas (ed.), *United Nations Sanctions and International Law* (Kluwer Law International 2001)

Judith Czako, Johann Human and Jorge Miranda, *A Handbook on Anti-Dumping Investigations* (Cambridge University Press 2003)

D.

Kenneth Dam, *The GATT: Law and International Economic Organization* (University of Chicago Press 1970)

William J. Davey, 'Dispute Settlement in GATT' (1987) 51. 11 *Fordham International Law Journal*

Arwel Davies, 'Reviewing Dispute Settlement at The World Trade Organization: A Time to Reconsider the Role/s of Compensation' (2006) 5. 1 *World Trade Review* 31

Ibek Debroy and Debashis Chakraborty (eds.), *Anti-Dumping: Global Abuse of a Trade Policy Instrument* (Academic Foundation 2007)

Andre De Hoogh, *Obligations Erga Omnes and International Crimes: A Theoretical Inquiry into the Implementation and Enforcement of the International Responsibility of States* (Martinus Nijhoff Publishers 1996)

Bertrand De Jouvenel, *De la souveraineté* (Génior 1955)

Nejdet Delener, *Strategic Planning and Multinational Trading Blocs* (Greenwood Publishing Group 1999)

Aluisio de Lima Campos, 'Nineteen Proposals to Curb Abuse in Antidumping and Countervailing Duty Proceedings' (2005) 39. 2 *Journal of World Trade* 250

Axel Desmedt, 'Proportionality in WTO Law' (2001) 4 *Journal of International Economic Law* 441
Yoram Dinstein, *War, Aggression and Self-Defence* (Cambridge University Press 2001) 159
Yoram Dinstein, 'International Law as a Primitive Legal System' (1986) 19. 1 *New York University Journal of International Law and Policy* 12
Pierre-Marie Dupuy, 'Le fait générateur de la responsabilité internationale des états' (1984) 188 *Recueil des Cours de l'Académie de Droit International de La Haye*
Pierre-Marie Dupuy, 'Responsabilité internationale des Etats' (1984) 187 *Recueil des Cours de l'Académie de Droit International de La Haye*
Pierre-Marie Dupuy, 'The Place and Role of Unilateralism in Contemporary International Law' (2000) 11. 1 *European Journal of International Law* 19
Rene-Jean Dupuy, 'Communauté internationale et disparités de développement' (1979) 165 *Recueil des Cours de l'Académie de Droit International de La Haye*
Rene-Jean Dupuy, *Le développement du rôle du conseil de sécurité* (Martinus Nijhoff Publishers 1993)

E.

Clyde Eagleton, 'Measure of Damages in International Law' (1929) 39. 1 *The Yale Law Journal* 39, 52
Piet Eeckhout, *External Relations of the European Union: Legal and Constitutional Foundations* (Oxford European Community Law Library 2004) 330
Claus D. Ehlermann, 'Six Years on the Bench of the World Trade Court' (2002) 36. 4 *Journal of World Trade* 655
Clarck Eichelberger, *Organizing for Peace: A Personal History of the Founding of the United Nations* (Harper & Row 1977)
Omer Y. Elagab, 'The Place of Non-Forcible Counter-Measures in Contemporary International Law', in Ian Brownlie, Guy Goodwin-Gill, Stefan Talmon and Robert Jennings, (eds.), *The Reality of International Law: Essays in Honour of Ian Brownlie* (Oxford University Press 1999)
Taslim O. Elias, *New Horizons in International Law* (Martinus Nijhoff Publishers 1979)
Frederic E. Emery, 'Economic Conflicts in Relation to War', in Victor H. Wallace (ed.), *Paths to Peace: A Study of War, Its Causes and Prevention* (Ayer Publishing 1957)

F.

Paolo D. Farah, 'Five Years of China WTO Membership: EU and US Perspectives About China's Compliance with Transparency Commitments and the Transitional Review Mechanism' (2006) 33. 3 *Legal Issues of Economic Integration* 263
David Fidler, Richard Pregent and Alex Vandurme, 'NATO, Cyber Defense, and International Law' (2013). Articles by Maurer Faculty. Paper 1672
Andreas Fischer-Lescano and Gunther Teubner, 'Regime-Collisions: The Vain Search for Legal Unity in the Fragmentation of Global Law' (2004) 25. 4 *Michigan Journal of International Law* 999
Mary E. Footer, *An Institutional and Normative Analysis of the World Trade Organization* (Martinus Nijhoff Publishers 2006)
Francesco Francioni, *Environment, Human Rights and International Trade* (Hart Publishing 2001)
Philippe Franceskakis (ed.), *L'entreprise multinational face au droit* (Litec 1977)

Thomas M. Franck, 'On Proportionality of Countermeasures in International Law' (2008) 102 *American Journal of International Law* 763.

Wolfgang Friedmann, *The Changing Structure of International Law* (Columbia University Press 1964)

Rosemary Foot, S. Neil MacFarlane and Michael Mastanduno, *US Hegemony and International Organizations: The United states and Multilateral Institutions* (Oxford University Press 2003)

G.

Francisco V. García Amador, Louis B. Sohn and Richard R. Baxter, *Recent Codification of the Law of State Responsibility for Injuries to Aliens* (Oceana Publications 1974) 91

Richard N. Gardner, 'Balance Sheet of Success and Failure', in Orin Kirshner (ed.), *The Bretton Woods – GATT System, Retrospect and Prospect after Fifty Years* (Sharpe Armonk 1994)

Mario Giuliano, Tullio Scovazzi and Tullio Treves, *Diritto internazionale, parte generale*, (Giuffré 2005)

Mohamed Gomaa, *Suspension or Termination of Treaties on Grounds of Breach* (Martinus Nijhoff Publishers 1996)

Leland M. Goodrich, 'From League of Nations to United Nations' (1947) 1. 1 *International Organizations* 3

Folkert Graafsma, 'Recent WTO Jurisprudence in the Field of Anti-dumping' (2001) 28. 3 *Legal Issues of Economic Integration* 338

Lorenzo Gradoni, *Regime failure nel diritto internazionale* (Cedam 2009)

Bernard Graefrath, 'Responsibility and Damage' (1984) 187 *Recueil des Cours de l'Académie de Droit International de La Haye*

Rodney Grey, *The Development of the Canadian Antidumping System* (Private Planning Association of Canada 1973)

H.

Marc Hansen and Edwin Vermulst, 'The GATT Protocol of Provisional Application: A Dying Grandfather' (1989) 4. 5 *Columbia Journal of Transnational Law* 263

David J. Harris, *Cases and Materials on International Law* (Sweet & Maxwell, 6th edn, 2004) 862

David Held, Anthony McGrew, David Goldblatt and Jonathan Perrathon, *Global Transformations* (Polity Press 1999)

Jean-Marie Henckaerts and Louise Doswald-Beck, *Customary International Humanitarian Law: Rules* (Cambridge University Press 2005) 518

Mehinard Hilf, 'Power, Rules and Principles – Which Orientation for WTO/GATT Law?' (2001) 111. 4 *Journal of International Economic Law*

Albert E. Hindmarsh, 'Self-Help in Time of Peace' (1932) 26. 2 *American Journal of International Law* 321

Judith Hippler Bello, 'The WTO Dispute Settlement Understanding: Less is More' (1996) 90. 3 *American Journal of International Law* 416

Anthony Honoré, 'Causational and Remoteness of Damage', in Andre Tunc (ed.), *International Encyclopedia of Comparative Law* (Mohr 1983)

Gary Horlick and Eric Shea, 'The WTO Antidumping Agreement' (1995) 29. 1 *Journal of World Trade*

Gary Horlick and Pa Clarke, 'The 1994 WTO Subsidies Agreement' (1994) 17. 4 *World Competition* 41

Keith Horsefield, *The International Monetary Fund 1945–1965: Twenty Years of Monetary Cooperation* (International Monetary Fund 1969)

Charles Howard-Ellis, *The Origin Structure & Working of the League of Nations* (The Lawbook Exchange 2003)

Robert E. Hudec, *Essays on the Nature of International Trade Law* (Cameron May 1999) 207

Gary C. Hufbauer and Jeffrey Schott, *North American Free Trade: Issues and Recommendations* (Peterson Institute 1992)

I.

Akira Iriye, *Global Community: The Role of International Organizations in the Making of the Contemporary World* (University of California Press 2002)

J.

John H. Jackson, *The Jurisprudence of GATT & the WTO: Insights on Treaty Law and Economic Relations* (Cambridge University Press 2000)

John H. Jackson, 'Direct Effect of Treaties in the US and the EU, the Case of the WTO: Some Perceptions and Proposals', in Anthony Arnull, Piet Eeckhout and Takis Tridimas (eds.), *Continuity and Change in EU Law: Essays in Honour of Sir Francis Jacobs* (Oxford University Press 2008)

John H. Jackson, 'Perception about the WTO Trade Institution' (2002) 1. 1 *World Trade Review* 103

John H. Jackson, *Sovereignty, the WTO and Changing Fundamentals of International Law* (Cambridge University Press 2006)

John H. Jackson, *Restructuring the GATT System* (Taylor & Francis 1990)

John H. Jackson, *The World Trading System: Law and Policy of International Economic Relations* (MIT Press 1997)

John H. Jackson, *World Trade and the Law of GATT* (Bobbs-Merrill 1969)

John H. Jackson, 'Reflections on Problems of International Economic Relations', in Michael Young and Yuji Iwasawa (eds.), *Trilateral Perspectives on International Legal Issues* (Transnational Publishers 1996)

John H. Jackson, William J. Davey and Allan O. Sykes, *Legal Problems of International Economic Relations: Cases, Materials and Text* (West Group 2002).

John H. Jackson, *The World Trade Organization. Constitution and Jurisprudence* (Royal Institute of International Affairs 1998)

John H. Jackson, 'Global Economics and International Economic Law' (1998) 1. 1 *Journal of International Economic Law* 1

Mark Janis, 'Individuals as Subject of International Law' (1984) 61. 17 *Cornell International Law Journal* 61

Wilfrid Jenks, 'Coordination in International Organization: An Introductory Survey' (1951) 28 *British Yearbook of International Law* 29

Wilfred Jenks, 'Conflict of Law-Making Treaties' (1953) 30 *British Yearbook of International Law* 401

Joseph M. Jones, *Tariff Retaliation: Repercussion of the Hawley-Smoot Bill* (University of Pennsylvania Press 1934)

Robert S. Jordan, *International Organizations: A Comparative Approach to the Management of Cooperation* (Greenwood Publishing Group 2001)

Christopher C. Joyner, *International Law in the 21st Century: Rules for Global Governance* (Rowman & Littlefield 2005)

Thomas Jurgensen, 'Crime and Punishment: Retaliation under the World Trade Organization Dispute Settlement System' (2005) 39 *Journal of World Trade* 327

K.

Hans Kelsen, 'Compulsory Adjudication of International Disputes' (1943) 37 *American Journal of International Law*

Hans Kelsen, *General Theory of Law and State* (Harvard University Press 1945)

Hans Kelsen, *Principles of International Law* (Holt, Rinehart and Winston 1966)

William Kerr and Laura Loppacher, 'Anti-dumping in the Doha Negotiations: Fairy Tales at the World Trade Organization' (2004) 38. 2 *Journal of World Trade* 211

John M. Keynes, *The Economic Consequences of the Peace* (MacMillan 1919 reprinted 1971)

Azhar M. Khansari, 'Searching for the Perfect Solution: International Dispute Resolution and the New World Trade Organization' (1996) 20 *Hastings International Law & Comparative Law Review* 183

Jong B. Kim, 'Fair Price Comparison in the WTO Anti Dumping Agreement – Recent WTO Panel Decisions against the "Zeroing" Method' (2002) 36. 1 *Journal of World Trade*

Charles Kindleberger, 'Commercial Policy Between the Wars', in Peter Mathias and Sydney Pollard (eds.), *The Industrial Economies: The Development of Economic and Social Policies: The Cambridge Economic History of Europe* (Cambridge University Press, Vol. III, 1989)

Frederic Kirgis, 'Some Proportionality Issues Raised by Israel's Use of Armed Force in Lebanon' (2006) *ASIL insight* 10.

Jan Klabbers, *An Introduction to International Institutional Law* (Cambridge University Press 2002)

Marek S. Korowicz, 'Some Present Aspects of Sovereignty in International Law' (1961) 102 *Recueil des Cours de l'Académie de Droit International de La Haye*

Marti Koskenniemi, *Study on the Function and Scope of the Lex Specialis Rule and the Question of 'Self-Contained Regimes'*, UN Doc. ILC(LVI)/SG/FIL/CRD.1/Add.1 (2004), para 134

Edward Krauland, 'The Challenge of Enhancing Global Security Through Multilateral Legal Architecture', in Marco J. Bronckers and Reinhard Quick (eds.), *New Directions in International Economic Law: Essays in Honour of John H. Jackson* (Kluwer Law International 2000)

Anne O. Krueger, 'An Enduring Need: The Importance of Multilateralism in the 21st Century' (IMF Singapore, September 19, 2006)

Anne O. Krueger and Chonira Aturupane, *The WTO as an International Organization* (University of Chicago Press 2000)

L.

Manfred Lachs, 'Legal Framework of an International Community' (1992) 6. 2 *Emory International Law Review* 329

Manfred Lachs, 'Views from the Bench: Thoughts on Science, Technology and World Law' (1992) 86 *American Journal of International Law* 673

Michael Laidhold, 'Private Party Access To the WTO: Do Recent Developments in International Trade Dispute Resolution Really Give Private Organizations a Voice in the WTO?' (1999) 12. 2 *Transnational Lawyer* 427

Pierluigi Lamberti Zanardi, *La legittima disfesa nel diritto internazionale* (Giuffrè 1972)

Pascal Lamy, 'The Place of the WTO and its Law in the International Legal Order' (2006) 17. 5 *European Journal of International Law* 969

Hersch Lauterpacht, *The Development of International Law by International Courts* (Stevens 1958)

Robert Lawrence, *Crimes and Punishments? Retaliation under the WTO* (Institute for International Economics 2003)

Yaji Lee, 'Destabilization of the Discipline on Safeguards? Inherent Problems with the Continuing Application of Article XIX after the Settlement of the Agreement on Safeguards' (2001) 35. 6 *Journal of World Trade* 1245

Yong-Shik Lee, *Reclaiming Development in the World Trading System* (Cambridge University Press 2006)

David W. Leebron, 'Linkages' (2002) 96 *American Journal of International Law* 5

Eric K. Leonard, *The Onset of Global Governance: International Relations Theory and the International Criminal Court* (Ashgate Publishing 2005)

Werner Levi, *Contemporary International Law: A Concise Introduction* (Westview Press 1979)

Aldo Ligustro, *Le controversie tra Stati nel diritto del commercio internazionale, dal GATT all'OMC* (Cedam 1996)

Anja Lindros and Michael Mehling, 'Dispelling the Chimera of 'Self-Contained Regimes' International Law and WTO' (2005) 16.5 *European Journal of International Law* 877

Andreas F. Lowenfeld, 'Remedies with Rights: Institutional Reform in the New GATT' (1994) *American Journal of International Law* 477

Andreas Lowenfeld, *International Economic Law* (Oxford University Press 2003) 249

Evan Luard, *A History of the United Nations* (Macmillan 1989)

Gustavo Luengo Hernandez de Madrid, *Regulation of Subsidies and State Aids in WTO and EC Law* (Kluwer Law International 2006)

M.

Francis Macmillan, *WTO and the Environment* (Sweet & Maxwell 2001)

Salah M. Mahmud, 'Mondialisation et souveraineté de l' Etat' (1996) 123. 3 *Journal de Droit International* 611

Peter Malanczuk, *Akehurst's Modern Introduction to International Law* (Routledge, 7th edition, 1997)

Irmgard Marboe, *Calculation of Compensation and Damages in International Investment Law* (Oxford University Press 2017)

Gabrielle Marceau, 'Conflicts of Norms and Conflicts of Jurisdictions: The Relationship between the WTO Agreement and MEAs and Other Treaties' (2001) 35 *Journal of World Trade* 1081

Gabrielle Marceau (ed.), *A History of Law and Lawyers in the GATT/WTO: The Development of the Rule of Law in the Multilateral Trading System* (Cambridge University Press 2015)

Gabrielle Marceau, *Anti-Dumping and Anti-Trust Issues in Free-Trade Areas* (Oxford University Press 1994)

Edward S. Mason and Robert Asher, *The World Bank Since Bretton Woods* (Brookings Institution Press 1973)

Greg Mastel, *Antidumping Laws and the U.S. Economy* (Sharpe 1998)
Mitsuo Matsushita, Thomas Schoembaum and Petros C. Mavroidis, *The World Trade Organization: Law, Practice, and Policy* (Oxford University Press 2006)
Petros Mavroidis, 'Remedies in the WTO Legal System: Between a Rock and a Hard Place' (2000) 11 *European Journal of International Law* 763
Petros Mavroidis, *The General Agreement on Tariffs and Trade. A Commentary* (Oxford University Press 2005)
Scott Mcbride, 'Dispute Settlement in the WTO: Backbone of the Global Trading System or Delegation of Awesome Power?' (2000) 32 *Law & Policy International Business* 643
Nathalie McNelis, 'What Obligations Are Created by World Trade Organization Dispute Settlement Reports?' (2003) 37. 3 *Journal of World Trade* 652
Donald McRae, 'The Contribution of International Trade Law to the Development of International Law' (1996) 260 *Recueil des Cours de l'Académie de Droit International de La Haye*
Donald McRae, 'The WTO in International Law: Tradition Continued or New Frontier?' (2000) 3. 1 *Journal of International Economic Law* 30
Edward McWinney, 'The Concept of Co-Operation', in Mohammed Bedjaoui (ed.), *International Law: Achievements and Prospects* (Martinus Nijhoff Publishers 1991)
Gerald M. Meier, 'The Bretton Woods Agreement – 25 Years After' (1971) 39. 2 *Stanford Law Review* 235
Stanley Meisler, *United Nations: The First Fifty Years* (Atlantic Monthly Press 1997)
Bryan Mercurio, 'Why Compensation Cannot Replace Trade Retaliation in the WTO Dispute Settlement Understanding' (2009) 8. 2 *World Trade Review* 315–338
Charles E. Merriam, *History of the Theory of Sovereignty since Rousseau* (Columbia University Press 1900)
John G. Merrills, *International Dispute Settlement* (Cambridge University Press 1998)
Patrick A. Messerlin 'Should Antidumping Rules be Replaced by National or International Competition Rules?', in Heinz Hauser and Ernst-Ulrich Petersmann (eds.), *International Competition Rules in the GATT-WTO System* (1994) 49(2–3) *Aussenwirtschaft* 351–374
Patrick A. Messerlin and Hilda Fridh, 'The Agreement on Safeguards: Proposals for Change in the Light of the EC Steel Safeguards' (2006) 40. 4 *Journal of World Trade* 713
Michelle Miller-Adams, *The World Bank: New Agendas in a Changing World* (Routledge 1999)
Bob Milward, *Globalisation? Internationalisation and Monopoly Capitalism. Historical Processes and Capitalist Dynamism* (Edward Elgar Publishing 2003)
Raleigh G. Minor, *A Republic of Nations: A Study of the Organization of a Federal League of Nations* (Oxford University Press 1918)
Andrew D. Mitchell, 'Proportionality and Remedies in WTO Disputes' (2007) 17. 5 *European Journal of International Law* 998
Andrew Mitchell, *Legal Principles in WTO Disputes* (Cambridge University Press 2008)
Bruce E. Moon, *Dilemmas of International Trade* (Westview Press 2000)
Riccardo Monaco, *Scritti di diritto delle organizzazioni internazionali* (Giuffrè 1981)
Gaetano Morelli, *Soluzione pacifica delle controversie internazionali, Ciclo di Lezioni* (Jovene 1991)
Gaetano Morelli, *Nozioni di diritto internazionale* (CEDAM 1976)
Felix Morley, *The Society of Nations – Its Organization and Constitutional Development* (The Brookings Institution 1932)

Herman Mosler, 'International Legal Community', *Encyclopaedia of Public International Law, Vol. II* (1995) 1251

N.

Pietro S. Nivola, *Regulating Unfair Trade* (Brookings Institution Press 1993)

Math Noortmann, *Enforcing International Law: From Self-help to Self-contained Regimes* (Ashgate Publishing 2005)

Emmanuel Nyahoho, Cédrick Lefebvre and Claire Malbouires, 'Les mesures antidumping: un phenomene commercial largement répandu' (2007) 38. 3 *Etudes Internationales* 361

O.

John O'Brien, *International Law* (Routledge 2001) 371

Lassa Oppenheim, *International Law A Treatise, Vol. II* (Longmans 1960) 134–144

Lassa Oppenheim and Ronald Roxburgh, *International Law: A Treatise, Volume 1* (The Lawbook Exchange, Ltd., 1920) 42

Federico Ortino and Ernst-Ulrich Petersmann, *The WTO Dispute Settlement System, 1995–2003* (Kluwer Law International 2004)

P.

Federica I. Paddeu, 'Self-Defence as a Circumstance Precluding Wrongfulness: Understanding Article 21 of the Articles on State Responsibility' (2015) 85. 1 *British Yearbook of International Law* 90

David Palmeter and Stanimir Alexandrov, 'Inducing Compliance in WTO Dispute Settlement', in Daniel Kennedy and James Southwick (eds.), *The Political Economy of International Trade Law: Essays in Honor of Robert E. Hudec* (Cambridge University Press 2002) 646–647.

David Palmeter and Petros Mavroidis, *Dispute Settlement in the World Trade Organization: Practice and Procedure* (Cambridge University Press 2004)

David Palmeter, *The WTO as a Legal System: Essays on International Trade Law and Policy* (Cameron May 2003)

Joost Pauwelyn, 'Enforcement and Countermeasures in the WTO: Rules Are Rules: Toward a More Collective Approach' (2000) 94 *American Journal of International Law* 335

Joost Pauwelyn, 'The Role of Public International Law in WTO Law: How Far We Can Go?' (2001) 25. 3 *American Journal of International Law* 535

Joost Pauwelyn, *Conflict of Norms in Public International Law: How WTO Law Relates to Other Rules of International Law* (Cambridge University Press 2003)

Emile-Robert Perrin, *Les grand problème internationaux* (Masson 1995)

Ernst-Ulrich Petersmann, *The GATT/WTO Dispute Settlement System: International Law, International Organizations, and Dispute Settlement* (Martinus Nijhoff Publishers 1997)

Ernst-Ulrich Petersmann, 'Dispute Settlement in International Economic Law – Lessons for Strengthening International Dispute Settlement in Non-Economic Areas' (1999) 2. 2 *Journal of International Economic Law* 189

Ernst-Ulrich Petersmann, 'From the Hobbesian International Law of Coexistence to Modern Integration Law: The WTO Dispute Settlement System' (1998) 1. 2 *Journal of International Economic Law* 179

Paolo Picone and Aldo Ligustro, *Diritto dell'Organizzazione Mondiale del Commercio* (Cedam 2004)

Frederick Pollock, *The League of Nations* (Stevens and Sons 1929 reprinted 2003)

Javier F. Pons, 'Self Help and the World Trade Organization', in Paolo Mengozzi (ed.), *International Trade Law on the 50th Anniversary of the Multilateral Trade System* (Giuffrè 1999)

Pitman B. Potter, *Introduction to the Study of International Organization* (The Century 1922)

Arnold Pronto and Michael Wood, *The International Law Commission 1999–2009: Treaties, Final Draft Articles, and Other Materials* (Oxford University Press 1999)

Q.

Rolando Quadri, *Diritto internazionale pubblico* (Liguori 1968)

R.

Willem Rappard, 'Vues rétrospectives sur la Societé des Nations' (1947) 71 *Recueil des Cours de l'Académie de Droit International de La Haye*

Michael Rauscher, *International Trade, Factor Movements, and the Environment* (Oxford University Press 1997)

Bob Reinalda and Bertjan Verbeek, *Autonomous Policy Making by International Organizations* (Routledge 1998)

Michael Reisman and Andrea Armstrong, 'The Past and Future of the Claim of Preemptive Self-Defense' (2006) 100 *American Journal of International Law* 526

Paul Reuter, *Institutions Internationales* (Presses Universitaires de France 1969)

David Richardson and Edward M. Graham, *Global Competition Policy* (Peterson Institute 1997) 224

Richard Rivers and John Greenvald, 'The Negotiation of a Code on Subsidies and Countervailing Measures: Bridging Fundamental Policy Differences' (1979) 11 *Law & Policy International Business* 1447

Pablo Martin Rodriguez, 'Safeguards in the World Trade Organization Ten Years After: A Dissociated State of the Law?' (2007) 41. 1 *Journal of World Trade* 189

Dani Rodrik, *Has Globalization Gone Too Far?* (Peterson Institute 1997)

James N. Rosenau, 'Toward an Ontology for Global Governance', in Martin Hewson and Timothy J. Sinclair (eds.), *Approaches to Global Governance Theory* (Suny Press 1999)

Shabtai Rosenne, *The Perplexities of Modern International Law* (Martinus Nijhoff Publishers 2004)

Jed Rubenfeld, 'Unilateralism and Constitutionalism' (2004) 79. 6 *New York University Law Review* 1971

John Gerard Ruggie, 'Multilateralism the Anatomy of an Institution' (1992) 46. 3 *International Organizations* 561

Ruth B. Russel and Jeannette E. Muther, *A History of the United Nations Charter: The Role of the United States, 1940–1945* (Brookings Institution 1958)

S.

Giorgio Sacerdoti, 'WTO Law and the "Fragmentation" of International Law: Specificity, Integration, Conflicts', in Merit E. Janow, Victoria Donaldson and Alan Yanovich (eds.), *The WTO: Governance, Dispute Settlement & Developing Countries* (Juris Publishing 2008)

Giorgio Sacerdoti, 'The Role of Lawyers in the WTO Dispute Settlement System', in Rufus Yerxa and Bruce Wilson (eds.), *Key Issues in WTO Dispute Settlement. The First Ten Years* (Cambridge University Press 2005)

Giorgio Sacerdoti, Alan Yanovich and Jan Bohanes (eds.), *The WTO at Ten: The Contribution of the Dispute Settlement System* (Cambridge University Press 2006)

Harald Sander and Andras Inotai, *World Trade after the Uruguay Round: Prospects and Policy Options for the Twenty-first Century* (Routledge 1996)

Philippe Sands, 'Unilateralism, Values and International Law' (2000) 11. 1 *European Journal of International Law* 291

Seema Sapra, 'The WTO System of Trade Governance: The Stale NGO Debate and the Appropriate Role for Non-state Actors' (2009) 11 *Oregon Review of International Law* 71

Oscar Schachter, *International Law in Theory and Practice* (Martinus Nijhoff Publishers 1991)

Henry Schermers, 'Different Aspects of Sovereignty', in Gerald Kreijen et al. (eds.), *State, Sovereignty, and International Governance* (Oxford University Press 2001)

Warren Schwartz and Alan O. Sykes, 'The Economic Structure of Renegotiation and Dispute Resolution in the World Trade Organization' (2002) 179. 31 *Journal of Legal Studies* 181–183

Georg Schwarzenberger, 'The Principles and Standards of International Economic Law' (1996) 117 *Recueil des Cours de l'Académie de Droit International de La Haye*

Georg Schwarzenberger, 'The Fundamental Principles of International Law' (1955) 87 *Recueil des Cours de l'Académie de Droit International de La Haye*

Thomas Sebastian, 'World Trade Organization Remedies and the Assessment of Proportionality: Equivalence and Appropriateness' (2007) 48 *Harvard International Law Journal* 337

Angelo Piero Sereni, *Diritto internazionale* (Giuffrè, vol. III, 1962)

Gregory C. Shaffer, 'The Role of the WTO Director-General and Secretariat' (2005) 4. 3 *World Trade Review* 438

Malcom N. Shaw, *International Law* (Cambridge University Press 2003)

Linos A. Sicilianos and Laura Forlati Picchio (eds.), *Les sanctions économiques en droit international* (Martinus Nijhoff Publishers 2002)

Bruno Simma, 'Self Contained Regimes' (1985) *XVI Netherlands Yearbook International Law* 111

Bruno Simma and Dirk Pulkowski, 'Of Planets and the Universe: Self-contained Regimes in International Law' 17 *European Journal of International Law* 483

Adinda Sinnaeve, 'The "Community Interest Test" in Anti-dumping Investigations: Time for Reform?' (2007) 4. 2 *Global Trade and Customs Journal* 157

Roberto Soprano, 'The Threat of Material Injury in Antidumping Investigations: A Threat to Free Trade' (2010) 11. 1 *Journal of World Investment and Trade* 67

Roberto Soprano, 'Doha Reform of WTO Export Credit Provisions in the SCM Agreement: The Perspective of Developing Countries' (2010) 44. 3 *Journal of World Trade* 611

Roberto Soprano, *L'Accordo Antidumping nel Diritto dell'Organizzazione Mondiale del Commercio* (Giuffrè 2013)

Roberto Soprano, 'WTO and the Financial Crisis: What Lessons Should We Learn?' (2011) 12. 1 *Journal of World Investment and Trade*

Roberto Soprano, Commentary of the 'China – Countervailing and Anti-Dumping Duties on Grain Oriented Flat-Rolled Electrical Steel from the United States' (2013) *Italian Yearbook of International Law*

Roberto Soprano, 'La rilevanza dei precedenti giurisprudenziali OMC come possibile rimedio al problema dello "zeroing"' (2008) 22. 2 *Diritto del Commercio Internazionale* 43

Roberto Soprano, 'Towards a New Bretton Woods? The Financial Crisis, the Doha Round and the Future of the WTO', in Maria Chiara Malaguti, Biagio Bossone and Susanna Cafaro (eds.), *Legitimacy and Effectiveness in Global Economic Governance* (Cambridge Scholar Publishing 2013)

Lucas E.F.A. Spadano, 'Cross-Agreement Retaliation in the WTO Dispute Settlement System: An Important Enforcement Mechanism for Developing Countries' (2008) 7. 3 *World Trade Review* 512

Holger Spamann, 'The Myth of 'Rebalancing' Retaliation in WTO Dispute Settlement Practice' (2006) 9. 1 *Journal of International Economic Law* 31

Clive Stanbrook and Philip Bentley, *Dumping and Subsidies – The Law and Procedures Governing the Imposition of Anti-dumping and Countervailing Duties in the European Community* (Kluwer Law International 1996)

Terence P. Stewart, *The GATT Uruguay Round: A Negotiating History (1986–1992), Vol. 1* (Kluwer Law 1993)

Karl Strupp, 'Le regies generates du droit de la paix' (1934) 47 *Recueil des Cours de l'Académie de Droit International de La Haye*

Peter D. Sutherland, 'Beyond the Market a Different Kind of Equity', *International Herald Tribune* (20 February 1997)

Hjörtur Sverrison, *Countermeasures, the International Legal System, and Environmental Violations* (Cambria Press 2008)

Arthur Sweetser, 'The Framework of Peace', in Harriet Eager Davis (ed.), *Pioneers in World Order: An American Appraisal of the League of Nations* (Ayer Publishing 1970)

Alan O. Sykes, 'The Safeguards Mess: A Critique of WTO Jurisprudence' (2003) John M. Olin Program in Law and Economics Working Paper No. 187

Alan O. Sykes, 'The Fundamental Deficiencies of the Agreement on Safeguards: A Reply to Professor Lee' (2006) 40 *Journal of World Trade* 979, 984

T.

William H. Taft, *Taft Papers on League of Nations* (Ohio University Press 2004)

Attila Tanzi, 'Is Damage a Distinct Condition for the Existence of an Internationally Wrongful ACT?', in Maria Spinedi and Bruno Simma (eds.), *United Nations Codifications of State Responsibility* (Oceana 1987)

Joel Trachtman, 'Bananas, Direct Effect and Compliance' (1999) 10. 4 *European Journal of International Law* 655

Michael J. Trebilcock and Robert Howse, *The Regulation of International Trade* (Routledge 3rd edition 2005)

Tullio Treves, *Le controversie internazionali – Nuove tendenze, nuovi tribunali* (Giuffrè 1999)

Tullio Treves, 'Piracy, Law of the Sea, and Use of Force: Developments off the Coast of Somalia' (2009) 20. 2 *European Journal of International Law* 399

Ennio Triggiani, *Gli aiuti statali alle imprese nel diritto internazionale e comunitario* (Cacucci 1989)

Nicholas Tsagourias, 'Cyber attacks, Self-defence and the Problem of Attribution' (2012) 17. 2 *Journal of Conflict and Security Law* 229

Ioan Tudorache, 'Multilateralism and the Maintenance of International Peace and Security' (2003) 9. 2 *Romanian Journal of International Affairs* 89

V.

Cherise Valles and Brenan McGivern, 'The Right to Retaliate under the WTO Agreement – The Sequencing Problem' (2000) 34. 2 *Journal of World Trade* 63

Ivo Van Bael and Jean-Francois Bellis, *Anti-Dumping and other Trade Protection Laws of the EC* (Kluwer Law International 2004)

Peter Van den Bossche, *The Law and Policy of the World Trade Organization: Text, Cases and Materials* (Cambridge University Press 2005)

Peter Van den Bossche, 'NGOs Involvement in the WTO: A Comparative Perspective' (2008) 11. 4 *Journal of International Economic Law* 717

Peter Van den Bossche and Iveta Alexovičová, 'Effective Global Economic Governance by the World Trade Organization' (2005) 8. 3 *Journal of International Economic Law* 667

Kim Van der Borght, 'The Review of the WTO Understanding on Dispute Settlement: Some Reflections on the Current Debate' (1999)14. 4 *American University International Law Review* 1223

Kim Van der Borght, 'Accession of the Russian Federation to the World Trade Organization: A New Player Joins the Trade Game' (2015) 40. 3 *Review of Central and East European Law* 321

Pitou Van Dijck and Gerrit Faber, *Challenges to the New World Trade Organization* (Kluwer Law International 1996)

Eelco N. Van Kleffens, 'Sovereignty in International Law' (1953) 82 *Recueil des Cours de l'Académie de Droit International de La Haye*

Edwin Vermulst, 'The 10 Major Problems With the Anti-Dumping Instrument in the European Community' (2005) 39. 1 *Journal of World Trade* 107

Edwin Vermulst, 'WTO Dispute Settlement with Respect to Trade Contingency Measures Selected Issues' (2001) 35. 2 *Journal of World Trade* 218

Francisco Orrego Vicuña, *International Dispute Settlement in an Evolving Global Society – Constitutionalization, Accessibility, Privatization* (Cambridge University Press 2004)

Jacob Viner, *A Memorandum on Dumping* (League of Nations 1926)

Tania Voon, 'Eliminating Trade Remedies from the WTO: Lessons from Regional Trade Agreements' (2010) *Georgetown Law Faculty Publications* 226

W.

Nii L. Wallace-Bruce, *The Settlement of International Disputes: The Contribution of Australia and New Zealand* (Martinus Nijhoff Publishers 1998)

Guiguo Wang, *International Investment Law: A Chinese Perspective* (Routledge 2014)

Paul Ward, *Sovereignty: A Study of a Contemporary Political Notion* (George Routledge and Sons 1928)

Malcolm Waters, *Globalization* (Routledge 2001)

Prosper Weil, 'Le droit international en quête de son identité' (1992) 237 *Recueil des Cours de l'Académie de Droit International de La Haye*

Nigel D. White and Ademola Abass, 'Countermeasures and Sanctions', in Malcolm Evans (ed.), *International Law* (Oxford University Press 2003)

Elizabeth Wilmshurst, 'Principles of International Law on the Use of Force by States in Self-Defence', Working Paper (1 October 2005). Reprinted in 'The Chatham House Principles of International Law on the Use of Force in Self-Defence' (2006) 55. 4 *The International and Comparative Law Quarterly* 963

Rüdiger Wolfrum, 'International Law of Cooperation', *Encyclopedia of Public International Law, Vol. II* (1995) 1242

Rüdiger Wolfrum, 'Fighting Terrorism at Sea: Options and Limitations under International Law', in Myron H. Nordquist, Rüdiger Wolfrum and Ronán Long (eds.), *Legal Challenges in Maritime Security* (Brill 2008) 21

Quincy Wright, *The Role of International Law in the Elimination of War* (Manchester University Press 1961)

Xiaochen Wu, *Antidumping Law and Practice of China* (Wolters Kluwer 2009)

Y.

Linda M. Young and John Wainio, 'The Anti-dumping Negotiations: Proposals, Positions and Anti-dumping Profiles' (2005) 6. 1 *The Estey Centre Journal of International Law and Trade Policy* 30

Z.

Maurizio Zanardi, 'Antidumping: A Problem in International Trade' (2005) 22. 3 *European Journal of Political Economy* 591

Maurizio Zanardi, 'Anti-dumping: What are the Numbers to Discuss at Doha?' (2004) 27. 3 *The World Economy* 403

Giuliana Ziccardi Capaldo, 'The Law of the Global Community: An Integrated System to Enforce "Public" International Law', in Giuliana Ziccardi Capaldo (ed.), *The Global Community. Yearbook of International Law and Jurisprudence 2001* (Oceana Publications/Oxford University Press 2001)

Giuliana Ziccardi Capaldo, *The Pillars of Global Law* (Ashgate 2008)

Giuliana Ziccardi Capaldo, 'Providing a Right of Self-Defense Against Large-Scale Attacks by Irregular Forces: The Israeli-Hezbollah Conflict' (2007) 48 *Harvard International Law Journal Online* 111

Index

For Product Safety Concerns and Information please contact our EU representative GPSR@taylorandfrancis.com
Taylor & Francis Verlag GmbH, Kaufingerstraße 24, 80331 München, Germany

www.ingramcontent.com/pod-product-compliance
Ingram Content Group UK Ltd.
Pitfield, Milton Keynes, MK11 3LW, UK
UKHW011017180926
475701UK00004B/787
* 9 7 8 0 3 6 7 5 8 8 1 1 3 *